A MOST DANGEROUS BOOK

A MOST DANGEROUS BOOK

Tacitus's *Germania*

FROM
THE ROMAN EMPIRE
TO
THE THIRD REICH

CHRISTOPHER B. KREBS

W. W. NORTON & COMPANY
New York   London

For information about permissions to reproduce selections from this book,
write to Permissions, W. W. Norton & Company, Inc., 500 Fifth Avenue,
New York, NY 10110

For information about special discounts for bulk purchases,
please contact W. W. Norton Special Sales at
specialsales@wwnorton.com or 800-233-4830

Manufacturing by Courier Westford
Book design by Brooke Koven
Production manager: Devon Zahn

Library of Congress Cataloging-in-Publication Data

Krebs, Christopher B.
A most dangerous book : Tacitus's Germania from the Roman
Empire to the Third Reich / Christopher B. Krebs. — 1st ed.
    p. cm.
Includes bibliographical references.
ISBN 978-0-393-06265-6
1. Tacitus, Cornelius. Germania. 2. Group identity—Germany
I. Title.
PA6706.G4K736 2011
936.3'02—dc22

                                                    2010049425

W. W. Norton & Company, Inc.
500 Fifth Avenue, New York, N.Y. 10110
www.wwnorton.com

W. W. Norton & Company Ltd.
Castle House, 75/76 Wells Street, London W1T 3QT

1 2 3 4 5 6 7 8 9 0

To my father,
Rudolf Bodo Jürgen Krebs,
on his seventieth birthday

CONTENTS

ILLUSTRATIONS

The reproduction of any illustrations is not permitted without the explicit permission of the copyright holder.

1. Mosaic in the entrance hall of the Villa Fontedàmo, © C. B. Krebs 2009, courtesy of Giovanni Baldeschi-Balleani.

2. Codex Aesinas, Vittorio Emanuele 1631, c. 66r. Biblioteca Nazionale Centrale di Roma.

3. Funerary inscription of Tacitus (Museo Nazionale Romano, Rome), © Livius.org, 2008.

4. Woodcut of Poggio Bracciolini (1380–1459): Jean-Jacques Boissard, *Icones quinquaginta virorum illustrium, doctrina & eruditione præstantium . . . cum eorum vitis descriptis* (Frankfurt, 1597–99), 108. Houghton Library, Harvard University, Typ 520 97.225.

5. Noah's son Tuysco, the German primogenitor: Giovanni Nanni (Annius of Viterbo, 1432–1502), *Commentaria super opera diversorum auctorum de antiquitatibus loquentium* (Rome: Silber, 1498), pi^v. Houghton Library, Harvard University, Inc 3888.

6. Tuisco, the father of all Germans: Johannes Turmair (Aventinus, 1477–1532), *Chronica, darinn nicht allein dess alten Hauss Beyern . . . Herkommen, Stam vnd Geschichte . . . , sondern auch der uralten Teutschen Ursprung, Herkommen, Sitten, Gebrauch, Religion, Mannliche und treffliche Thaten*

. . . *beschrieben* (Frankfurt: Feyerabend, 1580), ii^r. Houghton Library, Harvard University, Ger 9250.3.1.

7. A Germanic feast: Philipp Clüver (1580–1622), *Germaniae antiquae libri tres* (Leiden: Elzevier, 1616), 158. Houghton Library, Harvard University, GC6 C6275 616g.

8. Germanic farmer: Justus Möser (1720–94), *Osnabrückische Geschichte*, in *Sämmtliche Werke*, vol. 5 (Berlin: F. Nicolai, 1798), frontispiece. Widener Library, Harvard College Library, 47528.1.10.

9. SS runes: Cover of Photo Album B in the Himmler collection, Hoover Institution Archives.

10. Facial angle: Peter Camper (1722–89), *The Works of the Late Professor Camper* (London, 1821), Tab. vi. Boston Medical Library in the Francis A. Countway Library of Medicine, fNC760.C15.

11. Cephalic index: Hans F. K. Günther (1891–1968), *Rassenkunde des deutschen Volkes* (Munich: J. F. Lehmann, 1922), 28. Widener Library, Harvard College Library, Ger 330.435.

12. Masthead of the *Alldeutsche Blätter: Mitteilungen des Allgemeinen Deutschen Verbandes* 10 (1900), March 4. Center for Research Libraries, MF 10155.

13. Photograph of Heinrich Himmler (1900–45), from 1931/32: Heinrich Himmler Papers, Album A, Hoover Institution Archives.

14. Tacitean Motto of a Hitler Youth manual: Horst Wagenführ, *Gefolgschaft—Der germanische Kampfbund* (Hamburg: Hanseatische Verlagsanstalt, 1935), motto. Widener Library, Harvard College Library, KD41701.

ACKNOWLEDGMENTS

Many are those who have in one way or another helped to make this book come about.

First and foremost I would like to thank my teachers, sincerely and belatedly. I was fortunate to learn Latin at an early age, at first inspired by Elke Steinkrauß at elementary school (Grundschule am Weinmeisterhorn), then challenged by Walter Fietz at high school (Kant Gymnasium). There I also, somewhat naively, signed up for ancient Greek under Elisabeth Krause's guidance. When after a break from the classical languages I returned to studying them at university, I realized the depth of my debt. Even though English came last in my curriculum of languages, I had the good luck of receiving Gabriele Zigann's (now Tapphorn) instruction, which would eventually allow me to study in England and to live and work and write in the United States. In other areas my indebtedness is similarly profound: I would have walked a lot less surefootedly through 450 years of European history if I had not visited much of the territory before during many years of history lessons. Education should not be a privilege; but I feel very privileged.

It has also been my privilege to work more recently at two excellent libraries, the Harvard College Library, with Widener and its marvelous open shelves at its center, and, for almost a year, at the Bayerische Staatsbibliothek in Munich. Researching the impact of Tacitus's *Germania* involved browsing a great number of books, journals, and other documents, published over centuries in places far and wide, and these two libraries either counted the texts I needed among their respective collections or secured them through their smoothly running interlibrary loan systems. I feel particularly grateful to the staff at Widener and Houghton (Harvard's library for rare books and manuscripts): For no matter how obscure or rare the document I was interested in and no matter where I turned for help, I met only with cheer and competence. Other institutions that speedily met my requests for information or documents include the Archiv des Erzbistums München und Freising; the Hoover Institute; the Bundesarchiv Koblenz; the Bundesarchiv Berlin; the Biblioteca Nazionale Centrale di Roma; the Ufficio Turismo: Comune di Jesi; and the Ufficio Informazione e Accoglienza Turistica in Osimo.

Walking through Widener's stacks in search of references to and quotations from Tacitus's *most dangerous book*, I ventured repeatedly into areas outside my expertise. I am grateful for the guidance I received from the following: Giovanni Baldeschi-Balleani on the history of his family and the Codex Aesinas; Dr. Michael Carhart (Old Dominion University) on Christoph Meiners; Professor Andreas Gardt (University of Kassel) and Dr. Nicola McLelland (University of Nottingham) on seventeenth-century linguistic theories; Professor Roger Chickering and Björn Hofmeister (both Georgetown University) on the *Alldeutsche Blätter*. Particular thanks are due to Dr. Brian Vick (Emory University), who not only helped with various eighteenth- and nineteenth-century issues but also read and copiously annotated two of my chapters, and to Dr. Allan A. Lund as well as Heather Pringle for their generous help and careful readings of my chapter on National Socialism.

Finding Tacitean traces was one challenge; presenting them in a readable fashion the other. Many friends, including former and current students of mine, read and commented on individual chapters or helped in some other way during the process. My heartfelt thanks go to Sean Braswell, Tiziana D'Angelo (who often heard several versions of the same paragraph), Caitlin A. Donovan, Christian Flow, Edward A. Gargan, Christopher D. Johnson, Elizabeth D. Mann, Alex Rehding, Ryan Rowberry (who also lent a receptive ear to my ideas over many happy dinners), and my agent, Steve Wasserman. Andrew C. Johnston and Ryan B. Samuels not only read parts of the manuscript but also checked numerous references, and Rebecca A. Katz took it upon herself to peruse the whole, from the introduction to the epilogue, alerting me to inaccuracies and oddities, thus saving me from blunders. They all helped significantly to make this a better book, but none more than my editor, Amy Cherry, who, with a good sense of humor and much patience, saw me through this undertaking from beginning to end.

INTRODUCTION

The Portentous Past

Thus shall we be again, or at least some among us.
—Heinrich Himmler, *Diary*, 24 September 1924

WITH THE speed of those who know that their days are numbered, the SS detachment charged up the pebble-and-sand-covered driveway. Shaded by two dense lines of trees, it gave on to an opening. There, ten miles west of the regional capital, Ancona, on the Adriatic coast, and just south of Jesi with its perilous airport, the SS men now stood along with local supporters in front of the Villa Fontedamo. Three-storied, its front decorated by six pillars and a little balcony, and painted in light colors that would block the heat of summer afternoons, it seemed incongruously quiet. It was the fall of 1943. Allied troops had started their invasion of the south of Italy.

Agents of Heinrich Himmler, the head (Reichsführer) of the SS, the men pounded on and in no time broke down the door to step on a small floor mosaic. Its earth-colored tesserae indicated the year the villa was built: 1855. The Nazis stormed in to find the place unoccupied, and systematically searched the rooms and alcoves, inch by inch, story by story. Gradually descending into sheer vandalism, they damaged frescoes, paintings, and books. But with the object of Himmler's desire safely out of reach, they could not find what they had come for.

The villa's owner, Count Aurelio Baldeschi Guglielmi Balle-

1. Mosaic in the entrance hall of the Villa Fontedàmo. *C. B. Krebs*

ani, had installed his family in another of his domiciles in nearby Osimo. This ancient hilltop village, whose inhabitants refer to themselves as *i senza testa*, the "headless" (an allusion to a series of decapitated statues in the town center), had seemed the safest place: far enough from the airport and located above a multibranched cellar network accessible from his palazzo. For thousands of years these shafts, tunnels, and nooks hewn into the ocher sandstone had provided damp protection. Now they protected the count along with his wife and their two children, who were supplied with all the necessities due to the foresight of their chauffeur, Giuseppe Angeletti, and a local waiter, Riccardo Cerioni. When German soldiers banged on the door, echoes could be heard downstairs. The Baldeschi-Balleani had received "visits" before: from German nationalists in the 1920s, from National Socialists and Italian Fascists since the 1930s. Adolf Hitler himself had been interested in one of the family's possessions. But like the SS troops searching the Villa Fontedàmo, they all failed to obtain what after centuries of oblivion had suddenly fallen into a priest's hands, when, in 1901, the library of yet another palazzo of the Baldeschi-Balleani, in the center of Jesi, yielded the oldest extant manuscript of "one of the one hundred most dangerous books ever written."[1] Almost two thousand years after it was composed, five hundred years after it was rediscovered by manuscript hunters, Tacitus's *Germania* was once again and for the last time the object of dreams and desires. Given its history, it hardly mattered that the so-called Codex Aesinas, the hand-copied fifteenth-century manuscript of the *Germania* discovered in Jesi, escaped the Nazis' grasp: Tacitus's text had done its damage already.

HEINRICH HIMMLER, the Reichsführer SS and as such ultimately responsible for the execution of millions, did not go down in history as a bibliophile. Why, then, did the second most powerful man in the Third Reich bother about the *Germania*? With the world engulfed in war, why did he take such an interest in an almost two-thousand-year-old text, which the Roman historian Cornelius Tacitus had written in 98 CE "About the Origin and Mores of the Germanic Peoples," as the *Germania* is titled in the coveted manuscript? What made this ethnography of fewer than thirty pages so precious that he tried to steal it, even though it was illegible to anyone but specialists and the text itself available in modern Latin editions and translations throughout Nazi Germany—as it had been for four hundred years?

The *Germania* was taught in schools, amply quoted in Nazi articles, and a source of enthusiasm for countless National Socialists, from party foot soldiers to high-ranking leaders. The only comprehensive account from ancient times of the Germanic peoples, it was read as a report of the German past and widely celebrated as a "magnificent monument."[2] Unfortunately it is not a report, nor is it about the German past.

The *Germanen*, as I shall call the Germanic tribes to differ-

2. Codex Aesinas: The opening lines of Tacitus's *Germania*.
Biblioteca Nazionale Centrale di Roma

entiate them from the Germans, defy a single definition.* To the Romans following the trail of their general Gaius Julius Caesar, they were the unruly northern people east of the Rhine, roaming an area enclosed by the Baltic Sea to the north, the Alps to the south, and (usually) the Vistula River to the east. While Roman authors knew of numerous Germanic tribes like the Goths, the Suevs, and the Teutons, they conceived of them as one single eth-

---

* English differentiates between "German" and "Germanic" only in adjectives; the difference is crucial. I, however, speak of "Germans" (often qualified by "old," "ancient," and so on) in reference to the *Germanen* (singular, *–e*), whenever I translate texts or relay theories where the author himself speaks or thinks of "ancient Germans." The same considerations apply to the country: *"Germanien"* and "(ancient) Germany."

nic group bound by geography. To a modern linguist, on the other hand, "Germanic" refers to a branch of the Indo-European language tree, which sprouted modern German, English, Swedish, and other languages in due time. From this perspective the *Germanen* comprise all speakers of the Germanic language. Slightly different yet again, archaeologists first classified as "Germanic" all material finds in the north that were not of Roman origin; but then, around 1900, they recalibrated their methods and defined as *Germanen* those sharing the same material culture.[3]

There are two problems with this fuzzy picture. Roman writers, including Tacitus, show little concern for the material cultures of the Germanic tribes and even less for their languages. Most of the people whom they call *Germani* (the Latin form) might have spoken the same language and used similar objects, but we do not know. The three sources—ancient testimony, linguistics, and archaeology—simply yield no single people. But no matter how the *Germanen* are defined, they must not be considered as the ancestors of modern Germans, as quasi "ancient Germans." For even though Tacitus and other Romans describe the Germanic tribes as if they were a cohesive ethnic group forming a nation, they were not. From which *Germanen*, then, do the Germans descend? What commonality unifies them with their alleged ancestors? And what about those Germanic tribes living outside modern-day Germany, like the Goths whom the Swedes claimed as their original forebears? The timeline between the Germanic past and the German present is fractured: "The" *Germanen* were not early Germans. There were always a few readers of Tacitus who realized this; yet the majority from the fifteenth through the twentieth century studied the *Germania* through an ideological lens and valued it as the gateway to the German past.

Considered as the "dawn" of German history, Tacitus's text was taken to illuminate the life and mores of those ancient German days.[4] The light of dawn is mellow, and most readers formed a positive impression. No sooner had the *Germania* been retrieved from the murky library of a German monastery in the fifteenth century than it supplied what would quickly become the standard epithets for the German ancestors: simple, brave, loyal, pure, just, and honorable. When Himmler read the *Germania* twenty years before the above-described SS mission, it struck a rare chord in his soul: "Thus," like our Germanic ancestors, "shall we be again," he confided to his diary.[5] He was but one of many on a long list of readers, starting with the Italian humanist Giannantonio Campano, who in 1471 called upon his German audience to rise to what they had once been. Many centuries later Hitler himself was to consider "Germanic Revolution" as a title for *Mein Kampf*. Although the Führer, who in 1936 would ask Mussolini for the return of the Codex Aesinas, ultimately decided against this title, it would have reflected (only too aptly, for Hitler) an important ideological component for the many National Socialists who demanded a "homecoming" to former shores.[6] In order to reach this German neverland, they—as well as generations of Germanophiles before them—relied on Tacitus as their involuntary helmsman.

Tacitus's work wielded so great an influence over so extended a period of time—450 years in all—because "Germany" for many centuries was but a product of the imagination. Or, rather, the idea of "Germany" posed a question to which the *Germania* provided an answer. To be German meant to wonder what it meant to be German (to appropriate the words of the nineteenth-century philosopher Friedrich Nietzsche).[7] In defense of such self-scrutiny it could be said that it was a legitimate issue: Before the North German Federation and the southern German states joined to create the German Empire on January 18, 1871, there had been no German nation-state, and cartographers used to sigh in despair over the muddle in Europe's middle. Before the nineteenth century Germany existed only as a sentiment. With geographical and political unity clearly lacking among the hundreds of states, which until 1806 coexisted in the loose fold of the "Holy Roman Empire of the German Nation," the common past, shared culture, and mother tongue were called upon to substantiate the idea of a unitary nation. But even this cultural nation emerged from the political kaleidoscope only to those who already cherished the German idea. Modern scholarship has revealed this alleged cultural nation to be almost as variegated and multigrained as the political one: The *Volk* had lived happily outside a national culture and inside their communal boundaries, participating in regional traditions and speaking local dialects, which often bore little resemblance to German. Contrary to the fantasies of many nineteenth-century historians, a German nation-state was not politically or culturally predetermined; to think otherwise is to fall for the German teleological fallacy.

Yet to speak of "Germans" prior to 1871 can nonetheless be justified. The German nation as an "imagined community" among intellectuals existed in a paradoxical state of anticipation for four hundred years before its realization as a nation-state.[8] Ernst Moritz Arndt, a German nationalist who lived long enough to see the beginning of the German Empire, expressed this paradox to its fullest: "German people? What are you, and where are you? I seek and cannot find you."[9] Three hundred years before, in the very early sixteenth century, humanists living north of the Alps had already consciously called themselves "Germans" and urged their compatriots to study and rally to the defense of their *patria* against Italian obloquy. In Tacitus's *Germania* they found this *patria*—a brave people whom they claimed as forefathers. Their cultural and intellectual shortcomings, apparent in comparison with sophisticated Romans, were amply compensated for by their morality and fortitude: The German ancestors had in fact been superior.

The Germans' opponents changed—Romans yielded to Italians, Italians to the French, and the French to Jews—but the opposition remained a characteristic feature of the German national consciousness. Again and again, when the "German question" was asked, the Germanic past in general and the *Germania* in particular provided the answer. Heinrich Heine, a German Jewish poet of the nineteenth century, satirized this extended Q&A: "Where does the *Germane* begin? Where does he end? May a German smoke tobacco? The majority rules no. May a German wear gloves? Yes, but only those of ox-hide. . . . But a German may drink beer; indeed, he should drink it as a true son of *Germania*, since Tacitus mentions specifically German *cerevisia*. . . . Whoever descended from a French, Jew, or Slav . . . was sentenced to exile."[10] The poet, exiled himself, would not have been surprised when less than a century later National Socialism attempted a Germanic revolution.

Its Führer's claim to the contrary notwithstanding, the ideology of Nazism did not present itself to Hitler out of nowhere; nor is the Germanic myth the only component that can be traced back to the *völkisch* movement and even farther back through preceding centuries. In the formation of the core concepts of the National Socialist ideology—racism, the ideology of the *Volk* and its spirit, and the selfsame Germanic myth—Tacitus's *Germania* played a major role. Arnaldo Momigliano, a voracious reader and erudite authority on the history of ideas, suspected this. After the collapse of the National Socialist regime he gave the *Germania* high priority among "the one hundred most dangerous books ever written."[11] He was right. For the book that one enthusiastic Nazi recommended to "every thinking German" as a "bible" was not only quoted by Nazis in support of their ideological views. More importantly, admired through centuries as "a golden booklet" (*libellus aureus*), "an admirable work" (*un admirable ouvrage*), and "an immortal text" (*ein unsterbliches Werk*), it contributed central ideas to the formation of those ideological views in support of which it would then be quoted: The *Germania* is a most dangerous book not because it fitted the frame but because it had helped to form it. It fulfilled its own promise. While the National Socialist reception of Tacitus's "particular stroke of luck" in most regards continued previous trends, in one it differed notably: Inside and outside Himmler's SS there was an actual attempt to turn the Roman's description into German reality, the past into the future, *Deutsche* into *Germanen*.[12] One of the Nuremberg race laws—the so-called Law for the Defense of German Blood and Honor passed in 1936—prohibited marriages between Jews and Germans just as Tacitus's *Germanen* were believed to have restricted marriages with foreigners.

IDEAS RESEMBLE viruses: They depend on minds as their hosts, they replicate and mutate in content or form, and they gang up together to form ideologies. They spread vertically through generations as well as horizontally from one social group to another.[13] The *Germania* virus, imported in the late fifteenth century from Italy, exhibited various local symptoms in historical texts, linguistic treatises, political and cultural philosophy, law, racial theories, and even school texts, all of which were indicative of a serious disease. Then—after 350 years of incubation—during the latter part of the nineteenth century, it progressed to a systemic infection culminating in the major crisis of the twentieth century. Since then, after an initial avoidance, the text has been studied mostly for the sake of scholarship rather than ideology.

To write an intellectual epidemiology means to visit the patients and to inspect the various historical and cultural contexts in which this innocuous yet noxious text figured. From its tumultuous rediscovery by Italian humanists in the fifteenth century to the violent attempts to appropriate it from an Italian noble in the twentieth, the *Germania* spread throughout Europe in the fields of literature, science, and politics. Tacitus had written for his fellow senators, maybe even the Roman emperor and his advisers. They would, he assumed, get the gist of his brief treatise. Yet even among his contemporary audience and readership, comprehension varied. For the meaning of a text is mediated by its readers. It is their linguistic sensitivity, their familiarity with the literary tradition, their knowledge of present-day political and cultural concerns—in short, their ability and alacrity to hear what the text has to say—that determine its meaning. What is true of Tacitus's peers applies tenfold to readers outside that author's horizon. When, hundreds of years later, beyond the period uncharitably called the Middle Ages, readers turned to Tacitus's pages again, they lived in different worlds and thought in different words than his. The leading writers of the times read and often blithely rewrote the *Germania* according to their knowledge and interests, in the main arguing for Germanic superiority. In all those years few tried to listen to Tacitus as if they had been present when he delivered his *Germania* in Rome in 98 CE. Most, instead, read it in the light of their own concerns, but rarely in so crude a form as one avid Nazi who considered the laws concerning the "Jewish question" to be the most recent effort to restore the "racial purity" allegedly mentioned in Tacitus's little book.[14] While the Roman's words stayed (for the most part), their meanings changed according to the needs at hand.

The reception of the *Germania* varied not only over time; there were also variations at any given time. No tradition runs in a single stream. There are rills, runnels, and rivulets, making up different readings of the same text. The epilogue contains a glimpse of an alternative history, but for the rest I have settled on following the broadest branch: the one that took the *Germanen* to be the German forefathers, that idealized the past and declared it to be the guiding light toward a brighter future. The journey's end provides perspective: How did the ideas in Tacitus's text contribute to the discourses from which National Socialism would ultimately emerge? Like all travel, the one through history tracing ideas has its risks: With our eyes on the destination, we heed little of what does not seem to lead there, and we read much as a signpost, even though it may not be. This is generally known as the "mythology of doctrine," and in the case of Nazism has been decried as the

"Nazification of the past." Tacitus himself was, of course, no Aryan peasant, whose "racial bond with us [Nazi Germans] can explain his sympathy for our ancestors," nor did the *Germania* contain any National Socialist ideas.[15] Yet the "golden booklet" was called upon again and again to substantiate ideas that National Socialists would ultimately embrace as their own. *Ex nihilo nihil fit*—nothing comes out of nothing.

ONE NATIONAL SOCIALIST, Heinrich Himmler, took a particular interest in the *Germania*. His hunt for its oldest extant manuscript in the autumn of 1943 concludes the history of its ideological impact, just as a manuscript hunt in the fifteenth century marks its beginning. The SS mission epitomizes the fascination that captured not just the Reichsführer SS but also the National Socialist mainstream and centuries of previous readers. The failure to locate the parchment symbolizes the elusiveness of the ancient "Germany" described: a utopia, a word that literally means "nowhere." For the *Germania* is not a report: Tacitus had most likely never been to the banks of the Rhine. He wrote his work with recourse to previous Greek and Roman ethnographic writers, with one eye on Roman affairs and but a fleeting glance toward northern realities. The text that would be called upon to define the German national character was a Roman's imaginative reflection on human values and a political statement. This is undoubtedly one of history's deeper ironies.

A MOST DANGEROUS BOOK

1

The Roman Conquest of the Germanic Myth

It is the greatest honor, the greatest power to be at all times
surrounded by a huge band of chosen young men.

—motto for a 1935 Hitler Youth manual,
taken from the *Germania*

NOTHING GOOD was to be expected of a man who enjoyed
stabbing flies with a sharpened stylus. Those expectations
were not disappointed. Domitian, the last emperor of the
Flavian dynasty, wreaked a reign of terror on Rome. When he was
finally assassinated in 96 CE, the Roman aristocracy exhaled in
relief. Many among them, foremost the courageous, had fallen
victim to "that most savage beast," as a contemporaneous writer
described him.[1] Especially during the last years of his regime,
he had stifled life in the capital of the far-flung Roman Empire.
Survival was bought with submissiveness and silence, enforced by
informers who abolished any free exchange of thought and speech.
After fifteen years of fear—a time span during which "young men
had reached old age, old men almost the end of their days"—even
survivors were mere shadows of their former selves, as if "they had
survived themselves."[2] One of them was the leading Roman senator, the greatest historian in Latin literature, and the author of a
most dangerous book: Cornelius Tacitus.

Authors inevitably inscribe their own times into their written work. Every page in Tacitus's books carries the watermark of history. This is certainly true also of his second work, the *Germania*, whose opening words swiftly take the reader into the circumscribed territory north of the Alps: "*Germanien* in its entirety is separated from the Gauls [in the west] and from the Raetians and Pannonians [in the south] by the Rhine and Danube rivers; from the Sarmatians and Dacians [in the east] by mutual misgivings or mountains. The rest [in the north] is surrounded by the ocean."[3] These lines introduce a booklet of less than thirty pages, without title or preface and with an abrupt and ironic ending. Its first part presents the *Germanen* and their land in general; the second offers a panorama of the various Germanic tribes. Why, one might wonder, would a Roman senator, just months after the restoration of freedom of speech, consider "the Origin and Mores of the Germanic Peoples" a topic worthy of his attention and literary efforts, especially since he probably never even came near the land of his interest?

BAD EMPERORS MAKE GOOD WRITERS

> They choose kings for their nobility, leaders for their valor.
> —Montesquieu, quoting from the *Germania*, 1748

About Tacitus's times much is known, about him very little. The historian is reticent about himself, as befits someone whose name in Latin signifies "silent" (*tacitus*). Yet, in addition to the scant and scattered autobiographical comments in his writing, there are the remarks in the letters of his loquacious acquaintance Pliny the Younger (63–113)* and two highly fragmentary inscriptions: One, found in the late nineteenth century in Mylasa in the southwest of

---

* All dates are CE unless otherwise specified.

3. Funerary inscription of Tacitus. *Livius.org, 2008*

modern-day Turkey, uses Tacitus's name instead of a date (events were often dated by reference to the leading regional administrator at the time). The other, a few letters seemingly flung across the three remaining lines of a marble chunk from Rome, was only recently related to the historian: "CITO" in the first line and the Roman career sketched in the two lines below make it virtually certain to belong to Tacitus's funerary inscription, given that few Roman names end with -*citus* (of which -*cito* is the dative case), and Tacitus is the only one we know of with the required senatorial career.[4] From these literary and epigraphic sources, it is possible to reconstruct the major moments of his career. It should be borne in mind, however, that most dates are approximate, and that the fact that not even his first name is securely attested is indicative of the general uncertainty regarding him. What follows is not a portrait but a silhouette.

TACITUS SEEMS to have been born in one of the long-established Roman provinces: either somewhere in the southeast of France, known as Gallia Narbonensis, a region that was characterized as "more Italy than a province"; or in the north of Italy, referred to as Gallia Cisalpina (Gaul this side of the Alps), which in Tacitus's time was not a province anymore but part of Italia.[5] This amiable area, enclosed by the Pyrenees, the Alps, the Po, and the Mediterranean, and often favored by a light breeze carrying a faint whiff of the salty sea, was famous not only for the fertility of its soil and the prosperity of its economy but also for the morality of its inhabitants. Those looking for traditional Roman virtues—piety, simplicity, disciplined virtuousness—would find them here, where "the old ways were still retained," as Tacitus himself would write. It was an ideal recruiting place to fill Roman offices.[6]

Tacitus's father was a member of the equestrian class and dealt in finance, if he is the Roman knight mentioned by Pliny's uncle (which, again given the rarity of the name, is likely). Ambitious and sufficiently affluent, he provided his son with a thorough education and later the necessary means to establish himself in Rome. The historian's birth around 55 coincided with the beginning of the reign of the young emperor Nero (37–68), successor to his gauche great-uncle and adoptive father Claudius (10 BCE–54), whose life had ended over dinner—probably mushrooms, possibly poisoned, perhaps by his wife. The old and awkward Claudius, who was afflicted with a stammer, had been forced by his embarrassed family to spend years out of public view but then saw himself elevated to the rule of the Roman Empire. Nobody was more surprised than Claudius himself, and, as evidenced by a persiflage (the "Pumpkinification") written after his death, he never learned how to sit comfortably on the cushioned throne. Nero, the last emperor of the Julio-Claudian dynasty, a youthful and seemingly modest seventeen-year-old, stood in welcome contrast to his predecessor.

The young emperor's hesitant first steps augured well—and wrongly. There was hope that Nero would "provide happy times for his exhausted subjects and break the silence of the laws."[7] Indeed, because of the moderating guidance of his tutors—the

Stoic philosopher and prolific writer Seneca the Younger was one—Rome enjoyed tranquillity and stability for five years, a period celebrated as the golden *quinquennium*. The ruler pursued his literary, culinary, and sexual interests—moderately in comparison to later orgies—and had others rule. But when the influence of his tutors waned, and the spell of his designing mother, Agrippina the Younger, broke, his rule soon deteriorated to the arbitrariness of absolute power. The "long-meditated crime," the murder of his mother, marked a turn for the worst; her death ended the reign of the sister, wife, and mother of Roman emperors.[8]

Accusations, executions, and "suggested" suicides followed in ever-greater numbers. Rome burned, "whether accidentally or by the emperor's ploy was uncertain," but it was rumored that Nero had played his harp to the sound of the crackling fires.[9] Every Roman could see that the emperor's Golden Villa—a building complex hugging the Esquiline Hill, which stretched to the Palatine and occupied an area of at least one hundred acres—could not have been built if the fire had not cleared existing domiciles. The charred remains gave way to artificial lakes, lush pastures, and sparkling halls covered with marble, ivory, or gold veneers, and decorated with mosaics and frescoes. "Rome was turned into a house" whose grandeur was outsized only by its owner's ego.[10]

Money was spent with abandon. Dissatisfaction grew. Senators grumbled sotto voce that they had lost all but their lives—which actually reflected their luck. A series of conspiracies and rebellions ensued. The beleaguered emperor "murdered whomsoever he chose for whatever reason, indiscriminately and immoderately."[11] (Among the victims was Nero's former tutor Seneca, whose suicide Peter Paul Rubens famously depicted in the early seventeenth century.) But all to no avail. In 68 Nero was compelled by circumstances to forfeit both his throne and his life. At the time of the emperor's suicide, Tacitus was in his teens, about fifteen years old. To what extent he was privy to the developments in Rome is beyond the reach of historical inquiry (as is the true nature of Nero's reign, since ancient historical accounts are biased). Yet these were the future historian's formative years, and that he would later regard Nero's reign as tyrannical emerges from his second major work, the *Annals*, on which this account is based. It would not be his only encounter with tyranny.

Civil wars followed. The "long and single year" after Nero's death saw or, perhaps better, glimpsed four emperors: With the exception of the last, they all prayed to Roman gods already heeding their respective successor.[12] "The Roman capital was seized by Roman armies, Italy devastated, the provinces plundered." Tacitus's family was personally affected, since marauding Roman troops from the northern parts of Europe, where one of the short-lived emperors had been stationed, ravaged and burned their way to Italy, close enough to his home to cause anxious nights and tremulous days. Many years later he would learn that his wife's grandmother had been killed during those months of mayhem. After three luckless emperors (about whom Tacitus quipped that "whoever won would be the worse") peace, stability, and a new dynasty emerged from the east in the person of Titus Flavius Vespasianus (9–79).[13]

It is said that the ideal ruler does not want to rule. Vespasian qualifies. He was stationed in the Roman province of Judaea (covering modern Israel and the Palestinian territories) in order to quell the Jewish uprising when he learned of the developments in Rome. No sooner had he declared allegiance to the first of the fleeting emperors than he found out about his sudden death. He understood that now emperors "could be made elsewhere than in Rome" (until Nero all emperors had been acclaimed in Rome by the senate).[14] Reluctant, hesitant, ultimately compliant, he agreed, when asked by the Roman governor of neighboring Syria, to make his bid for the emperorship. Vespasian was a chary man not least because of his recent experience of the vicissitudes of fortune, inflicted by Rome's arty emperor, Nero himself: After Vespasian had dared either to fall asleep or leave during a recital by Rome's self-declared greatest talent, he was demoted. (The Roman biographer Suetonius reports that a woman gave birth, not daring to leave the performance of the "artiste" who ruled over life and death.[15]) But rebellious activities in Judaea made it necessary for Nero to fall back on one of his most successful and seasoned commanders, who had proved himself in places as diverse as Britain and Africa. About to reach his sixties, Vespasian found himself in a position of important command once more, and in possession of the means necessary to rule Rome and the world: soldiers.

Once word spread of Vespasian's move, further support was tendered: The governor of Egypt joined with him, and other leaders and their legions followed suit. In the east, from the north to the south, a storm rapidly gathered that would descend on Rome. With his allies fighting the battles, the future emperor waited in the south of the Roman Empire, securing Egypt, the granary of Rome. Among his staunch supporters he could count on his older son, Titus, soon to be his coregent, but at that time left in charge of the siege of Jerusalem. His younger son, Domitian, on the other hand, "used his father's fortune only for his abandon."[16] But this was written after the assassination of the tyrant, with hindsight scoring easy points.

Vespasian's procession into Rome marked the beginning of the Flavian dynasty. It was perhaps during the early years of his reign that Tacitus, still a very young man, moved to Rome in order to add the finishing touches to his education. Schooling at the time comprised three phases: First, privileged pupils learned reading and writing, often in Greek as well as in Latin, from a *litterator*, who was not afraid to use a rod. Then, roughly from the age of eleven, they studied with a *grammaticus* for a fuller appreciation of Greek and Latin literature, many parts of which had to be committed to memory. The *grammaticus* would also introduce them to the elaborate rhetorical system. Thereon, from the age of fifteen, the students would be trained by a *rhetoricus* in the art of speaking well. Finally there would be a period of practice and probation: An experienced and reputable public figure would take the young man under his wing, generally serving as an example but more specifically acquainting him with political leaders, introducing him to the courts, and explaining procedures. A solid rhetorical education was of utmost importance in a society in which those who could not speak well could not hope to attain public office: "To be wordless and inarticulate was considered shameful."[17] It is therefore not surprising that the young Tacitus would studiously listen to conversations between leading elders, as he would relate later in one of his minor works, the *Dialogue on Oratory*. It would not be long before he had become one of Rome's eminent orators, and other young men would follow him.

If his writing is indicative of his speaking, Tacitus was armed with irony and sarcasm. Pliny the Younger, that prolific letter writer, would praise him as "most eloquent" and his style as "majestic."[18] Almost from the outset, Tacitus must have made memorable impressions. His public appearances attracted the attention of the emperor himself, who was always on the lookout for talent to fill the many administrative positions in Rome and its far-reaching empire. Success followed swiftly. With the ambition of the provincial who finds himself in the coveted center of the world, Tacitus married into a well-respected family and took the traditional career path.

Vespasian was sixty-one years old by the time he became emperor. Political stability required the prospect of continuity, if only of a dynastic kind, for the specter of powerful commanders once again competing for the vacant throne had to be banished. As soon as his older son, Titus, entered Rome in 71 after his successful and destructive campaign to capture Jerusalem and its temple, Vespasian formally declared him partner in power. He received, like his father, the title *Caesar* and was put in charge of the Praetorian Guard, which was stationed near Rome. Though responsible for the protection of the emperors' lives, the guard had repeatedly abetted in their murders. (In essence a guardian was found for the guard.) During the next several years of his reign, the father groomed the son to become his successor, allowing him to add administrative experience to his ample war record. But fate intervened: Only two years into his sole rule after his father's death in 79, Titus passed away. On his deathbed he is reported to have said, "I have made but one mistake."[19] A fortunate man, no doubt, felicitous even, since nobody knows which momentous mistake he regretted.

Probably during Titus's short-lived emperorship, Tacitus was elected *quaestor*, an office overseeing financial affairs in Rome or one of the provinces. The appointment marked the first major stop on the Roman career path and carried automatic entrance into the Roman senate. The word *senatus*, derived from the Latin for "old man" (*senex*), means literally "council of elders." In the republic it had served as the highest and most important governing body; in the empire its significance varied, but it remained the highest council, even if only to be ignored by an overbearing emperor. With his accession Tacitus had entered the hallways of power, where he would walk for three decades.

WHEN DOMITIAN (51–96), Vespasian's younger son, took over as emperor in the early eighties, rumors circulated that he had caused his brother's illness by poison. If so, envy must have been the motive, since Domitian lacked what Titus had: military success, acknowledgment as an administrator, and amiability. Foremost, the victory in the Jewish war had established Titus as a competent commander. His triumph was celebrated by a still extant arch displaying his achievements as much as Domitian's shortcomings. While his brother had enjoyed the partnership with their father,

Domitian had merely held a few consulships and minor priest-hoods, and he must have sensed his position to be one of powerless-ness veiled by the pretense of responsibility. And, as is indicated by the anecdote of his stabbing of flies, it seems likely that Domitian lacked social skills as well. Once, after he had spent several solitary hours, the guard posted in front of his door was asked by a passerby whether there was anybody with the emperor. "Not even a fly," was the apt response.[20]

According to historical tradition, the new emperor brought to his reign paranoia and an inferiority complex (the latter often accompanied by an exaggerated self-assertiveness). He was quoted as saying that nobody believed an emperor's fear of a conspiracy until he was proved right by his own death. Later in his reign he preferred walking through colonnades whose surface was so highly polished that he could see his reflection—and, more importantly, what was happening behind him. Fear triggered fear. Senators soon also watched their backs.

Unaccomplished and overeager, he embarked on military cam-paigns, only to meet senatorial disdain. The north and east, the areas around the Rhine and the Danube, were the major military trouble spots during Domitian's reign. As early as 83 he celebrated his first triumph over the Chatti (a Germanic tribe), *before* they had been conquered. Malicious contemporaries added the gibe that he preferred celebrating victories to winning them. They hinted that the captives, who were traditionally displayed during a triumphal procession in Rome, had in this case been purchased and dressed up to pass as prisoners of war.[21] To them it seemed scarcely justi-fied that Domitian had coins minted that included the abbrevia-tion of *Germanicus* in the emperor's titulature. (This might have provided a reason for Tacitus to write his *Germania* two years after the assassination in order to disclose that all of *Germanien* was not yet conquered.) However, other evidence suggests that the maligned emperor's campaigns did indeed secure possessions for

Rome: He established two Germanic provinces, began the construction of the Roman dam against barbarian surges (known as the *limes*), and stabilized the Danube region through a treaty with the powerful king Decebalus. But Domitian's senatorial opposition would rather have died than have given him credit; and many, according to Tacitus, did.

Equally zealous was the emperor's self-appointment as *censor*, an office that supervised morals and chastised bad conduct. From the beginning of his rule Domitian wanted to cleanse Rome. To judge from contemporary writers, reasons would not have been lacking. His execution of the Vestal Virgins, highly regarded female priests in charge of the sacred fire of Vesta, the goddess of the hearth, is only the best-known example of his draconian approach to upholding Roman mores. Accused of the loss of her virginity, the head of the Vestals was buried alive—and with her Domitian's reputation: Under his rule "even peace was brutal."[22]

An autocrat and micromanager, Domitian made his biggest mistake with his conduct in the senate. He liked to be addressed as "Master and God," the offensive word being *dominus* ("master"), which had led other emperors to avoid it. Whenever the "Master and God" was so addressed, the senate was reminded of its slavish position, the more painful as it still cherished the illusion of power. But its time would come. After the "master's" assassination by members of his court—his exiled-and-then-recalled wife among them—the senators had the last word when they decreed the "damnation of memory" (*damnatio memoriae*). The tyrant's name was erased: His statues were demolished or recycled (by replacing their heads), and inscriptions with his name obliterated, just as if he had never existed. (Sometimes, however, obliteration guarantees remembrance: As every visitor of the Sala del Maggior Consiglio in Venice knows, the blackened portrait of the fifty-fifth doge, Marino Faliero, is always among those—and often the only one—commented upon in guidebooks.) In the end Domitian's fate was not to be forgotten but to be remembered as a villain. Senatorial writers like Tacitus ensured that for centuries his reign would be deemed despotic. They have determined his infamy to this day. Like the reign of Nero (to whom satirists compared Domitian as the "bald Nero"), Domitian's cannot be characterized with ultimate certainty: Sycophancy taints contemporary writing, and loathing permeates subsequent accounts.[23]

In the preface of his literary debut, a biography of his father-in-law, Agricola, written in 98, Tacitus states that fifteen years had been cut out of men's lives by Domitian's rule. Those are precisely the fifteen years during which he steadily climbed one career rung after another. In one of his few personal remarks the "silent one" informs his readers that in 88, in addition to discharging his duties as a *praetor* (Rome's second highest republican office), he had held an office in the college of priests, known as the *quindecimviri* (the "fifteen men," a name retained even when they had been increased to sixteen).[24] Their duties consisted mainly of consulting Greek oracles in times of adversity and organizing the secular games, as happened in 88, almost seven years after Domitian had succeeded his brother, Titus. Since this post was usually allotted to meritorious older statesmen or young noblemen whose greatest merit was their lineage, Tacitus's attainment gives evidence of either exceptional service or exceptional patronage or—and perhaps most likely—a combination of both. Usually such a position boded well for future advancement, certainly in his case. Subsequent to the offices he held in Rome, Tacitus left for a governmental post in the provinces; the whereabouts are uncertain. Then in 97, shortly after Domitian's death, he attained the consulship, the summit of political ascension during the republic and still the highest office in the empire—albeit mostly representative. Tacitus, who was about forty, may have been nominated by the detested tyrant himself.

But this period of advancement came at the expense of silence, and silence abetted wrongdoing. Ultimately it was not the tyrant's hands that were bloody but "our hands that dragged [the statesman and willful philosopher] Helvidius to his incarceration."[25] Integrity, it seemed, should have prevailed over fear. But at the same time Roman respectability necessitated public service, as a Roman should "think of what benefited the fatherland first, one's parents second, oneself last."[26] Protest against the emperor at the expense of the empire (and often the protester's life) met Tacitus's outspoken criticism *and* secret admiration.

Tacitus's first work, which goes beyond the boundaries of a normal biography, reflects on this question of how to be virtuous in "times so savage, so hostile to virtuousness."[27] He tries to demonstrate that human values can persist in an inhuman system, that "good men can exist even under bad rulers." His father-in-law serves as an example of someone who contributed without collaborating with the regime. Deeper motives might have been at play, however. Perhaps Tacitus wanted to make this claim in his own defense as well. If so, he seems to have failed to convince himself. The self-accusatory tone resounds too loudly in his first work, published just after Rome had emerged from the long shade and brighter times seemed to lie ahead. The date of publication itself contained a message: Silenced voices could speak again, now that it was possible "to think what you wanted and to say what you thought."[28] Later Tacitus would return to the Flavian dynasts, whose reign along with the preceding fleeting emperors he addressed in his first major historical work, the *Histories*. He frankly acknowledges in the preface that he had worked his way up under their emperorships, not hiding his advancement under Domitian. But what else could he have done? Every reader in Rome must have known that the writer who claimed to be a dispassionate critic of the system had contributed to it.

But the Flavians, and particularly Domitian, affected Tacitus in yet another way: Although interpreters of texts run the risk of ridicule when they tie a text too closely to the author's life (if poets of a certain kind drank all the wine and loved all the women they versify, they would not have any time for their poetry), there can be no question that his existence under Domitian shaped him as a writer. If he had been born at the end of the tyrant's reign, gaining political consciousness during the early years of the "best emperor," Trajan, and living a happy life through to the days of the wise Marcus Aurelius (the last of the five good emperors, who died in 181), he might still have become a writer, but a very different one—perhaps not even a historian. Tacitus the historian presupposes Domitian the tyrant. His biting words about senatorial slaves must have gnawed away at his own sense of pride.

Tacitus's interest in how values depend on social and political circumstances would accompany him throughout his literary career. It is one of the questions he also addresses in his second minor work, the *Germania*.

AN ARMCHAIR ETHNOGRAPHY

> The tribes in *Germanien*, not tainted by intermarriage with any other nations, exist as a distinct unadulterated people that resembles only itself. Consequently, all of them even share the same physical appearance . . . fierce blue eyes, tawny hair, huge bodies.
>
> —Tacitus's *Germania*, quoted by
> Houston Stewart Chamberlain, 1899

A tyrant's assassination is decided by its aftermath. "The best day after a bad emperor is the first," and only a better successor justifies the deed.[29] Marcus Cocceius Nerva (30–98), the senate's choice as Domitian's successor, was recommended by his considerable political experience as well as age and childlessness, the latter particularly welcome given the most recent example of dynastic deterioration. He duly distanced himself and his policies from his hated predecessor and swore that senators would not be killed. After years of despondency "the spirit finally returned" in Rome.[30] Nerva rang in the happiest and most prosperous period, as the eminent historian Edward Gibbon saw it. Five emperors, all adopted by their predecessors because of their promising talents, would oversee peace and prosperity for almost a century in an empire that now, at its greatest expanse, comprised all of western Europe, the north of Africa, the Middle East, and the territory west and south of the Black Sea. Nerva, well into his sixties in 96, was the first to adopt a successor. It was a timely move: Fifteen months after he had commenced his rule, he died, and Marcus Ulpius Trajanus (53–117), governor of the province of Upper Germany, took the throne.

Trajan did not rush to Rome but remained in his province to consolidate what Domitian had begun: the upper and lower Germanic provinces and the *limes*. Meanwhile, in Rome, no one knew the new emperor's intentions. A contemporary poet begged the Rhine to return the emperor "to his people and his city."[31] But many aristocrats may have wished that in accordance with the Roman credo "to spare the subjected and to battle down the proud," he would finally cross the Rhine and conquer all of *Germanien* (including the territory east of the river).[32] No fewer than 210 years had passed since *Germanen* and Romans first faced off in the north of Italy. After the many triumphs Roman leaders had celebrated over the as-yet-*unconquered* enemy, now—maybe—there stood a competent general on the bank of the Rhine?

Said *Germanen*, however, did not know that they were living in *Germanien*. The Romans had determined the boundaries. Julius Caesar, conqueror first of Gaul, then of the Roman republic, defined the Rhine as the borderline between Gallic and Germanic tribes—between those whom he beat into compliance and those who exasperated him by their resistance. He was the first, it seems, to distinguish between these two tribal groups (many later writers would consider them one Celtic people again). The *Germanen* as one people living in *Germanien* were invented by Caesar: Intentionally ignoring Germanic settlements west of the Rhine, he defined *Germanien* as the territory to its east, calling the inhabitants *Germanen*, as if they formed a political union. But the numerous tribes, factious and discordant, could hardly share a meal unmarred by brawling (Tacitus would later pray for this Germanic contentiousness to continue, "as fate could provide no greater favor" to the Roman Empire).[33] Caesar's motivation for this geographical and ethnical realignment was political, and politics would continue to color Roman interest in northern Europe. But of the many who wrote about *Germanien*, the senator Tacitus was the only one to write a monograph.

LIKE JULIUS CAESAR but different from contemporary political usage, Tacitus marked the Rhine as *Germanien*'s western borderline (thus basically excluding the two Roman provinces). While well aware of the numerous tribes, which step forward one by one in the booklet's second part, he (again like Caesar) conceived and spoke of them as one people. Readers learn about this Germanic people—its emergence and appearance as well as mores, customs, and institutions—in the first part of the *Germania*. Nobody, Tacitus postulates, would move to their country, as it is "wild in its scenery, harsh in its climate, and grim to inhabit and behold."[34] His Mediterranean eyes found little that appealed in a land he described as "horrid because of its forests and ugly because of its marshes." But this land, Tacitus continues, brought forth from its soil the god Tuisto. This earthborn god had a son, Mannus, whom ancient Germanic songs—"their only form of history"—commemorated as the original founder of the Germanic people. (Modern linguistics has revealed that Tuisto's name contains the Germanic word *twi*, which means "two" and may reflect the god's hermaphroditic nature, whereas his son's name, Mannus, signifies "human being.")[35] Sprung from the earth itself, the autochthonous *Germanen* remained isolated from other people, Tacitus adds, because of the repulsive nature of their country. In the single most influential paragraph, quoted above in this section's epigraph, he concurs with those who believe in the indigenousness and ethnic purity of the Germanic people, attributing to it the physiognomic features Greek and Roman writers considered characteristic of northerners.

To avoid a disconnected sequence of characteristics that would resemble a shopping list, Tacitus uses a stylistic device (particularly practiced within the ancient ethnographical genre) of associative connections, which weave the texture tightly together without harsh transitions. He starts with a discussion of the Germanic territory, placing *"Germanien* in its entirety" at the very beginning of his book (the Latin language resembles LEGO blocks in that its word-bricks can be arranged in almost any order). He then moves on to "the *Germanen"* and ends their portrait, in itself stringently structured, with a reference to their climate and their soil. The following chapter begins with "land" (*terra*), which is then described and discussed with regard to its metal resources, then leading to a description of weaponry and continuing with an account of their soldiery, supplemented by a profile of their leaders. The *Germania* is an exquisitely spun narrative; its author was not a novice.

Tacitus unfolds Germanic life in some detail, in both the private and the public spheres, expanding on those human values in which he took a distinct interest: freedom, fortitude, morality, and simplicity. They could still, it seemed, be found, if not in Rome, at least in *Germanien*. The—often only implicit—antithesis between Roman life and life in *Germanien* pervades the whole of Tacitus's account. *There* they know "no ostentation of style," as evidenced by their rudimentary habitation, minimal weaponry, and merely functional utensils: They hold earthen- and metalware "in equally *low* esteem" (a typical example of Tacitean conciseness: The *Germanen* care equally little about either).[36] *There* they resist luxury and its twin vice, decadence. The sword dance is the only spectacle they know, and lush and lascivious dinner parties take place only in—Rome. Since simplicity fortifies morality, and lack of temptation prevents deviation, instances of adultery are as rare as their punishment is severe: "Their hair shorn, and stripped naked," adulterous women are thrown "out of the house in the presence of their relatives." As so often in Tacitus's work, a timely epigram concludes the description of sexual restraint: "There good habits carry more weight than good laws elsewhere." Deprived of its context, it would flutter on the banner of German humanists in their struggle to redeem their allegedly barbaric past.

Among this people "nobody laughs off vice; and to corrupt and to be corrupted is not called 'modern times.'"[37] They are neither "cunning nor shrewd," are awed by the "magnitude of celestial powers," which they worship accordingly in large open spaces, and are prepared to die for the sake of honor and loyalty. Their loyalty, which receives Tacitus's particular attention, reaches beyond the intimate circle of friends and family: Men join the following (*comitatus*) of a Germanic leader, vying for his respect and trust. The leaders, who contend with one another for power and prestige, provide for their followers, who in turn are sworn to fight until released by death. "To return from battle surviving one's leader [was considered] shameful and a disgrace for life." Almost two millennia later, members of the SS would wear this German motto engraved on their buckles: *Meine Ehre heißt Treue* ("My honor is called loyalty").

Germanic life is devoted to military valor and fortitude, and "rest is odious to this people."[38] They are warriors, "created," as the fifteenth-century humanist Giannantonio Campano would write on the basis of Tacitus's description, "by nature for warfare and military discipline." Upon entering society as an adult, the young man receives a shield and spear (the *framea*), thus learning what contributions to society are expected of him. Even the dowry, which the husband, not the wife, brings into the marriage, includes weapons (along with other items like oxen and horses); quite simply "nothing is done without weapons." As warriors they defend their freedom, inside and outside their country: not even their kings reign absolutely. Tacitus summed up his historical survey of more than two hundred years of Germano-Roman wars with characteristic sarcasm: The *Germanen* had been "the object of triumphs rather than victories." There was no question that "the Germanic desire for freedom [had] prove[d] fiercer than the Parthian monarchy" (the latter being Rome's most threatening enemy in the east).

Tacitus could not anticipate that his list of Germanic virtues would help future Germans to define their national character as simple, loyal, brave, and moral; the less so as the values that some later generations would idealize and embrace are highly ambivalent in his rendering. For the bravery with which the *Germanen* defend their freedom comes at the expense of any other cultural pursuit, and Tacitus sets off their capacity for war against farming, which the Greeks and Romans held to be a higher form of occupation. While the *Germanen*'s urge for freedom keeps Rome's disciplined legionaries at bay, it also causes bloody discord among the tribes themselves. And while the simple lifestyle fosters morality, it deprives them of literacy and more often than not descends into sheer primitiveness. Most of the values found among the *Germanen* are clearly contingent on their simple lifestyle: Men and women are brave and moral not out of choice but necessity, and in most aspects they resemble stereotypical representatives of an early period characterized by low cultural development. Tacitus's portrait of the *Germanen* casts human values in a nuanced light that reveals their tensions, interdependencies, and darker sides. Some genuinely negative traits also appear: Because of a strange contradiction in their nature, "the same people love idleness and detest peaceful quiet"; they either fight or laze.[39] If they had alcohol in sufficient supply, they would defeat themselves drinking. They gamble recklessly, betting their homes, their wives, themselves.

Later readers of Tacitus, interested in underscoring the barbaric nature of the *Germanen*, would draw on these facets only, which sympathetic readers would in turn simply ignore. Both readings are equally inadequate, for Tacitus's canvas contains many colors.

Whether readers turned to the *Germania* to condemn the Germanic barbarians or to commend them as moral warriors, Tacitus's text was widely read as a historical source on authentic Germanic life until the beginning of the twentieth century. Karl Trüdinger, who died young during World War I, had written his thesis at the University of Basel on the history of Greek and Roman ethnography. Published in 1918, it situated the *Germania* within the ancient ethnographical tradition, which provided a series of questions that ethnographers were expected to address. When Tacitus discusses the origin and "purity" of the Germanic tribes—to choose a conspicuous example—he fills in the established ethnographical table: The *Germanen* are autochthonous (as opposed to immigrants) and ethnically pure (as opposed to mixed). Trüdinger was careful to differentiate between standardized questions and answers. But Eduard Norden, a contemporary of his and the greatest scholar of Latin literature of his times, almost simultaneously published a study that demonstrated how various characteristics ascribed to the *Germanen* had "wandered" from one foreign people to another. The most famous example of such a "wandering motif," as Norden called them, is the characterization of the *Germanen* as a "people like no one but itself."[40] While many centuries later this would be seized upon as a genuine observation and used as an argument for the purity of the Aryan race, it really is just a Greek, then Roman, stereotype of many foreign people that other authors had previously attributed to the Egyptians and Scythians, to name but two. However, the prevailing sentiment inside and outside academia at the time was such that the insights gained by Trüdinger and Norden were ignored or vilified, and the *Germania* retained its status as a first-class historical source.

In comparison with other Greek and Roman accounts of foreign people—like the ones produced by the speedy general Caesar, who came, saw, and wrote digressions on the Gauls as well as the *Germanen*—the *Germania* appears as a mosaic of Greek and Roman stereotypes, arranged by a writer who most likely never went north of the Alps, and whose concern was of a moral and political rather than a scientific nature. Not an eyewitness but a reader, Tacitus for his portrait culled from many literary sources, enriched by details obtained from merchants, soldiers, and others with firsthand knowledge. This is not to say that the *Germania* is utterly useless as a historical source. But the *Germanen* who roam Tacitus's pages are in many ways typical representatives of the northern barbarian, sketched within the Greek and Roman ethnographical tradition by a writer with at least one eye toward Rome and the empire. Later celebrated as an accurate reflection of authentic German people, the *Germania* was written by a Roman in Rome for Romans. It was only later that this snapshot of a particular cultural period would be turned into the German people's own national profile.

In 98 the Romans had once again a political interest in *Germanien*. Contrary to Domitian's propaganda of his Germanic triumphs, those barbarians were still free. Did Tacitus hope that his *Germania* would help to persuade the emperor to strike blows against the *Germanen*? This seems most likely.[41] But even though his motivation was political, his interests were decidedly philosophical. He shows sympathy for their raw bravery, moral integrity, and passionate striving for freedom. But there is also sadness: Not all desirable values can be had at the same time. Sleeping on the ground makes hardy soldiers, but who would want to dispense with the comfort of a bed?

Whatever Tacitus's ultimate intention, Trajan soon turned away from the Rhine to the Danube, which he rightly considered the more troublesome frontier. The Romans never conquered Germanic territory. But where their legionnaires failed, their writers succeeded: Tacitus's *Germania* would determine the Germanic myth for centuries.

THE PATHOLOGY OF POWER

It is recorded that even Germanic women would occasionally take up arms and renew their men's battle efforts.

—Giannantonio Campano, paraphrasing the *Germania*, 1471

When, after his designation as emperor, Trajan finally returned from *Germanien* to Rome in 100 to deify his adoptive father, his comportment showed civility. The senate, relieved, cooperated and in due course reciprocated. It dedicated a column in his honor, once he had completed two major campaigns in Dacia (a territory that included the Danube, the plateau of Transylvania, the Vistula, and the eastern shore of the Black Sea), thus taking the Roman Empire beyond the Danube toward its greatest expansion (reached soon after, when it also included the province of Arabia). The column—a marble narrative of Trajan's military achievements, which can still be seen north of the Forum Romanum near the Piazza Venezia—would also serve as his tomb upon his death. Burial inside Rome was an exceptional honor, in Trajan's case merited not only by foreign but also by domestic accomplishments. He introduced government officials (*curatores*) who controlled the finances inside and outside Rome, like Pliny, Tacitus's good-humored correspondent, who served in the province of Bithynia (central-northern Turkey) and communicated his problems, questions, and suggestions to the emperor's chancellery. When faced with the Christian sect, Pliny asked for advice and received a comparatively moderate directive: to insist on legal proceedings and to desist from harassment.[42]

Circumspection also characterized the emperor's use of Dacian booty: It financed improvements of the infrastructure throughout the empire; and in Rome, the largest of the imperial public places, the Forum Trajanum, surrounding the Basilica Ulpia, rose to magnificence. As with previous emperors, architecture propagated greatness. But in his building projects as much as in his administration Trajan showed a genuine concern for the people. Most symbolic was the construction of public baths on the grounds of Nero's "Golden Villa," which, torn down, supplied some of the material for them. Once again the emperor presented himself as a public servant. His many achievements did not go unnoticed, as he was soon unofficially and then officially praised as *optimus*, "the best."[43]

A natural death is an emperor's ultimate honor. Trajan died on his sickbed in 117 after almost twenty years in power. Unlike Domitian, he had been an affable autocrat. Just before he died— and with some intriguing qualms—he adopted Publius Aelius Hadrianus (76–138), in whose able hands the Roman Empire would continue to enjoy peace and prosperity. Even in his final act Trajan had done well. Later Roman generations could only hope that their emperors' prayers to be "luckier than Augustus" (who felicitously had overseen the metamorphosis of the Roman republic into the rule of the first man: the *principate*) and "better than Trajan" would be heard.[44] Tacitus himself in the preface of his *Agricola* explicitly includes the *optimus princeps* in his expression of gratitude for the happiest age. It seems strange, then, that he decided not to write about this happy reign.

TACITUS'S PUBLIC SERVICE continued under the new regime. Pliny relates two oratorical performances of his: as a eulogist at a funeral in 97, and as a prosecutor in 100. Little is known about the following years. But it seems likely that he remained politically active, since he became governor of the province of Asia in

112–13, as revealed by the above-mentioned inscription at Mylasa. The provinces of Africa and Asia were the most prestigious ones, and Tacitus must have been sufficiently prominent and involved to be chosen. Other details of his last two to three decades, including his date of death, cannot be ascertained. But one fact is certain: During those years he painstakingly labored over his major historical works. He emerged from Domitian's troubled reign to become Rome's supreme historian, outstanding for his creative style, vivid depictions of tyrannical regimes, and reflections on the secrecies of rule (*arcana imperii*). A few years after the *Agricola* and the *Germania*, he composed the third of his minor works (or "historical attempts," as they are also called), another contemplation of freedom: the *Dialogue on Oratory*. Seemingly discussing the decline of oratory, it uses its topic as a lens to focus on freedom of speech—its conditions, consequences, and political ramifications. His major works would then depict a world in which such freedom was replaced by selective silence paired with adulterated eloquence.

The *Histories*, which span from the long year of short rules (69) to Domitian's death (96), are "rich in calamities, savage in its battles, torn by civil strife, and violent even in peace," as its preface warns the reader (translators often find themselves at a loss when challenged by Tacitus's dense style; here the characterization gradually slips from the work to the times).[45] Rome had lost its traditional virtues. Appealing to a long-gone sense of duty, Galba, the first of the four emperors in 69, declared: "I choose my soldiers, I don't buy them"; soon after, he paid for this attitude with his life. Tacitus reports pithily "that he was a capable leader, as all agreed, if he had not led." The occasional act of decency and glimpse of brighter times notwithstanding, the *Histories*, completed toward the end of the second century's first decade, show that "the gods do not care about our carefree safety, but our punishment." One can only imagine what Tacitus's portrait under the reign of Domitian might have looked like; unfortunately, of the (probably) twelve books that covered twenty-eight years, only the first four and the opening of the fifth have survived to the present (in the form of a manuscript of the eleventh century, which is called the Second Medicean, named after the library of Lorenzo de' Medici, to which it belonged). They account for less than two years. *Habent sua fata libelli*: Books have their fate too.

The *Annals*, the second major work and for many people Tacitus's crowning achievement, continue the analysis of the political system that elevated one to absolute power, leaving justice to chance and circumstances. Contrary to what he had indicated earlier, Tacitus did not write about his own times under the good emperors Nerva and Trajan. Instead he went farther back, embarking on an archaeology of tyranny. He started with the death of Augustus (in 14), who—though seemingly only "the first among equals"—had commenced the rule of the first man; and he ended with the death of Nero, the last of the Julio-Claudian dynasty, whence the (earlier written) *Histories* continued. Maybe Tacitus's interest in the "relation and causes" of historical events led him deeper into the past and the secrecies of power and human frailty;[46] or maybe he found it safer not to write about these "happy times," except in allusions inserted into his portraits of tyrants now long dead? In any case the *Annals* are primarily a study of one-man rule, its deleterious impact on those to whom "the gods gave supreme judgment over affairs," and those to whom "only the glory of obsequiousness was left." They paint vivid portraits of the sour Tiberius, the maladroit Claudius, and the histrionic Nero. Roman rulers are benign before they rule, and the pretense of morality is the best to be hoped for. But neither Tiberius nor Nero, who "defiled by acts both permitted and proscribed [and] omitted no outrage," maintained their initial effort. Under such circumstances freedom could be found only in inner emigration or outside the empire, for example, among the *Germanen*.

Rome, on the other hand, resembled "a funereal community," run by sycophants, ruled by the emperor.[47] Tiberius's mother is warned by an expert in political machinations that "secrecies of the imperial family, confidants' advice, and soldiers' services should not be made public; and Tiberius should not dissolve the power of the *principate* by referring everything to the senate. To rule implied that the account could be balanced only if rendered to one." In his *Annals* Tacitus provides his readers with a long and damning copy of that balance sheet; but of the eighteen books in total (whether and when they were finished is uncertain), only books 1–6 and 11–16 have come down to us (thanks to two manuscripts from the ninth and eleventh centuries). Of the reign of Caligula, the mad emperor who held his horse Incitatus in such respect that he considered appointing it consul, not a single sheet is left.

Tacitus is "the greatest possible enemy to tyrants," as John Milton called him.[48] He is also a white-gloved character assassin who has no blood on his hands. His weapon of choice is innuendo. He reports rumors: Concerning the death of Augustus, "*some* suspected crime on the part of his wife."[49] He offers damaging alternatives: The emperor and his mother did not partake in their relative's funerary ceremony, "deeming it would belittle their sovereignty to lament openly—or lest, with everyone's eyes examining their demeanor, their falsity be understood." He can master insinuation by mere juxtaposition: Nero's orgies are lit by the fire of torches; next we hear about the fire in Rome—but of course "whether accidentally or by the emperor's ploy was uncertain." With such insinuations, who needs incriminations?

His revelatory character portrayals, political analyses, and sour moralism have fascinated readers for almost two millennia, his effect on the political discourse of the late sixteenth and seventeenth centuries being such that the period is referred to as the era of "Tacitism." Undoubtedly much of his impact is owed to his razor-sharp style, with which he dissects the ailing Roman body politic. Sparkling and serrated, it has stimulated writers as late as the twentieth century, including its greatest Tacitean: Sir Ronald

Syme. The twentieth-century historian may have had himself and his debt to the Roman historian in mind when he wrote: "Men and dynasties pass, but style abides."[50]

This highly original style is disconcerting: It is characterized by brevity bordering on obscurity, swift-footed ironies that do not wait for the slow, syntactical asymmetries, and bottomless ambiguities. The conciseness often leaves the reader breathless and frequently concentrates content in unforgettable one-liners: "he chose to be accused of a crime *perpetrated* rather than *commenced*."[51] He avoids smoothness and parallel constructions, shuns common words, and disappoints readers' expectations at every turn of the page. Nero embarked on "the long-meditated crime," because Poppaea, his mistress and later wife, spurred him on by "regular rebukes and sometimes by way of jests." Tacitus could have written "with regular rebukes and occasional jests." But the symmetry is avoided, and readers are kept on their toes. Equally asymmetric is his presentation of facts, the most complex and important of which are often presented as a mere appendix. He is a difficult writer, who leads readers to discover that they were misled, and undermines what is stated by what he suggests. But it may serve as a small sign of the force of his style that the modern phrase "conspicuous by its absence" is originally Tacitean.[52]

BECAUSE OF the poetic power of his language, Tacitus has been called one of the few great poets of the Roman people; he is also undoubtedly one of their greatest satirists. He casts a cold eye on human foibles and feebleness, standing in men's midst, yet at a distance. He comments wittily, in a sad voice suffused with anger. And yet he cannot help but cling to an unfaltering belief in human dignity beyond the daily fray. One may briefly wonder what he would have made of the use to which his *Germania* was put centuries after his death.

2

Survival and Rescue

Where is Tacitus?
—Coluccio Salutati, 1392

S ILENCE IS almost all we hear of Tacitus for much of late antiquity and the Middle Ages. Then, toward the end of 1425, a year otherwise conspicuous for its lack of conspicuousness, Poggio Bracciolini (1380–1459) in Rome sat down to compose with "a hasty hand" one of his many letters to his lifelong friend Niccolò Niccoli in Florence. Secretary by profession, humanist by passion, Poggio reeled off letters that detail his life in general and his hunts for manuscripts in particular. This time he had grand news. As a skilled writer, he knew to withhold this tidbit for last for his correspondent, another bibliomaniac:

> That's all—almost. I've kept the honey until the end. A certain
> monk, a friend of mine, from some monastery in Germany, sent
> me a letter in which he writes that he's found a few volumes of the
> kind we're interested in. Among these volumes there's Julius Fron-
> tinus and works of Cornelius Tacitus heretofore unknown to us.[1]

Almost fifteen hundred years after it had been composed, the *Germania* would be read—again; and after centuries of silence Tacitus would speak—again. But his survival had been perilous. Through the vagaries of time he reached the safety of the fifteenth century with only one single manuscript of his minor works remaining. If by fire burned, sunlight bleached, or rain weltered, his most dangerous book would certainly not have been the object of Heinrich Himmler's desire five hundred years farther on.

A QUIET PASSAGE

The Saxons most carefully guarded their race and nobility and did not taint themselves casually by intermarriage with any other tribes, let alone inferior ones; they tried to generate a distinct, unadulterated people that resembles only itself.
—Rudolf of Fulda, ca. 865

Posterity is lavish with oblivion. It seems miraculous that a text like the *Germania*, written two thousand years ago, can be read to this day. Its transmission from one century to another in the form of handwritten apographs began with early copies produced in Tacitus's own time. Even though we do not know the specifics, we can reconstruct the likely dissemination.

After finishing the *Germania*, Tacitus probably sent it to a friend, possibly his voluble correspondent Pliny the Younger, with whom he was in the habit of exchanging work. This first reader held in his hands a roll made of papyrus; on its inner side one of Tacitus's slaves would have reproduced the original with a reed or bronze stylus, inked in one of several recipes (the Romans used ingredients ranging from carbon soot to cuttlefish ink). "I read your book [probably part of Tacitus's *Histories*]," Pliny writes in one billet, "and with as much diligence as I command commented on what I believe should be changed and what should go."[2] With such guidance Tacitus revised his *Germania*, which would then be copied and sent out again to a wider circle of friends, once more soliciting comments. It is likely that he also gathered his *amici*—friends, senators, and some of his clients—for a reading, discussion, and last review.

With these last changes incorporated, the book would have its final release: more copies would be distributed to a greater number of acquaintances, in widening circles like those caused by a skipping stone. In its wake Tacitus's text reached private and public libraries like the magnificent Ulpian library, which after its completion as part of Trajan's forum in around 110 was the greatest of the four major libraries in Rome. The *Germania* might also have been available in bookstores, which clustered near the city center and sported excerpts pinned on posts for passersby, whereas the actual book rolls, prone to wear and tear, were safely kept inside. Individual copies had to be written by hand—probably in the *capitalis* script, capital upright letters combining thin lines with broad strokes and juxtaposed rather than strung along—and no two were likely to contain the same errors. On the whole the scant evidence suggests that books were not a pricey commodity, and bookstores existed even in towns the size of Lyon. Perhaps Tacitus negotiated with a bookseller just as Pliny the Younger relates he himself had done in one of his letters. Whatever the actual details, the *Germania* must have circulated soon after its composition, as traces of it can be spotted in other written work.[3]

IT IS A COMMONPLACE: Literary accomplishment grants immortality, and the Fates are forced to spin the author's thread of life beyond death—grudgingly, it must be said, in Tacitus's case. Pliny the Younger, with enthusiasm energized by similar hopes for himself, had predicted "that your [Tacitus's] *Histories* will be immortal,"[4] and with the work its writer. But Tacitus survived in tatters. Passing through the centuries, his texts suffered major losses and to all appearances resurfaced in the Renaissance each in one manuscript only. The copying of manuscripts guaranteed a text's transmission: No autographs of Roman authors survive, and very few manuscripts as old as the fourth century are still extant. Whatever was not transcribed by a slave's or (later) monk's slanted hand would be lost to oblivion, and the author's thread would finally snap. Tacitus is a difficult author. His work was not included in the canon of school authors, and was therefore not frequently replicated. A doubtful source relates that Marcus Claudius Tacitus, a short-lived emperor of the slowly disintegrating Roman Empire (275–76), ordered the reproduction and distribution of Tacitus's works. Claiming, falsely, descent from his namesake, he expressed his fear that the author "might perish from readers' negligence."[5] True or not, such fear would seem fitting; perhaps only one and a half centuries after his death, the Roman historian's permanence was already insecure. And it might have been in the context of this brief spell of imperial attention that his works, like other texts deemed worthy of preservation, were transferred from papyrus rolls to codices of parchment (in form resembling modern books). During this period, from the third to the fourth century, the minor works were—literally—bound together.[6]

Then followed years of darkness or, insofar as reading and transcribing manuscripts guaranteed the author's voice to be heard, silence. Generally the transmission of individual works through the centuries are variations of the same form, often compared to an hourglass: Manuscripts of an author's work like Virgil's *Aeneid* or Ovid's *Metamorphoses* circulated fairly widely and in good frequency in the late Roman Empire. Until the middle of the sixth century, amanuenses continued to produce new apographs, thus filling the hourglass's upper bulb. But from 550 to 750, the so-called Dark Ages that form the hourglass's neck, reproduction of secular texts came almost to a standstill. Take the case of Rome's national poet Virgil, who is exceptional in that manuscripts (or leaves thereof) exist that predate this period: six from the fourth century (the marvelous illuminated *Vergilius Vaticanus* being one); five from the fifth, and three from around 500. But then more than 250 years pass before, under the aegis of Charlemagne (747–814), Carolingian scholars and scribes resumed reproduction in the second half of the eighth century. Their searches for dust-clad parchments of all-but-forgotten texts lifted classical authors from neglect, as happened to Tacitus and his *Germania*. Many, however, were less fortunate.

THE POLITICAL LANDSCAPE of continental Europe underwent tectonic shifts during the eighth century. Once Charlemagne had commenced his reign in 768, he continued his grandfather and father's expansion of Frankish rule; his lands would soon reach from the Spanish March south of the Pyrenees to the English Channel and from the region of the Saxons west of the river Elbe to north-central Italy, the kingdom of the Lombards. From his capital, Aachen, where today Germany abuts the Netherlands and Belgium, Charlemagne ruled over a European empire evocative of its Roman predecessor, with which he was officially associated when in 800 he was crowned emperor by Pope Leo III. Coins soon celebrated him in the abbreviated legend as KAROLVS IMP(erator) AVG(ustus). Like Augustus, the first Roman emperor, Charlemagne also presided over a blossoming of literary culture, which—like his dynasty—took its name from his grandfather's: the "Carolingian renaissance."

Across Charlemagne's empire various languages could be heard. The regions west and south of the Rhineland on the whole conversed in a crude and late version of Latin steadily morphing into the Romance languages. In the lands east of the Rhine, Latin served in office, but Germanic dialects were spoken at home. One dialect—a form of Frankish—was spoken by the versatile emperor himself, who was, however, also conversant in Latin. Charlemagne took a personal interest in the promotion of Latin and learning, which went beyond what biblical exegesis and the administration of the empire required. He had his children taught in the liberal arts, knew how to read, and late in life tried his hand at writing—though to little avail, according to his biographer Einhard.

Bad emperors fear those cleverer than themselves; good ones use them. Charlemagne surrounded himself with men of letters recruited for their talents from all corners of his empire and brought to the palace school in Aachen, which for a short time came to resemble an Alexandrian sanctuary of learning. Among those scholars the pious and erudite poet Alcuin (735–804), originally from York in Northumbria, played a leading role as the emperor's key adviser in intellectual and educational matters. New schools were founded and the curriculum standardized: "Let schools for teaching boys the psalms, musical notation, singing, computation and grammar be created in every monastery and Episcopal residence . . . and if there is need to copy the gospel, psalter or missal, let men of full age do the writing, with all diligence."[7] Rare and neglected manuscripts were brought forward. Copyists sitting in scriptoria transcribed them in a new font, the Caroline minuscule: Simple and neat, its rotund letters easily distinguishable, the words separated by even spaces, the font disseminated from Alcuin's school in Aachen throughout the empire. It was this period, this first wave of rediscoveries, that carried most extant classical texts to the shores of posterity. What Carolingian scholars rediscovered and reproduced was most likely to survive until today—often after another rediscovery in the fifteenth century, as in Tacitus's case.

One of those monasteries requested to spread literacy and learning had been founded in Fulda, in what is now the central German state of Hesse. Around 795 Baugulf, Fulda's second abbot, received the imperial missive sent out by Charlemagne to all his monasteries concerning "the cultivation of letters." Therein the emperor recommended that the suitably talented also study letters, "so that those who strive to please God by living correctly do not neglect to please him also by speaking correctly." Promoting grammar as an act of piety, he admonished his subjects to undertake these grammatical studies "so that the mysteries of the holy scripture be more easily and correctly grasped."[8] It is near Fulda, which Charlemagne personally visited, that the only extant codex of the *Germania* would be rediscovered in the fifteenth century; and it is at Fulda that the most extensive use of the *Germania* before the age of humanism appears.

THE IMMORTALITY of one is often bought by the anonymity of many. Rudolf of Fulda here represents the long line of mostly nameless monkish scribes to whose candlelit transcriptions the preservation of classical texts is owed. Illustrations show them bent over their sloping desks, skillfully wielding their quills—and, it may be added, sometimes compensating with calligraphic diligence what they lacked in linguistic competence. Their feel for Latin varied considerably over the centuries and across the regions, as is often revealed in their marginal explanations—glosses—some in Latin, others in a vernacular. Rudolf, devout and devoted, had studied with the learned Rabanus Maurus, himself a student of Alcuin's and later, from 822 to 842, the fifth abbot of Fulda.

In Fulda, Rudolf worked with his teacher toward the transformation of the monastery into a center of learning and a transmitter of classical culture. Within the walls of the library and the school, the scratching of parchments could increasingly be heard. Rabanus and Rudolf tirelessly searched for classical curios and directed a scriptorium in which scribes produced beautiful copies in the Anglo-Saxon script, imported from Ireland and Great Britain. The style was characterized by the letters' gradual diminution from the left to the right of each line; it soon gave way, however, to the Caroline minuscule. Rabanus and Rudolf's endeavors met with success. Before long they oversaw a collection of two thousand manuscripts. For centuries the monastery would be a library of great standing. It also counted an extremely rare copy of Tacitus's *Germania* among its precious items.[9]

Rudolf, who was also a writer (most notably of hagiographic works), in 863 upon request agreed to compose an account of the transfer of the relics of the martyr Alexander from Rome to Wildeshausen (in Saxony) in 851. These relics were buried in a newly founded church to lay to rest lingering pagan beliefs (the Saxons had resisted Charlemagne's power and Christianization for almost thirty years). Rudolf began his narrative by going back to the Saxons' heathen past: "The Saxon people, as ancient times record, emerged from among the English inhabitants of Britain, sailed across the ocean, and were driven to the German shores in their vital effort to find shelter." Using this historical perspective, he wishes his "prudent reader" to see the heathen Saxons in some detail so as to make him "realize from how great a darkness of errors they were freed by the mercy and grace of God."[10] Close inspection reveals that these bygone heathens are dressed in Tacitean garb. Rudolf had lifted three chapters from the *Germania*, with changes mostly consisting of turning Tacitus's present tense into the priest's past tense. In Rudolf's narrative the Saxons no sooner arrived than they established themselves apart from others, trying to turn themselves into "a people that resemble[d] no one but itself." Tacitus, whose chapter 4 will be very influential, is here adapted for the first time, even though the Saxons are presented as immigrants (not indigenous as Tacitus's *Germanen* are).

Rudolf borrowed more material from Tacitus. The Saxons, like Tacitus's *Germanen*, lived a simple, moral, and honest life. They would have found true happiness "if they had not been in ignorance of their creator." Rudolf adds how they venerated "Mercury foremost among the gods," and "on certain days even with human sacrifices." Tacitus's (partly) noble *barbarians* have become Rudolf's noble *pagans*. Times change, and texts with them.

The monastery in Fulda is the scene of another major development, for which Tacitus also seems to have been crucial. Until the ninth century, the Latin *theodiscus* was used as the proper name for

Germans. Linguists have shown how it is related to the Germanic word *theudo*, which means "the people." Since the Latin is rooted in a vernacular word, the usage seems quite natural. But then, in the *Annals of Fulda* in 876, *Teutonicus* appears. Although it has no connection to the German language, it replaced its predecessor and became the standard Latin term for "German" until humanists replaced it with *Germanus*. Why a foreign term should successfully replace a well-established one baffled scholars. But it seems as if the reception of Tacitus, who writes about the German tribe of the "Teutones," led to a usage of the term in reference to all the German tribes.[11]

Rudolf, however, does not mention a single German people and apparently has no notion of them as a cohesive ethnic group. He speaks of the Saxons simply as one of those tribes living in German territory. His adaptation of the *Germania* was limited to the Saxon tribe and therefore stands in marked contrast to those that would appear in the fifteenth century, when the *Germania* would serve to define the common German ancestor. This may be one reason why Rudolf's call upon Tacitus receded without resonance; his adaptation seems to be the only one in all the Middle Ages. For the *Germania* to develop its singular impact, different circumstances would be required. And so Tacitus's text would once more float on the sea of time, buoyed above the bottom of oblivion, eventually to be snatched up by the humanists' hands.

THE INTANGIBLE FIND

> Cornelius Tacitus is still silent in the Germans' midst.
> —Poggio Bracciolini, 1428

After Rudolf's stealthy borrowing, Tacitus grew quiet again; not quite silent, however, as passages from the *Germania* are quoted in works written during subsequent centuries. Some Tacitean quotations suggest that in the twelfth century there existed a copy of the minor works at the Abbey of Monte Cassino, which housed one of the finest medieval libraries and a busy scriptorium about eighty miles south of Rome. If there was, it was lost to neglect; not so the copy Rudolf had used at Fulda.

The Carolingian scribes had long been dead when, half a millennium later, Latin authors would once more be in need of rescue. One of them was Quintilian, Tacitus's contemporary and the author of the most comprehensive Roman handbook on rhetoric:

> There is no question that this glorious man [Quintilian], so elegant, so pure, so full of morals and of wit, could not much longer have endured the filth of that prison, the squalor of the place, and the savage cruelty of his keepers. He was sad and dressed in mourning, as people are when doomed to death; his beard was dirty and his hair caked with mud, so that by his expression and appearance it was clear that he had been summoned to an undeserved punishment. He seemed to stretch out his hands and beg for the loyalty of the Roman people, to demand that he be saved from an unjust sentence.[12]

Quintilian's appeal—vividly rendered in a letter by Poggio Bracciolini dating from 1416—did not fall on deaf ears. Like Poggio, many Italian humanists traveled far and wide in their hunt for manuscripts, rummaging through northern European monasteries, to find, free, and copy maltreated Roman classics. One of them was Tacitus. Later in the second half of the quattrocento, he could be seen in Italy, clean-shaven and in proper attire, as his minor works, the *Germania* among them, were copied and circulated among eager humanists. Having survived imprisonment, he escaped, albeit narrowly, perishing.

The humanistic community heard of Tacitus's minor works in the early 1420s. A southern breeze carried rumors to Poggio in

London, where the unhappy Italian froze in the service of Cardinal Beaufort. Far from his Mediterranean home in order to earn a living, he depended on letters from fellow humanists for news and comfort. One of them let him know that the archbishop of Milan, Bartolomeo Francisci de la Capra, was believed to have found unknown writings by Roman historians. Poggio was not quick to acknowledge somebody else's success, and his expressions of excitement are undercut by skepticism. Who could believe, he wrote on June 10, 1422, that a man like the bishop, so ambitious in nature, would rely on the whispers of rumor to spread his discovery? He would have shouted it out loud! And how come a man in his position, "bolstered by the emperor's patronage" and dealing with "barbaric donkeys," did not obtain those books with ease, if only to have them copied? Even he, Poggio, when traveling in Germany, always had a copyist at hand. He concludes that far from having made an actual discovery, the bishop had spread "hearsay as facts."[13] Poggio would not believe it unless he saw it. But a few years later, more than just believing in the unseen, he would chase it.

THE STYLE IS SAID to be the man. Readers of Poggio's letters will recognize the writer from illustrations. On them he stands slightly pudgy, clean-shaven and in scholarly attire, and with a spark of interest in his eyes and an ironic grin stretching the corners of his mouth. He has a furrow of determination on his forehead, an eyebrow slightly raised, perhaps in surprise. His familial background certainly had not predestined him for a scholarly career, and his work would reveal the discipline and dedication inspired by his adolescent days of dearth. When, in 1416, he retrieved from under the dusty layers of centuries Quintilian's above-mentioned work, consisting of twelve books on "the training of an orator," he copied it in a sweep of fifty-four days. Tenacity, talent, and training made him a leading humanist and manuscript hunter, whose activities are amply documented in his collected letters.

FLOREN·T· ·IOAN·
FRANCISC·
POGGIVS·

Felle armata tibi manus est ; multog̃ cachinno
Tinxisti et nudo scripta proterva sale.

4. Woodcut of Poggio
Bracciolini (1380–1459).
*Houghton Library, Harvard
University, Typ 520 97.225.*

In fifteenth-century Italy *umanista* signified a student and, in turn, teacher of classical culture. The term, derived from Cicero's notion of *humanitas*, originally applied to a person versed in the "liberal arts" (the *studia humanitatis*). But beginning with Francesco Petrarca (1304–74), who, disdaining the Middle Ages, fervently sought out classical writers like Rome's greatest speaker, Cicero, a humanist came to be known as one with a lively, almost existential interest in classical culture, especially Roman and to a lesser extent Greek.[14] Petrarch's efforts focused on the rediscovery and restoration of classical literature. Bent over a manuscript or—better still—a grouping of several manuscripts of the same work, he would try to establish the original text and its meaning—the classical author's *ipsissima verba*—exposed, as they had been, to the risk of corruption during centuries of copying. The extant manuscripts of the *Germania*, to give an example, offer both *barditum* and *baritum* in the later enormously influential passage where Tacitus writes about Germanic battle songs: Which variant is the right one? Beyond these scholarly endeavors, humanists aspired to compose works that could compare to the classics. A particularly popular genre was epistolography, the artful writing of seemingly artless letters, like the ones by Poggio's careful "hasty hand." For humanists, correspondence did not simply substitute for conversation. Written with at least one eye on as-yet-unborn readers, diligently copied, collected, and mourned when lost, such letters allowed their writers "to speak to posterity in [their] lifetime."[15]

Poggio's lifetime was characterized by boundless bibliomania. The passion for classical texts kindled humanists' desire for rediscoveries, sometimes improperly pursued. The sole surviving manuscript of the opening books of Tacitus's *Annals* was stolen from the monastery of Corvey in North Rhine–Westphalia and then acquired for a small fortune by Pope Leo X. (Instead of returning the original, known as the First Medicean, the pope—stifling his feelings of penitence—sent the angered monks an embellished print along with a papal indulgence.) Among those occasionally ruthless literary scouts, Poggio ranked prominently, as his contemporaries acknowledged. Untroubled by morals, he would focus on the task at hand: When he found a quinternion (a gathering of five sheets folded in the middle) containing unknown Latin epigraphs, he slipped it up his sleeve. His industry was rewarded more than once: After scavenging another time in libraries in the German lands, dark and derelict places to Italian eyes, he related, excited and proud: "I want you to know that by my diligent efforts I have found many remains of the great men of the past. For twice now I have traveled through Germany alone. Very recently I have had a triumph: I have found seven orations of M. Tullius, which had been lost before."[16] His finds delighted some, disgruntled others. Fellow humanists greeted one another's discoveries with words of enthusiasm and envious thoughts. But no one underestimated their significance, and Poggio received his share of appreciation: "Your deeds will not be passed over in silence or be wiped from memory, but the story will persist that what was regarded as gone beyond recall was recovered through your industry and restored to us."[17]

AFTER HIS RETURN from London, Poggio held the office of apostolic secretary in Rome. He handled the pope's correspondence, briefed him on curial issues, and drew up decisions. In the summer of 1425 a German monk approached him in this official capacity. The monk must have suspected that he could help the cause of his monastery by offering rare texts from its library to a known bibliophile. When he, properly instructed, returned home to his monastery, he compiled an inventory of the works he had been able to unearth in its library, among them those "of Cornelius Tacitus heretofore unknown."[18] When Poggio read his emissary's report around the end of October, he might have remembered the rumors about the previous discovery by the bishop of Milan, which he had disdained. If so, he omitted mention of it in the letter he sent on November 3 to the Florentine Niccolò Niccoli (1364–1437), his friend, patron, and fellow enthusiast. In his account of the events of the summer he does not provide the names of the monk or the monastery. Such lack of detail might express lack of trust; and Niccoli, provoked by this reticence, would complain in due course. For now all Poggio disclosed was that the anonymous German was prepared to part with these texts in exchange for others, which were to be procured by Niccoli. Poggio included in his missive the inventory the monk had written and urged Niccoli to reply speedily, adding that the sooner he received a response, the sooner he could obtain the coveted texts. Nobody, except perhaps the monk, could foresee that such haste would not be necessary.

The patina of secrecy that coats the letter—a *certain* monk from a *certain* monastery—was scraped off five hundred years after the letter's composition. Though Poggio only mentions the clergy-man's cloister as Hersfeld (located in the center of Germany among verdant hills), other documents reveal that Heinrich von Greben-stein was the mysterious man.[19] His abbot repeatedly sent him on ambassadorial tasks to Rome from 1422 to 1429 in order to settle disagreements between the monastery and the local municipalities. Behind the screen of official errands he pursued his second agenda. For both missions he dealt with Poggio. Heinrich emerges from his letters, which ramble in a curious mixture of a Rhine dialect and Latin, as a devout and slyly naive representative of his abbot's inter-ests. In his efforts he claims to be impeded by financial obstacles, which may indicate that he intended to auction off the manuscripts to the highest bidder to increase his income (or the funds of the monastery). While tempting Poggio, he seems also to have been offering his humanistic commodities to others.

On June 26, 1426, a few weeks after the correspondence between Poggio and Niccoli, Guarino of Verona (1374–1460) wrote to a cor-respondent in Bologna: "What about this news of men reborn and brought forward into the light of day that you send me with won-derful amiability? O, if I could see Cornelius Tacitus himself, the friend, fellow, and colleague of my Pliny, and talk to him in per-son!"[20] And with a quiver of excitement he, a well-respected teacher and translator of Greek, added an appeal for further informa-tion. It came forth from Panormita (1394–1471), whose sobriquet (referring to Palermo, his Sicilian place of birth) served instead of his family name, and who had recently come to both fame and infamy. The cause célèbre was the publication of his *Hermaphro-ditus*, a collection of explicit erotic epigrams, one of which advises "women and chaste virgins" to turn and flee. The formal elegance attracted, while the obscenity repelled. Topics "so indecent and improper" were presented "so gracefully and orderly," in the words of Poggio, who, revealing conflicting interests—here morals, there aesthetics—hastens to voice his concerns for the author's soul.[21]

For unknown reasons, this naughty darling of the Muses knew to report that "Cornelius Tacitus on the origin and location of the Germans has been found."[22] In his response to Guarino's request he also listed the other texts on offer: Tacitus's *Agricola* and *Dialogus*, and fragments by the Roman biographer Suetonius among them. This is the earliest comprehensive account of the Hersfeld codex, named after its alleged place of origin, to have survived (it may be based on Heinrich's own inventory). But much history passes in twilight, and there are weighty reasons to assume that this codex actually came from neighboring Fulda—where, as we know, the *Germania* was used in the ninth century, and a great library held copies of numerous classical authors. Hersfeld, on the other hand, had neither such a library nor, as far as we can tell, a copy of the *Germania*. But Hersfeld's abbot was the brother of Fulda's curator, and Heinrich von Grebenstein might have offered the manuscript as if it belonged to his monastery, trusting that it could be obtained from Fulda should the necessity arise.

Panormita expressed his confidence to Guarino: "These and innumerable others, that are already circulating, and furthermore others (maybe) that are not in currency, are all together in one place. . . . They will be sent to a close confidant of mine any day now, and from him to me next and speedily; you will be next in line to hold these truly illustrious men reborn in your hands." But nothing was to come of it. Where he obtained this information we can only speculate. It might have come from the monk himself, the auctioneer, or possibly from Poggio, the interested buyer. Heinrich complained about his finances not only to his abbot but also to Poggio, and was known to discuss his precious pieces with other humanists. Then again, it seems less likely that Panormita had received this information from Poggio. For why would he, so eager for glory, be so forthcoming with a potential rival, when he was so secretive in his communications with his friend Niccoli?

Poggio continued his policy of secrecy in his correspondence.

Nine months passed; nothing, apparently, transpired. All Niccoli in Florence heard was that letters had been sent from Rome and in due time received by the man in Hersfeld. Niccoli must have suspected that it said a great deal that so little was said. Poggio's secrecy wore him out, and his threadbare patience turned into irritation by September 1426. Poggio, impervious in his response, parried with mockery:

> As for the German books I will say no more; just this: I am not asleep—that's your habit—but vigilant. And if that certain someone [*quidam*] keeps his promise, as I hope he will, the book will get here, either by force or consensus. I even have made an effort to obtain an inventory of this very old monastery in Germany, where a great number of books are kept. But you will learn no more lest you annoy me with your sarcasm.

Niccoli's sarcasm, apparently, had stung; Poggio stung in turn with a tease: "*You* will learn no more." Unfortunately, neither do we, as a consequence.[23]

More months of silence followed. The next episode unfolded in the late spring of 1427. Niccoli somehow learned that his friend in Rome had entertained a clandestine visitor. Disappointment and distrust must have filled his quill, as can be surmised from Poggio's response in May:

> I had, as you write, mentioned to our Cosmus that this monk from Hersfeld had said to somebody else that he had, just as I had written to him, brought an inventory of further books according to my note. Later upon my diligent search for that man he came to me, bringing his inventory—with many words but without substance. He is a good fellow, but unacquainted with our studies, and mistaking whatever he finds unknown to himself as equally unknown to us. And so his list bulges with books we

already have. . . . But I will send you the part of his inventory which contains that volume of Cornelius Tacitus as well as others that we are missing. . . . From greatest hopes conceived from his words I have fallen. That was also the reason why I did not bother so much as to write to you. For if something noteworthy had occurred, or something deserving of Minerva, I would not only have written to you but flown to notify you. Now this monk is in need of money.

Poggio added that he had offered to help, but only upon receipt of the coveted manuscripts, and that negotiations were in progress. He followed up with a more personal defensive note:

I am surprised by what you write, that you suspect I am hiding works listed in the inventory lest they become public. How did that idea get into your head? Haven't you known me "ever since my fingernails were tender"? Would I wish anything concealed from you who have always shared not only all of my deeds but also my thoughts? Don't you know that it is the companion who makes the possession of something good pleasant? Far be it from me to wish anything not to be a common possession that was written for all.[24]

Emphatic words, garnished with a learned quotation from a Ciceronian letter.

More time passed in the medley of mishaps. Niccoli continued to wait to hear what his friend had arranged and perhaps accomplished, his impatience growing. Finally, at the end of September, he once again asked—only to learn: "About Cornelius Tacitus who is in Germany I know nothing; I expect a response from that monk." The new year, 1428, revived old expectations, which were again thwarted that fall. And so, three years after the initial excitement about "works of Cornelius Tacitus heretofore unknown to us," Poggio could write no more than that "Cornelius Tacitus is still silent [*silet*] in the Germans' midst. And I have no bit of news about his works from that quarter."[25] Though disappointed, Poggio could not help but play with words: the tacit Tacitus. His addressee surely appreciated the pun, if not its point.

NEWS OF SORTS reached Florence in the spring of 1429, the fourth year of Poggio's quest:

> The monk from Hersfeld came—without the book. I gave him a serious talking-to for it. He promised to return with speed— he is, you must know, currently litigating on behalf of his monastery—and to bring along the book. He has asked me for various favors. I said that I would do nothing unless we received the book. And so I hope that we will [soon] be in possession of that one too; for he needs my help.[26]

Harried rather than hurried, as it turned out, the monk would fail to deliver once more. The *Germania* remained out of Poggio's reach. This is the last time the monk and his elusive manuscript are mentioned in his correspondence. Poggio's patience finally wore out. So much ado for nothing. However, his secrecy, lack of enthusiasm, and untimely resignation led some scholars to suspect that Poggio had actually obtained the manuscript and then kept it hidden. Scholarly casuistry supplied the motives. But a letter by Poggio's son, Jacopo, provides evidence that his father had in fact not obtained the *Germania*. Exit Poggio.

Niccolò Niccoli undertook a final attempt. He would not have been able to spend his fortune (and substantial parts of the Medicis') on assembling the finest library in Florence if he had been prone to resignation. To acquire eight hundred volumes—such was his marvelous collection—required dedication. He followed up on the few hints given him by his at-first reticent and now-resigned friend. When in 1431 two cardinals—Giuliano Cesarini and Niccolò Albergati—left for France and Germany, Niccoli supplied them with a list of literary treasures to look for. Known as the *Commentarium Nicolai Nicoli in peregrinatione Germaniae*, nothing except for a mention in a letter might have remained of it today.[27] But at the beginning of the twentieth century the list was discovered as an appendix to a manuscript of philosophical works by Cicero. A fortunate find, it gives valuable insights into the rediscovery of classical texts. The description it contains of the codex of Hersfeld is more comprehensive than the one Panormita sent Guarino in 1426, and must therefore be based on the second inventory Niccoli received from Poggio.

But all, it seems, was to no avail, even though, early in 1433, Niccoli heard about the codex once more, this time from the Council of Basel (1431–49), which was organized by dissenters pressing for church reform from within.[28] There a third group was on the scent. But the prey eluded these hunters too. When the manuscript finally came to light, Niccoli had been dead for almost two decades.

RETURN TO ROME

Cornelius Tacitus's book on "the origin and situation of Germany" is found; seen in Rome in 1455.

—Pier Candido Decembrio

The second act of the rediscovery of Tacitus's minor works—which resembles a play written by a dramatist with a preference for multiple plots—opens with a surprise. Pier Candido Decembrio (1399–1477), secretary in the pope's service, makes mention in his journal of viewing the *Germania* with the anticlimactic words quoted above. An experienced bibliophile, he adds the *incipit* (the opening line or two) and the *excipit* (the closing clause) of Tacitus's "book on the origin and situation of Germany," and equally delineates the *Dialogus*, the *Agricola*, and Suetonius's fragments, providing numbers of *folia* (leaves) for each.[29] His entry agrees almost entirely with Nicoli's in his *Commentarium*. Overnight, it seems, the manuscript came to light, most likely through the efforts of Poggio's rival: the official papal manuscript hunter Enoch of Ascoli.

At one point Poggio, a basilisk in controversies, thought it necessary to remind Enoch "that you do not possess sufficient talent or eloquence for it to behoove you to stir against me with false incriminations."[30] The man thus advised was no stranger to aversion and adversity. He had been born in Ascoli Piceno in central Italy in the early 1400s to a family whose low income only temporarily impeded his high aspirations. Lacking in money, but abounding in talent, Enoch obtained patronage and ultimately in Florence became a student of the industrious Francesco Filelfo, an authority on Greek as well as Latin authors. There he acquired the necessary humanistic skills and contacts, meeting among the other students the two later popes Pius II and Nicholas V. It was Nicholas who would several years later call him to Rome in order to teach rhetoric and poetry before dispatching him to search for manuscripts in the 1450s.

Nicholas V had been a scholar before he donned papal attire. Appearances change, character abides. During his tenure he continued his efforts "to retrieve books that were believed lost," envisaging no less than a Roman library that could rival the celebrated collection in Alexandria.[31] He commanded a contingent of literary scouts, including Enoch, who was dispatched on a trip to the north in 1451 to explore sites in Germany and Scandinavia. Poggio, in his role as the pope's secretary, wrote the letter of introduction. Nicholas therein asseverated "that to search and transcribe any books [by Greek and Roman authors] we send Enoch of Ascoli, our esteemed son, a man versed in Greek and Latin letters."[32] Recipients were asked to support the learned man in his needs and efforts.

Poggio allowed his scorn to pour forth in a private letter: "I have little hope that Enoch will produce anything good."[33] And *if* he discovered anything, Poggio continued, he would have good fortune rather than his intelligence and diligence to thank for it. Enoch seems to have been fortunate when he visited the northern monasteries, where, we may assume, his eyes fell on a state of neglect similar to the one a friend of Poggio's had described:

> When we carefully inspected the nearby tower of the church of St. Gall in which countless books were kept like captives and the library neglected and infested with dust, worms, soot, and all the things associated with the destruction of books, we all burst into tears, thinking that this was the way in which the Latin language had lost its greatest glory and distinction.[34]

Enoch returned in the company of those he had freed, carrying a piece of the glory of the Latin language, Tacitus's minor works, as preserved in the manuscript that Heinrich from Hersfeld had offered thirty years before. But evidence is scant and eristic, and once again what seems plausible must stand in for what is known as fact.

Two tiny notes provide a lead. When in March 1460 Giovanni Gioviano Pontano (1429–1503), the most important humanist in fifteenth-century Naples, had finished the transcription of several texts, the collection of which is known as the Codex Leidensis Perizonianus, he annotated that these books were "recently discovered and brought to light by Enoch of Ascoli."[35] Pontano's copy contains all the texts of Heinrich von Grebenstein's codex, except for the *Agricola*, severed, it seems, from the others sometime between the papal secretary Decembrio's viewing of it in 1455 and Pontano's copying of it. A historical inquirer's first impulse should be to credit contemporary evidence, but witnesses may err or lie. Pontano's testimony has met with misgivings, partly because elsewhere, on other matters, he provides patently erroneous information. More important, no other contemporary humanist mentions Enoch's discovery of Tacitus.

But the disputed witness receives some support from a Benedictine monk north of the Alps. Sigismund Meisterlin was working on his history of his hometown, Augsburg, the *Cronographia Augustensium*, when Enoch, traveling back to Italy in 1455, visited his cloister, Saint Ulrich and Saint Afra.[36] Meisterlin refers to his conversations with Enoch in his own work; and even though he makes no mention of Tacitus or the *Germania*, his familiarity with it or—at the least and perhaps more likely—its content seems indisputable. For in his investigation into Augsburg's beginnings, he rejects the common assumption that its originators were to be found among those who had fled Troy's smoldering ruins (known as the Trojan genealogy). Instead he proposed a novel idea: The Suevs, the original inhabitants, had been indigenous. It could be coincidental that Meisterlin was the first to use the Tacitean genealogy, which would have been in the text that his visitor was rumored to be hiding in his luggage, or, and more likely, Enoch could have shared information he had obtained from reading the newly found precious manuscript.

When Enoch finally returned to Rome, he learned that his patron, Nicholas V, had died (March 24, 1455). With the demise of the pope, his primary source of remuneration was gone. Enoch mourned, then searched for a buyer wealthy enough to meet his asking price (which was not small: At a time when a priest received an annual allowance of 4 fiorini, Enoch asked for 200–300). Carlo de' Medici, an illegitimate child of Cosimo the Elder employed at the Holy See in Rome, details these developments in a letter to his half-brother Giovanni in Florence. He portrays Enoch as weary and guarded, a man who even refused to show his finds to anybody, unless they put up the money first. Yet it seems safe to surmise that upon his return to Rome Enoch granted an inspection to his colleague in papal service Decembrio, who confided his impressions to his journal.

Others were less privileged, and based on what they could ascertain about Enoch's recent acquisitions greeted them with scorn. In the eyes of Carlo de' Medici—and "many learned (*dotti*) men" agreed—only four texts qualified as valuable. The remainder were worthless: *Tutto il resto non vale una frulla.*[37] Among the four exceptions is, as a later letter reveals, the text by Suetonius, which had accompanied the *Germania* in the manuscript offered by Heinrich from Hersfeld. But though Suetonius suggests a Tacitean presence, nobody attests to it. And if "the rest" had included any of Tacitus's writing, it would certainly have been considered "worthy," or at least worthy of mention.

Enoch left a mystery when he died in 1457. Maybe Pontano was mistaken after all. But how was it that Sigismund Meisterlin knew of the *Germania*? The final act, suitably brief and similarly inconclusive, offers more information but still falls short of a solution. Enter Enea Silvio Piccolomini.

THE SOIL on Enoch's grave had hardly settled when Piccolomini, the cardinal of Siena, inquired of Carlo de' Medici whether the recently departed had left behind "certain books," either with the Medici or elsewhere. Piccolomini had known Enoch since their student days in Florence, and he might have been privy to details undisclosed to others. If he enjoyed such privileged knowledge, he does not allude to it in his otherwise detailed correspondence. However, less than two months after his solicitation of this information, he incorporated Tacitean passages in his treatise on Germany that could only have come from the codex of Hersfeld or a copy of it. This suggests that his inquiry about Enoch's books led him to the *Germania*.

How, when, and why this acquisition happened is unknown. But Piccolomini's involvement with Enoch and his discoveries is also suggested by a comment in a letter almost twenty years later. In 1475 Jacopo, the aforementioned son of Poggio Bracciolini, claimed: "Cornelius Tacitus reached Italy due to the efforts of the pope Pius [the former Enea Silvio Piccolomini]."[38] Jacopo is quickly disproved by chronology: Tacitus was seen in 1455 in Rome, but Piccolomini did not commence his papacy until 1458. But the error may point to the truth: Jacopo may have remembered Piccolomini's most elevated position instead of the cardinal's office he occupied at the time.

After three acts that center around Poggio Bracciolini, Enoch of Ascoli, and then—briefly—Enea Silvio Piccolomini, the curtain falls, but the audience is left without closure. Contradictory evidence requires careful weighing. On the scales of probability Enoch carries the most weight. We know that he journeyed through Germany in search of manuscripts, that he conversed with Meisterlin on his way back, and that just at the time of his return, Decembrio in Rome reported—if only to himself—that "Tacitus . . . has been found." Within the same report figures Suetonius, who was cited in the Hersfeld codex as accompanying Tacitus and is later mentioned in reference to Enoch's finds. These works attracted the attention of Piccolomini, who a few weeks later would become the first to quote from the *Germania* in his soon-to-be-published treatise. Within this scenario several leaps of inference are necessary: Enoch upon his return showed his discovery to Decembrio but pleaded for confidentiality, prompting the latter to confide to his journal but no one else. Subsequently Enoch separated and sold the *Agricola* to keep himself afloat, since his patron, Pope Nicholas V, had died. What exactly happened to the *Germania* (along with the *Dialogus*) and how it ended up in Piccolomini's hands escapes even the most inquisitive eyes.

The mosaic remains imperfect. But perhaps one day another tessera will be discovered and let us know the whole story.

3

The Birth of the German Ancestors

First of all, we need to show what Germany once was, and
what it is today.

— Enea Silvio Piccolomini, 1458

WINTERS IN Rome are brisk. Not cold, not gray, but
crisp and clear—in all, very different from the hiemal
season in Germany. On February 1, 1458, the cardinal of Siena, none other than Enea Silvio Piccolomini, reminisced
about the many chilly nights he had spent north of the Alps, all
bundled up, earning a living by his skillful quill. It had been a long
time, too rarely interrupted by visits to "the soft and pleasant air
of Italy . . . where spring is all but perpetual."[1] Now back in Rome,
his face puffy with comfort, he composed the dedicatory letter to
his latest work, which would soon be known under the abbreviated
title that applied to merely a third of the whole work—but the most
significant third. This *Account of Germany* included Piccolomini's
experience-sated description of Germany (the first such from a
humanistic hand) and a bookish depiction of the Germans' ancient
past. This past contained the first paraphrase of Tacitus's *Germania*
in early modern Europe, brief and vague and highly consequential.
Unlike Rudolf of Fulda in the Carolingian era, Piccolomini used
the *Germania* to identify *Germanen* and contemporaneous Germans as the same people at two different moments in history. Thus

was born the *Germane* as the German ancestor. This misconceived notion of an ethnical continuity would last into the twentieth century, when the Nobel laureate Heinrich Böll (albeit hesitatingly) read the *Germania* as one of the oldest sources offering information about the German ancestors.

When the *Germane* was thus born in the second half of the fifteenth century, two empires cast their long shadows over Christian Europe: the thriving Ottoman Empire from the east and the Roman Empire from the past. Italian humanists, more often than not in ecclesiastical employment, regarded themselves as Roman descendants and trustees of the classical heritage. They used their rhetorical training and knowledge of the ancient world to glorify the Roman past and extend its glory into the present: "We lost Rome, we lost rule and dominance. . . . [And yet] ours is Italy, ours is France, ours are Spain, Germany, . . . and many other nations. For the Roman Empire still exists wherever the Roman language holds sway."[2] The Roman Empire lived on not just as the cultural model for Italian and more generally European intellectuals but also—according to the theory of the "transfer of rule"—in the Holy Roman Empire of the German Nation. After the fall of Rome to Germanic tribes in 476, centuries passed before Charlemagne around 800 united Europe once again within the boundaries of his Carolingian empire. In its wake the long-lived Holy Roman Empire came into being: Centering around the German "nation," it incorporated various subterritories from the Netherlands into the northern parts of Italy and was widely believed to have inherited dominion from its Roman predecessor.

But Italian humanists, the uncontested vanguard in Renaissance culture, scorned the German way of life. To many the north of Europe looked like a primitive wasteland, stretching into history as far back as they could read. Agostino Patrizzi (1435–94), a papal legate traveling in Germany in the 1470s, expressed in his travelogue an exceptional impression, tellingly couched: "Germany is (much more than our peers [*nostri homines*] believe) magnificent, beautiful, and—as far as prosperity and culture are concerned— very different from the ancient place that Caesar, Strabo, Tacitus, and others describe."[3] Change could reasonably be expected to have occurred over a period of almost fifteen hundred years. (After all, who today would read *Beowulf* to learn about modern Scandinavia?) Yet most of Patrizzi's peers had a view constricted by the classical tradition and prejudice. They read the three ancient testimonies Patrizzi mentions as an indictment of the Germans' barbarous past and considered present day Germany to be similarly inhabited (in Poggio Bracciolini's words) by "barbaric donkeys."

However, European unity was needed against the Turks, who in 1453 seized Constantinople (modern Istanbul), "one of the two lights of Christendom," and threatened the whole of Europe.[4] In describing Germany, even those humanists who harbored scorn hewed closely to the current political needs; such opportunism determined the German past too: The *Germane* would be dressed up as a hirsute heathen in bear hides or as an indigenous warrior valiantly armed, depending on the role he had to play. Right from the start the *Germania* served politics.[5]

LOUTS THEN, NOW GENTLEMEN

The description of Germany given by Cornelius Tacitus is even beastlier than those [of the other ancient authorities].
—Enea Silvio Piccolomini, 1458

The son of aristocrats cherishing memories of their bygone fortune, Piccolomini grew up near Siena in the Tuscan countryside, where "suave shades and silvery sparkling wells and lush grass and happy pastures attract poets."[6] Talent and lack of money led him from the University of Siena across the Alps, all the way to

Scotland. His career marked the triumph of the new humanistic training: Versed in the Roman classics more than in the Bible and schooled in rhetoric, he made a living by writing. A merchant of words, like so many humanists, he began his career as a secretary and diplomat in Basel, the Swiss city split by the Rhine that then hosted the Council of Basel (1431–49). Dissatisfied with Eugene IV, who was also subject—in theory—to the council's authority as "highest judge," the council fathers elected Felix V as an antipope, causing the so-called Schism of Felix V.[7] Piccolomini served under both banners for a while, but ultimately—after he had burned his bridges to both papal camps—in the chancellery of the German king and emperor Frederick III. As the liaison between the Holy Roman Empire in Vienna and the Holy See in Rome, he ended up spending more than twenty years in German-speaking territory, gathering impressions, composing most of his works, and spreading the humanistic word. (Modern scholarship regards him as an "apostle of humanism.") He liked the German people well enough; but they, "no lovers of letters," lacked his cultural refinement. Like many other contemporary Italians cast onto northern shores, he compared himself to the exiled poet Ovid, who, under Emperor Augustus, atoned near the Black Sea for the insouciance he had shown in Rome.[8]

While still in the service of Frederick III, Piccolomini delivered his most famous speech, "The Demise of Constantinople and the Preparation of War Against the Turks," at the Diet of Frankfurt.[9] Europe was still in shock because of the loss of its cultural center in the East to Mehmed II in the wake of the first concerted employment of cannons. The conquering sultan, who had "washed his hands in Christian blood," now had to be confronted. Piccolomini's oration on October 15, 1454, was meant to arouse the Germans to join in a crusade. It held its listeners spellbound for two hours (according to the speaker, who in his retrospective notes elaborated how nobody dared to clear his throat; others held a different view).

He implored them in the name of the absent Holy Roman Emperor not to "abandon the Christian community." He urged them to follow in the footsteps of their forefathers, who had been towers of fortitude. Were they not just like them? Piccolomini let his audience know what he saw when he looked at them: war-experienced soldiers, for whom it would be an easy pastime to fight the Turks. Thus would they show themselves to be the true Germanic offspring and worthy recipients of Roman rule. "For you are the great, you are the bellicose, most powerful, most courageous Germans, received into the grace of God. To you it was given to extend your empire far and wide and to resist the Roman force; you thus excel over all other people." But his many words were all for naught. When the delegates left, it was not to join the crusade.

The speech succeeded nevertheless. As one in a series of three, it quickly circulated in at least fifty handwritten copies and became a classic of its kind. Before long, quotations of it garnished German humanists' texts.[10] The German forebear it presented, an upright defender of Western civilization in shining armor, pleased northern readers—even though the portrait was blatantly opportunistic. But it did not contain any reference to Tacitus's *Germania* (which reached Rome only a year later, in 1455). It was Piccolomini's other, negative image of the German past as occupied by fur-clad and uncouth nomads that would prove more consequential in the end.

UNLIKE OVID, Piccolomini ultimately returned from his "exile." Back in Italy as the newly appointed cardinal of Siena, he lost no time positioning himself for his bid for the papacy. He was no stranger to ambition; and those ambitions, he knew, continued to rest on Germany. For prominence and influence in Rome a cardinal required a powerful family, papal benevolence, and/or foreign support. Piccolomini used his German connections—he accompanied Frederick III to his official coronation in Rome and sat as a guest of honor at his table—to curry the favor of the ailing pope Calixtus III (1455–58). He was proud that in German matters the pontiff turned to him "more than any other cardinal"; and in his own view he "always acted on the Germans' behalf."[11] But some of those beneficiaries viewed the cardinal's input differently.

Martin Mayer, the secretary to the bishop in Mainz, sent Piccolomini a letter. After expending a few congratulatory words on his recent election to the cardinalship, he warned him of widespread German dissatisfaction with papal policy. The secretary, an acquaintance from former days, added a list of grievances, including Rome's disregard for conciliar decrees and its selling benefices (offices that came with property) to the highest bidder, dealing in indulgences for sins, and reckless taxation.

A thousand ways are thought up by which the Roman Church ingeniously squeezes us for gold (as if we were barbarians). This has turned our once famous [German] nation, the queen and mistress of the world after she secured the Roman Empire with her virtue and her blood, to a maid and tributary, lying in squalor and mourning her fate and her poverty for so many years.[12]

Rome's greed degraded the German nation. Piccolomini must have sensed that he was included in this charge: Upon his election as cardinal, he had been granted by the pope benefices totaling two thousand ducats to compensate for the limited means he had inherited from his parents. While the cardinal presented himself as carrying German interests close to his heart, his critics might have thought his wallet lay closer.

In response to Mayer's communication Piccolomini felt compelled to write not just a letter but an epistolary treatise comprising three volumes. "I had no sooner opened and scanned [the letter] than I got angry. . . . I decided to refute the charges that [the German clergy] level against the Curia."[13] Yet it was not anger that fueled his writing. Rather this latest expression of German protest provided him with an opportunity to remind his senior fellow cardinals of his hard-earned expertise in German affairs and to pose as a staunch defender of the Roman church—just like the pope he hoped soon to be. Piccolomini enriched his voluminous response, a covert campaign effort, with ample demonstrations of his knowledge of conciliar and ecclesiastic issues and of his proficiency in the Bible. (He might have deemed such scholarship necessary in the light of his rather late religious calling: Before his ordination as subdeacon at Vienna in 1446 at the advanced age of forty-one, he—poet, lover, and scholar—had behaved in ways that he later piously regretted.)

In line with this hidden agenda, Piccolomini dedicated the work, later published as *An Account of the Rites, Site, Mores, and General Condition of Germany*, to the influential cardinal of Messina, Antonio de la Cerda.[14] In the accompanying letter to the dedicatee, in part quoted above, he pretended that his epistolary treatise had been composed in immediate reaction to Mayer's written complaint, a copy of which he included as a preamble to his response. But this copy had actually been written by Piccolomini himself (the original letter by the Mainz-based secretary has not survived), and the *Account of Germany* was not the first but the fourth response. Three conciliatory communications had already been sent to Mayer privately. They show Piccolomini at great pains to soothe German anger and to speak sympathetically like the advocate of their interests he claimed to be, sounding none of the impatience and scorn that characterize the cardinal in his *Account of Germany*, in which he presents himself as the stalwart of his church. Piccolomini had lived off rhetoric for most of his career. He once again depended on this art of persuasion in a treatise addressed to Mayer but sent to his fellow cardinal, which advertised his competence and loyally defended the church against accusations. The famous sketches of the past and present of Germany follow the same logic:

They were contrived to benefit the defendant rather than to reflect realities.

In order to discuss the charge of Rome's causing German decline, Piccolomini proposed to look into the past. Mayer's homeland should be revealed "as it was then, and as it is today."[15] How could one judge any development otherwise? Much history, the cardinal continued, extended beyond the historian's clear sight; but beginning with Julius Caesar past conditions were discernable. The suggested historical comparison seems congenial; Mayer would nonetheless have had to object. For it was not ancient times that he had in mind when he spoke of former glory, but the great medieval empire in the coercive hands of Charlemagne (whom German writers liked to claim as their ancestor). But Piccolomini, well aware of this, postponed the difficult discussion of the fall from medieval greatness, employing a common rhetorical strategy known as "substitution." In general it allows a respondent to address the most sensitive issue *after* his opponent's overall argument seems sufficiently dismantled. In this particular case Mayer was swiftly shown to be wrong—in what he had not meant.

As for this ancient past, the cardinal challenged anybody merely to browse the authoritative classical texts. No one could fail to realize that the German ancestors had been a horde of illiterate, bestial brutes, vegetating in a primitive environment. Three authorities, aligned chronologically from the fifties BCE to about 100 CE, serve to profile these barbarians. First, Gaius Julius Caesar, the general who came, saw, and quickly left Germany. His digression on the *Germanen* in the *Commentaries on the Gallic War* in Piccolomini's version presents men "considered" bellicose and trained in arms. But their lives were spent on toil and hardship; mostly naked, scantily covered by hides, little interested in agriculture, forfeiting permanent shelter. Next Strabo of Amaseia (Amasya in modern Turkey), the Greek historian and geographer under the reigns of Augustus and Tiberius, was made to concur. From the Latin translation of his *Geographica*, Piccolomini chose sloth (*ignavia*) and scarcity (*inopia*) to characterize the life of these Germanic nomads. And in Tacitus, last, the ambitious cardinal found still more fodder for his argument:

> The description of Germany given by Cornelius Tacitus is even beastlier than those [of the other ancient authorities]. . . . At that time your [Mayer's] ancestors' life differed preciously little from brutes' beastliness. For in the majority they were herdsmen, inhabiting woods and groves, and living a life of rude indolence. . . . They had no solid towns, nor were settlements surrounded by walls; no fortresses could be seen resting on high mountaintops, no temples built of carved stones.[16]

A long list of lacks followed, pilfered from Tacitus. Reflections on the scarcity of gold, silver, and fine fabrics led to the concluding remarks that "[these aspects] merit praise and must be preferred over our contemporary mores. But this lifestyle was characterized by illiteracy and the absence of legal enforcement and of the study of fine arts. Even their religion was barbarous, absurd, and—to use the proper terms—beastly and brutal. *This* is what your Germany looked like *(Talis tua Germania fuit)*." In the midst of paraphrase the only quotation from Tacitus's work that approached exactitude reemphasized barbarity: There could be no question that the *Germanen* "often offered up human sacrifices." Piccolomini's account did his bidding—from the turn of its pages stirred a waft of filthy furs and foul-smelling food.

The Germanic past as cast by the Italian rhetorician is heathen black. Positive aspects of the Germanic lifestyle—qualities like liberty, hospitality, fortitude, and morality, which Piccolomini found both in Tacitus and in Caesar—are either omitted or qualified in his account. No doubt, he admitted, their mores must be praised; but, he quickly added, they came at a high price, like the lack of legal enforcement. This last point is extrapolated from one of Tacitus's most memorable sententious statements: "There, good habits carry more weight than good laws elsewhere."[17] But while the Roman historian had implied that the Germans needed no laws because of their excellent sense of decency, Piccolomini eclipsed the context and presented lawlessness as still more evidence of Germanic backwardness.

From the depressing past the reader's gaze is then directed to far more pleasant present sights. The next panel displays a landscape, where farmers harvest bountiful crops, merchants trade refined goods, and artists and scholars host the Greek and Roman Muses. Piccolomini outlines how the German territory in the fifteenth century extended farther than that of ancient Germany, and praises its busy cities—an accurate description insofar as increasing urbanization was one development of the time. But he indulged in hyperbole and offered a catalog of grand dimensions, listing seventy-three city names, and employed "detailed description," another rhetorical technique meant to involve the reader emotionally through vivid details. Nowhere, he concluded, were the cities "cleaner or more delightful to behold" than in Germany (save, he murmured, for a *few* Italian cities). The muddy swamps and gloomy woods of Tacitus had yielded to this urban look. Gone were the days of paganism and human sacrifice; coarseness and illiteracy had vanished. Instead God was revered, and the liberal arts pursued. He lauded Germans' martial talents, honed, as he appended, since their early infancy. Of course he could have invoked this last talent as easily when he spoke of the ancient Germans. But the rhetorician's look at reality is utilitarian. It was in Piccolomini's interest for the differences between past and present to be categorical, with the two times representing all but two different countries.

The concluding rhetorical question, "Which place in Europe can now compare itself to Germany?" allowed for one answer only: None (except, maybe, for Italy). And to whom did the Germans owe this radical alteration from barbarous nomadism to prosperous civility? Why, the Roman church, of course. As a final stage act, the versatile writer raised ancient Germans from their graves in a rhetorical ruse known as the *sermocinatio*. There they stood and blinked in wonder, failing to recognize their own country. Their befuddlement was the ultimate expression of how everything had changed—but for the better. The Germans, however, instead of being grateful, were reproachful, and thus, the cardinal opined, preposterous.

A GERMAN READER would be quick to realize that it benefited Piccolomini, "as an Italian," to magnify the German present; the same observation applies to the barbarized past.[18] Yet in spite of the equally obvious rhetorical nature of the hirsute barbarians evoked from Tacitus's pages, German humanists were angered and provoked to study the *Germania* and to attempt their own illustrations of Germany. Prints of Tacitus's text—as well as their places and numbers—signal Piccolomini's importance. When the *Germania* was printed in Germany for the first time in 1476, few German readers seem to have noticed. Then, in 1496, the incendiary *Account of Germany* appeared. Four years later, in 1500, the second edition of Tacitus's booklet north of the Alps was published in Vienna, already bespeaking familiarity with Piccolomini's work. Over the next five decades it would be printed mostly in German-speaking countries, amounting to as many as six thousand copies, an impressive number for the time.

When the *Germanen* were born, anger was the midwife.

INDIGENOUS GERMAN WARRIORS

> You have not mingled with others but bonded among your-
> selves. . . . You have always been the indigenous people of
> Germany. . . . The lifestyle that your forefathers had from the
> very beginning, you keep till the last.
>
> —Giannantonio Campano, 1471

Piccolomini succeeded in his bid for the papacy in 1458, and as Pope Pius II made the Turkish threat one of his priorities. He was in the midst of his preparations for a crusade, when, feverish and ill, he died in 1464. Paul II succeeded him. The new pope was known to be ill disposed to the policies of his predecessor, whose humanistic interests had drawn his suspicion and whose proté-gés made him impatient. The Turkish war also held his attention rather than interest, until in 1470 Negroponte fell into the hands of Sultan Mehmed II. The loss of this Venetian stronghold on the Aegean island of Euboea stirred the Venetian-born pope into action. He asked the German emperor Frederick III to convene the Imperial Diet in Regensburg. Held in this borough in the east of Bavaria in 1471, it was intended once more to enlist German military forces for a crusade.

In preparation Frederick III requested that the Sienese cardinal Francesco Todeschini-Piccolomini—a nephew of Pius II who later became Pope Pius III—be the head of the papal delegation. He was recommended by his avuncular line and his connections to German leaders, who, still chafing at curial impositions, were disinclined to cooperate. In turn the cardinal needed a speaker who commanded the talents required to soothe, please, and stir an audience so that it would "seize arms and throw itself at the savage enemy for the preservation of the Christian faith."[19] Giannantonio Campano (1429–77), a member of the cardinal's circle, a cleric, and an accomplished orator, was quickly chosen to fill the position. A professor of rhetoric at the University of Perugia, born, according to legend, on Campanian fields under a laurel tree, Campano owed his career to his scintillating talent, "by which," contemporaries agreed, "he was most compelling."[20] His rhetorical and literary skills not only attracted the attention of Pope Pius II, whose autobiography Campano would edit, but also secured him appointments to a series of official delegations. The delegation he joined for Regensburg was special, however; for it included, among others, Tacitus. Both Cardinal Todeschini-Piccolomini and his Campanian speaker played an important role in the dissemination of the *Germania*, its manuscripts as well as its content. For Todeschini-Piccolomini lent the handwritten copy he had inherited from his uncle to German humanists for copying; Campano, on the other hand, made ample use of Tacitus's text in his speech at Regensburg. While this speech failed to lead Germans to the crusade, it succeeded in bringing them to a different view of their past.

Contemporaries compared Campano to Ovid, Rome's smartest poet, and to Cicero, Rome's greatest orator. And "of all the speeches he composed," Campano's editor, Michele Ferno, would later write, the one at Regensburg "was the most ornate by far and the most persuasive."[21] It is unfortunate, then, that it was never delivered. Disagreements among the diet's participants led to its premature dissolution. But the speech soon circulated in handwritten copies and—from around 1487—in print to work its belated influence on its German addressees. No sooner was it made public than it became a classic, considered on a par with Piccolomini's famous oration in Frankfurt.

COMPOSED FOR the diet "in order to excite the German leaders against the Turks and to praise the Germans," the Regensburg address belongs, as its descriptive title indicates, to the deliberative genre, while containing heavily encomiastic elements.[22] Yet it lined up its arguments neither neatly nor logically. Rather, not unlike a symphony, it sounded the major motifs—Germanic military prowess and power, glory, nobility, freedom, and fortitude—now softer, now louder, but almost through the whole of an arrangement that aimed for the arousal of an apathetic audience: "Now, now you must rise!" For nothing less was at stake than the rule of the Holy Roman Empire and the continuance of the Christian faith. Vividly Campano reminded his audience of their enemy and the atrocities already suffered: the terrified howling of men and women, gloom and anxiety, and "boys who serve as slaves to their Turkish masters—those, at least, who were not strangled in their cradles." In the presence of such danger the Germans, more than anyone else, were obligated to step forward and fight. Their obligation was their past: "I beseech you by the most glorious shadows of your ancestors [*per gloriosissimas umbras patrum vestrorum*]: make sure that Germany is Germany [*Germania Germania sit*] and that it commands those fighters now whom it commanded then."

For this heroic past Campano purloined persuasive details from the *Germania*, even though he left his source unnamed. He described men and women alike as bold warriors, whose martial devotion showed even in their marital commitment: A bridled horse, a spear, and a shield were exchanged for a dowry. The men often left to seek glory, always bringing their weapons; the women were ever ready to restore wavering spirits in battle and to attend to the injured. Jointly they protected German freedom, fighting off Roman aggressors. Campano's speech, like Piccolomini's, reveals the rhetorician at work: His techniques are rearrangement, exaggeration, and—where needed—fabrication. It was not enough that Germanic women, as in the *Germania*, participated in battle from a distance by their pleading: Campano made them seize weapons and join in the hand-to-hand combat. And not only did he omit the *Germanen* in his list of peoples practicing propitiatory human sacrifices—even though he found them mentioned in Tacitus—he also turned them into a beacon of religiosity, people who revered Mars, the god of war, as the highest divinity, before they, as Christians, surpassed all other peoples in faith, piety, and the erection of magnificent churches. Never mind that Tacitus had specified Mercury, the god of commerce, as the supreme ruler in the Germanic pantheon, and had made a point of the absence of religious edifices other than groves. Campano's rhetorical task required that Germanic power and piety be emphasized; and so, while Tacitus's *Germanen* simply undertake nothing unarmed, the versatile speaker played up the point by having them armed even when entering temples.[23] Just like that, with a few strokes of a quill, the German ancestors as portrayed by Tacitus were no longer barbaric but exemplary in their bravery and religious piety.

In the same vein Campano assured his audience of their ancestors' concord, even though Tacitus had feasted his eyes on bloody inner-Germanic conflicts, praying for the continuation of self-hatred among Rome's enemies, since that would protect the empire.[24] Yet Campano needed peace among the German ancestors, because current regional leaders, obstinately disagreeing with one another, should overcome their difficulties and move jointly against the common foe. Unperturbed by all past and present evidence to the contrary, and in an attempt to emphasize their harmony, he reminded his listeners of their name: "You are called *Germani* because of your brotherly spirit." Though it seems most likely that *Germani* was a term appropriated by Caesar in reference to all the peoples east of the Rhine, humanists (like their classical predecessors) discussed its deeper significance—as if the name said it all. The Latin *Germanus* can mean "related." On the grounds of this etymology the Germans were said to be brothers—not of the neighboring Gauls, as some humanists (on ancient authority) suggested, but among themselves, as Campano (and others) affirmed. "You have not mingled with others but bonded among yourselves," Campano insisted. "You have scorned commerce abroad and foreign marriages; born under this very sky, you have always been the indigenous people of Germany, not immigrants from elsewhere; and the lifestyle that your forefathers had from the very beginning, you keep till the last."[25] The ancient Germans were pure warriors. Tucked into this elaborate explanation of national union is the first quotation of Tacitus's most dangerous paragraph: *Germania*, chapter 4 (with parts of chapter 2 inserted).

Geography thus guaranteed that the present audience descended from the heroes of times past. The Germanic and the German warriors, bound by the same territory and traditions, formed a continuous line. When Campano considered his German audience, he saw *Germanen*: the same huge bodies, threatening eyes, and terrifying voices. He did not hesitate to credit it with the glorious victories of days gone by, and he goaded it on: "Are you then going to dither about fighting the Turks, you, whose ancestors are known to have taken up arms once against the tempests of the sky and rising waters?"[26]

IN ONE of the many letters Campano sent to acquaintances back home in Italy, he related how he composed his speech with great diligence, even though he felt as if he was polishing a pearl to be cast before swine. For it was of the kind, he confessed in another correspondence, "which Italians would read, Germans fail to understand."[27] (This was, as it turned out, a vain worry, since he never had the opportunity to test his audience's appreciation.) Looking around in Regensburg, he did not, it seems, see much to his liking. In a German environment that was so changed, so splendid, and so welcoming to the eyes of his Italian fellow legate, the secretary Patrizzi (quoted above), Campano was full of hostility, numbed by the cold, warmed only by memories, and in isolation unrelieved. He continued to send a stream of letters, some of which pleaded that he be allowed to return promptly, lest he die among those already dead but still farting, the more likely as he could not stomach the food, its coarseness surpassed only by the brutish companions assaulting his table. In these epistles the German present and past were equally barbaric. Campano's two versions of Germany, the one in the speech and the one in the letters, thus have little in common except for their rhetorical instrumentality: the former written to flatter and fire the German audience, the latter to entertain their Italian addressees. For the letters were sent to men steeped in the classics and as such on familiar footing with the most famous of all exiled poets, Ovid. One reader, Campano's editor Ferno, considered them "incomparably witty," written *as if* Campano had stayed in Tomis, Ovid's purgatory.[28] But though Campano's playful wit italicized his complaints, those italics were invisible to the eyes of many German readers. When they ran their eyes over the epistles, published as part of the complete works in 1495, they seethed with anger. They found therein another example of the widespread Italian contempt for northern "barbarism," in which alcoholism, gluttony, and coarseness left no room for finer tastes. Campano's billets, written with the stiletto, were thus answered with the battle-ax: Their author was abused as "an effeminate man, sodomite, masturbator, and *irrumator*."[29]

Yet, even though the correspondence scandalized readers north of the Alps, they were too flattered by the Regensburg address not to read, employ, and quote this "enemy and bad-mouther of the Germans."[30] Circulating in German hands, it unveiled the possibility of an exemplary past, and helped readers to a different reading of Tacitus and a fuller appreciation of specific Germanic values, like the motif of being indigenous.

NOAH'S NEW SON

> And Tuysco—according to the testimony of Berosus as well
> as Tacitus—was the progenitor of the Germans.
>
> —Annius of Viterbo, 1498

Approximately at the same time as Campano's letters appeared,
another scandal, but on a grander scale, came to pass elsewhere.
Late in the summer of 1498 the *Commentaries on the Works of Various
Authors Discussing Antiquities* were issued from the presses of
the printer Eucharius Silber in Rome.[31] A collection of ancient historical texts, previously thought lost, the *Antiquities* (*Antiquitates*)
filled the 216 folia of the Roman edition with a novel account of
prehistoric times before and after the Flood, of nations founded
by Noah's sons on soil still soaked with rain. Their editor, the
scarcely known Annius of Viterbo, had added explanatory notes, an
introductory outline, and a concluding summary. The European
republic of letters was soon abuzz with talk about their revelations:
how the Etruscans were the true founders of Italy, once ruled by
Noah himself, and how Romulus had not given his name to the city
of Rome—as was commonly believed—but had been named after
the city (which, in turn, owed its name to Roma, the daughter of
the mythical Italian king Italus). For Germans these rediscovered
texts contained sensational information as well. They learned that
they descended from Tuysco, identified as a previously unknown
son of Noah's. Upon closer inspection, however, Annius himself
appears to have adopted Tuysco from Tacitus's text.* This particular instance is indicative of the nature of the *Antiquities* as a whole,
whose slyly understated title hid what to this day counts as a masterpiece of artful forgery.

---

* The manuscripts of the *Germania* offer both "Tuysco" and "Tuisto" as names for the
Germanic god (cf. p. 254, n. 35). Most readers and editors of Tacitus prefer "Tuisto," and
so will I, unless "Tuysco" is used by the author I discuss—as is the case here with Annius.

All over Europe families, tribes, and nations vied to claim the earliest origins. "There is hardly a people," a German humanist wrote, "which does not delight in displaying its age or its faraway origin."[32] This quest had tradition: Already during the Middle Ages the glorious city of Troy had enjoyed great popularity as a genealogical origin, rivaled only by Noah's progeny. Fleeing from its smoldering ruins, Trojans were thought to have wandered far and wide, founding cities and fathering peoples: most famously the dutiful Aeneas, who, "an exile by fate," in the words of the Roman poet Virgil, "was the first to reach Italy and the Lavinian shores from the beaches of Troy, much tossed on land and sea."[33] Another Trojan, Francus, as the seventh-century *Chronicle of Fredegar* demonstrated, was the eponymous forefather of the Franci, whom the French aristocracy claimed as ancestors; French kings in particular prided themselves on uninterrupted Trojan descent. They were joined by the Britons and the Normans, who also took great pride in similar lineages. Rulers, like the Hapsburg Holy Roman emperor Maximilian I; municipalities, like the city of Augsburg; and other authorities financed research into their age and origin. Fabricated stories naturally abounded.

Among the counterfeiters none was greater than Annius of Viterbo (1432–1502). Born Giovanni Nanni, he Latinized his name in the humanistic fashion to Annius and included his town of birth. A brother of the Dominican order, thoroughly trained in theology and biblical exegesis, and with a reputation as an astrologer, he became an official papal theologian, a *Maestro del Sacro Palazzo* of Alexander VI, toward the end of his career. By the time he turned to the writing of the *Antiquities*, his most famous work, he had already dabbled in the art of forgery. Casting an envious eye on the old and esteemed histories of Athens and Rome, this hometown patriot had contrived several inscriptions, some of which he had had chiseled in stone, buried, and then felicitously dug up by a group of workers. Readers of the epigraphic tract, which he had hastened to publish, learned the astonishing news that Viterbo in Lazio, forty-five miles northwest of Rome, had actually been founded in biblical times by the Italian god Janus, a heathen appellation for none other than Noah. This fantastic foundation ensured his city's seniority over Rome and thus greater dignity. The *Antiquities*— similarly inspired by jealousy—pursued the same patriotic purpose but much more audaciously. The venture amounted to nothing less than the rewriting of world history from three generations before the Flood down to the foundation of Troy; it was a project in which talent was rivaled only by vanity.[34]

In editing these seventeen texts, which centered geographically on Europe but treated Africa and Asia too, Annius asserted in the preface that he had adhered to the truth unadorned. They would, he impressed on his readers, display the glorious antiquity not just of his country but of the whole of Europe. Yet in this imaginative volume, all but one of the alleged authors, ranging in time from Alexander the Great in the third century BCE to the second-century CE Roman emperor Antoninus Pius, were the editor's alter egos. Their beguiling names stood for "exceptional learnedness," as a later critic noted, and called for reverence, which was inspired also by the presentation of the materials: In the Roman incunabulum a dignified Gothic type highlights the allegedly authentic snippets, about ten lines in length, which are surrounded by the editor's erudite comments.[35] These editorial glosses, quotations, and references helped readers understand the fascinating facts and figures, not least by relating them to extant classical texts, like Tacitus's *Germania*. Texts and comments wove biblical stories and classical myths into a tapestry of history from antediluvian times. The single most important text—five books full of lists of prehistoric kings and Noachide family trees—appeared near the end of the anthology and contained the mention of the Germanic progenitor Tuysco.

IN HIS INTRODUCTORY REMARKS to this longest and most spec-
tacular "discovery," Annius introduced the "author" as "Berosus
born a Babylonian, in status a priest" to his humanistic readers.[36]
They thus learned what they already knew in part from ancient
authorities like the encyclopedist Pliny the Elder and the historian
Flavius Josephus, both of whom had lived during the first century
CE and mentioned Berosus in their works. The real Berosus had
indeed been a Chaldean priest, who early in the third century BCE
not only excelled in astrology but also wrote a Babylonian history
(in Greek) in three volumes, of which fragments remain to this
day. Their content overlapped with the Old Testament; Noah figured therein. Such facts preceding his fiction would, Annius rightly
calculated, increase credibility. He therefore also emphasized that
Berosus had been the curator of the library at Babylon, which the
Chaldeans had kept up to date ever since the days of Adam (Annius
is here playing on a medieval legend of an antediluvian book). But
for all of his buildup, this pseudo-Berosus shared with his real
namesake little other than the name—as a circumspect critic a century later scornfully noted.

With great diligence Annius laid out the content of Berosus's
now five volumes, obtained, he claimed, from an Armenian Dominican master. First, a summary of the Chaldean priests' reports on
the time before the diluvial flood, followed by genealogies of the
progenitors who repopulated the world after the rain had abated.
This second part segued into an account of the age of Janus, identified with Noah, whereas the fourth and fifth parts related the antiquities of various early kingdoms, like the Assyrian. Tuysco appeared
in the midst of the postdiluvial genealogies, where he joined Noah's
sons Shem, Ham, and Japheth as a half brother. He was "the progenitor," Annius added in his commentary, "of the Germans, as
Berosus as much as Cornelius Tacitus testify."[37] Ever alert to his
readers' difficulties, Annius suspected that many of the names of
Tuysco's offspring in Berosus's work might appear "rather obscure,"

and he quoted in full Tacitus's chapter on Germanic indigenous beliefs about their origins. It had not been cited or used previously:

> [The Germanic tribes] celebrate in olden songs—which is their only form of historical record—Tuysco, an earth-born god, and his son, Mannus, as their people's origin and founders. To Mannus they attribute three sons, from whose names the coast tribes are called Ingaevones; those of the inland, Herminones; and all the others, Istaevones. Some, with the freedom of conjecture permitted by antiquity, assert that the god had further descendants, and the nation further appellations, as Marsi, Gambrivii, Suevi, Vandilii, and that these are genuine old names.[38]

The heathen god appeared to have a biblical lineage. This was welcome information. By grafting Tacitus's earthborn but somewhat uprooted Germanic god Tuysco onto Noah's family tree, the *Antiquities* told German readers who they were in relation to the other European people and their respective originators. True, all Europeans were descendants of Noah, but Berosus knew further to report that Noah favored and adopted Tuysco's offspring, preferring them to his other equally nation-founding progeny. In this regard the Germans (along with the Sarmatians, peoples located in the eastern Balkans and the south of European Russia) excelled over the other European peoples, as is emphasized by the heading of this portion of Annius's text.[39]

Tacitus's text, which Annius drew on to contrive the Chaldean account, is quoted in the commentary to authenticate the fabrication. The cunning of this strategy is attested to by its impact on the skeptical reader Sebastian Münster, author of the first German cosmography. Whatever his other suspicions, Münster reassured himself that—with regard to the Germans at least—Berosus could not be doubted, corroborated as he was by Tacitus's account.[40] Similarly supported by Tacitus was Berosus in his fourth book, which

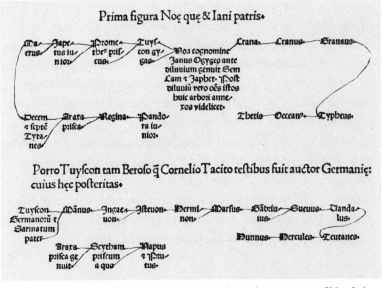

5. Noah's son Tuysco, the German primogenitor (according to Annius of Viterbo).
Houghton Library, Harvard University, Inc 3888.

unfolds "the old times of the kingdoms of the entire world."[41] The German territory said to have been under the rule of Tuysco and his offspring converged with the ancient territory delineated at the beginning of the *Germania*. But certainly the most brilliant (or impudent) move is Annius's observation that Berosus refers to the "Germans" as "Tuyscons." He interprets this nomenclature as evidence that the Chaldean priest lived before the Roman Caesars, since it was only in the days of Gaius Julius, the first Caesar, that the Germans became known as such.

On the tandem of author and commentator an acute reader within a few decades quipped: "While the one milks the he-goat the other holds out the sieve."[42] Yet for more than 250 years the "editor's" confabulations would continue to circulate among excited but duped intellectuals. An Italian translation and adaptations in other vernaculars and media, including art, quickly joined the (at least) twenty-five editions printed by 1551 in France, Germany, Italy, and the Netherlands.[43] By Renaissance standards it was an international best seller. Some editions dispensed with Annius's comments, printing the unannotated "original" texts, endowing them with still more authority. (This was the case with the second edition, *Seventeen Volumes of Various Antiquities*, which appeared in Venice late in 1498.) Most readers suspended their skepticism concerning Annius's works because of their alluring content, the seeming sobriety of their presentation, and the editor's professed espousal of philological standards. But above all it was patriotic enthusiasm that led them—German, French, Italian, Spanish, and Netherlandish—to refer to Berosus where they should have referred to his editor and commentator, Annius. Credulity granted credibility.

IN THE RHETORIC of the past Piccolomini, Campano, and Annius all relied on Tacitus's *Germania* as an account of German history, yet each with a different purpose: as a historical illumination of cultural change; as evidence of ethnic continuity; or simply as prehistory. Whether the primeval origin of the *Germanen* was specified or not, whether Tuysco (Tuisto) was mentioned as progenitor or not, the creed that solidified toward the turn of the sixteenth century was of the contemporaneous Germans as Germanic descendants. During the Middle Ages, German genealogies had for the most part been dynastic and tribal: of the Hapsburgs or the Bavarians but not of the Germans. The rediscovery of the *Germania* changed this for good. When behind the shrouds of time it revealed the *Germanen*, the German ancestors emerged.

4
Formative Years

[Cornelius Tacitus] ranks as the second founder of Germany.
—Franciscus Irenicus, 1518

GERMAN HUMANISTS embraced the *Germania* as a belated gift from Rome, a truly "golden booklet," passed on to them by their Italian counterparts.[1] Written by a classical pen, it shed much-needed light on their past, about which so little was known. Tacitus shone a bright candle into the dark, and its shadows mesmerized German eyes: Indigenous and pure, their ancestors had lived a hard but free, simple but moral life as tall, fair, and flaxen-haired men and women of war. Hardly flawless but certainly laudable, they held up well against their intellectually superior Roman contemporaries: What they lacked in cultural refinement they more than made up for by moral rectitude. In a literary culture ruled by Roman antiquity, they allowed Jacob Wimpfeling, the Alsatian author of the first history of Germany, to declare in 1505 that "we may pride ourselves on being descendants of our German ancestors."[2] The *Germania* helped him, along with many others within the humanistic community, to settle their forebears' character—the virtues more than the vices—and it allowed them to dream up a common German nation: Alsatians, Bavarians, and Saxons were "all branches of one single tree," another humanist exclaimed; and that tree was rooted in the Tacitean past.[3]

At the turn of the sixteenth century, a time of dramatic cultural change because of Gutenberg's invention of the printing press, nationalistic sentiments flared across the Holy Roman Empire. Headed by another Hapsburg emperor, it continued its existence as a clumsy body of disparate territories at a time when France, England, and Spain centralized and nationalized political power. Maximilian I (1459–1519), who had succeeded his father, Frederick III, in 1493 and would in turn be followed by his grandson, Charles V, in 1519, suffered a constant shortage of money and thus—in an age of mercenaries—military power. He encountered the domestic resistance of territorial rulers, who were independently minded and averse to being overruled, and learned that what Enea Silvio Piccolomini had said of his father's reign also applied to his: "The title of emperor [was] held in greater esteem abroad than at home."[4] Retaining its romantic allure, but bereft of real power, the empire continued to face threats not only from the Turks, who encroached on its territories, but also from inside its imperial boundaries: The "common German fatherland" felt the two wings of the Roman yoke settling on its neck.[5] The Holy See insisted on its privileges, filling German ecclesiastical vacancies at will and for its own profit; all the shepherds cared about was to shear their German flock, a humanist sneered at a time when the Reformation was beginning to divide the Christian community. Meanwhile the Roman law code superseded the German common law and by imperial decree had to be applied within the empire's borders. These were unsettling times for budding nationalists.

With the empire hobbling on feet of clay—to adapt another of Piccolomini's remarks—the notion of a German nation gained ground.[6] German humanists, while ensconced in their regional communities and simultaneously committed to supranational humanistic ideals, increasingly spoke of "all Germans," "all of Germany," and the above-quoted "common German fatherland." For many it coincided with the Holy Roman Empire of the German

Nation. But in the glaring absence of a political union, this "German nation" was defined culturally and with particular recourse to the common and morally superior past. As a consequence, during Maximilian's reign numerous humanists like Jacob Wimpfeling turned to writing their own histories—mostly in Latin, however, as the times demanded.

For the European republic of letters was still ruled from the south. For more than a century Italian humanists had confidently promoted the paradigmatic culture of the Roman classics and mastered Latin—the uncontested lingua franca—with unrivaled ease and elegance in their own compositions. Accomplished and proud, many expressed uncharitable opinions of other nations. German humanists in particular, committed as they were to the same aesthetic ideals, chafed under stereotypical accusations of a brutish existence bearable only because of inertia and widespread alcoholism, inclinations that had been already imputed by Tacitus. Though some retaliated in kind—denouncing Italian culture as notable primarily for the masturbation and sodomy practiced among its contributors—more sober voices emphasized cultural change: how the marshes and woods that Tacitus described had yielded to a "resplendent and prolific" urban scene.[7]

Yet the patriotic enthusiasm about the present notwithstanding, the humanists' attitude to their patria remained ambivalent. They held their vernacular, "a barbaric tongue," in low esteem (formal instruction in German was not given at the time, nor were there any grammars regulating its usage until the 1530s); and cultural progress was measured by proficiency in Latin, depth of knowledge of Greek and (mostly) Latin texts, and the production of literary works that emulated Latin models.[8] For German humanists, joining the republic of letters implied the adoption of a Latin(ized) name: Wolfgang chose a literal translation of his first name's two parts, "wolf" and "walk," Lupambulus; Wodka—with redeeming irony—settled on Abstemius, whereas *Gockenschnabelius* merely enlarged his vernacular name* with a Latin ending. Through their literary efforts in the Latin language, the nine Muses should be invited to move from the Tiber to the Rhine. Then Germans would have inherited not just the Romans' military but also their cultural rule. It may seem paradoxical, but with regard to culture this early form of German nationalism was Romanocentric.

AT THE CENTER of these efforts stood the German arch-humanist Conrad Bickel. In the course of his student years he had started to call himself Celtis, a rare Latin word signifying "chisel," and added a hellenized "middle name" so as to become Conradus Protucius Celtis. As Celtis he poeticized his calling: Apollo, the Greco-Roman god of poetry, at his birth divined that the newborn would further his fine art in Germany, and many fictive years later mandated that the young man "sing about the four regions of his fatherland."[9] Not naturally compliant but prudent enough to obey a god, Celtis spent much of his life (1459–1508) as poet and patriot in pursuit of these two assignments. He traveled for a decade in Germany, gathering impressions; taught Latin literature at various universities; and founded sodalities where humanists gathered. At the turn of the sixteenth century, nearly every German humanist of any repute was somehow enmeshed in his activities. Contemporaries praised him as a mediator of Roman culture, and his inaugural speech at the newly founded Bavarian University of Ingolstadt in 1492 quickly came to be one of German humanism's programmatic texts. Therein he admonished his audience to "turn first of all to those studies which can render your minds more gentle and cultivated," the liberal arts. They should then employ their skills to research and write about the history and geography of their common patria.[10]

For the past, no matter how prosperous the present, still resembled

---

* It signifies the cockerel's (*Gockel*) beak (*Schnabel*).

a wasteland. Unlike the Romans, the ancient Germans had failed to follow up with the quill what they had accomplished with the sword; no historical account existed from an indigenous hand. Much deplored, this "lack of writers" seemed to confirm the Italian verdict that when looking at the German past all inquisitive eyes could find was that there was nothing to be found.[11] To add insult to injury, the little that was known was owed to Greek and Roman writers. German humanists, however, believed the latter in particular had magnified "victories and honor on behalf of their people, although the Germans were braver and more honorable."[12] Fortunately there was "our Cornelius," to whom an exceptional status was readily granted.[13]

Tacitus's role in the inchoate nationalistic discourse is beyond exaggeration. It was commonly agreed at the time that no one "would know of a single letter concerning the Germans' origin, if it had not been recorded by Cornelius Tacitus—albeit a Roman," as the preface to a 1541 German history would acknowledge.[14] To enhance the authenticity of *this* Roman's singular testimony, most readers insisted that he had visited the territories east of the Rhine. The more enthusiastic went even further, turning Tacitus's foreignness—"a Roman, not a German," and thus, in fact, "the enemy"—into an advantage: Why would he have praised their ancestors, unless what he had to write was unavoidably true?[15] Yet, despite their grateful excitement over his "most elegant description in his *Germania*," sixteenth-century readers were left wondering what an ancient German would have reported of his own.

As "true lovers and defenders of their fatherland," German humanists soon set out to remedy past negligence and "write about their ancestors' myriad glories."[16] A comprehensive description of Germany by a German pen was the more needed as foreign writers continued to "hiss at German virtue like snakes" and to spray their poisonous lies.[17] Celtis, who like many others ultimately blamed Roman and Italian writers for Germany's bad reputation, wrote, as part of an unfinished larger project, a Latin poem as an accompaniment to his own edition of Tacitus's *Germania*. Soon circulating under the title *Germania generalis*, it provided a bright sketch of Germany in 283 hexameters, mixing cosmogony, history, geography, and ethnography. In the section "on the situation and mores of Germany," Celtis was, according to a friend, "more eloquent and splendid" than even Tacitus.[18] In it he described how his contemporaries still embraced their forefathers' values; but they had enhanced their skills, "making a living through various crafts, like tying a growing vine to bare stakes, and cutting fertile fields with a four-horse plough." He elaborated how it was now common "to turn to the teaching of Minerva, well-spoken and learned, or to pilot sailing ships over the shifting sea." Celtis's poem depicted an ideal world in which high culture and high morals conjoined. Together with Tacitus's *Germania*, it formed a diptych, past and present side by side, which in the winter of 1501 served the arch-humanist as the basis for a lecture series on Tacitus's text. It was the first such north of the Alps.

Others had read and used Tacitus before. However, even though first traces of the *Germania* appear in the work of German humanists as early as in the 1450s near the Bavarian city of Augsburg, its elevation to Germany's founding document did not occur before the turn of the century. The change from scattered readings to a widespread and continuous engagement with the *Germania* coincided with the publication of Celtis's edition-cum-accompaniment. His poem resounded with the soon commonly held Germanic beliefs, and in its interplay with the *Germania* edition typifies the dominant ideological—as opposed to philological—approach to the Germanic past. No single aspect demonstrates this more clearly than a particular change Celtis made in Tacitus's text. Where the original speaks of "human sacrifices" (*humanis quoque hostiis*), he detected a scribal error and emended the problematic first word, suggesting "his sacrifices" (*huius quoque hostiis*). It made next to no sense, but it dispensed with the barbaric practice that Enea Silvio Piccolomini had pointed to in his *Account of Germany*, published less than five years before.

When Celtis, Wimpfeling, and their cohort glanced backward at

their past, they saw the Germanic myth, characterized by autochthony and purity, liberty, bravery, and loyalty, as well as simple morality. Contrary to most recent Italian incriminations, their ancestors
were a people that "by the qualities of the mind and the body excelled
over all other nations" and deserved to be emulated.[19] The rhetoric of
the past that Piccolomini had begun was to be continued.

SINCE TIME IMMEMORIAL

> They are . . . indigenous: They do not draw their beginnings
> from another people, but were issued under their sky.
> —Conrad Celtis, 1501

The chivalrous emperor Maximilian I had been forced to retire to
Tyrolean Innsbruck (nestled in today's west-Austrian mountains) by
German princes who refused to cooperate at the imperial council
in Nuremberg. His freshly crowned poet laureate, Heinrich Bebel
(1472–1518), had had no choice but to follow suit. Now, on May
30, 1501, he stood before the court to deliver his Latin oration in
token of his gratitude for his recent coronation and in praise of the
emperor as well as the German people. Yet Bebel, a teacher of rhetoric and poetry at the newly founded University of Tübingen, started
by recounting for his audience his nocturnal vision: In his dream a
woman had appeared—old, too imposing and majestic to be human,
yet in tatters and emaciated. Germany, for that was the apparition,
had complained to him about the state of affairs, in particular the
princes' insurrection (fresh in the mind of all present). Such strife,
she warned, had sundered empires before; and she pleaded for help
to regain her former greatness. Having relayed his nation's present
sorrows, Bebel turned to its great past for consolation. He knew
that he had the undivided attention of his emperor. For Maximilian
I maintained a staff of historians charged with tracing his family's
beginnings back to the Trojans and even to Noah's offspring.

Unsurprisingly, Bebel placed great emphasis on the origin and age of the German people in his long catalog of its virtues and accomplishments; he did not, however, stray from the Rhine region. "We are no immigrants, no," he asserted. "Nor is the origin of Germany to be found in the dregs [*colluvies*] of peoples collected from everywhere." Where then, his audience might have wondered, did they come from? "We were born on the same soil which we cultivate now, and our place of residence is our place of origin."[20] Unlike Giannantonio Campano, whose Regensburg address Bebel knew well, the poet laureate supported this solemn claim with an extensive citation from the genealogical parts of the *Germania* and an explicit reference to Tacitus (his favorite witness, albeit a Roman, foreigner, and enemy, as he would frequently remark). He went on expounding on his nation's venerable age—hinted at in his description of the old woman (*verula*) of his dreams—and called on the Chaldean priest Berosus in Annius's fabricated edition for proof. It was true, Bebel conceded, that "many cities and nations took great pride in their origin and age," but none more rightly in his opinion than the Germans.[21] Their indigenousness made them special.

Bebel was—even more than the court expected of its poets laureate—prolific and vociferous in his propagandistic support of the empire, which to his eyes by and large tallied with Germany. Born in Justingen, a town in the all-but-impotent Duchy of Swabia, he was fiercely proud of his region's history and heritage: The Swabians were the finest Germans. But his patriotism extended much further, as his Latin phrase *patria me Germania* visually and elegantly indicates, wherein the German fatherland encloses the first-person *I*. This sense of belonging not only bonded him to the southwestern regions of the empire, which he did not leave even for the humanist's obligatory journey to Italy; it also prompted him to defend the reputation of his countrymen, whenever threatened by half-truths and slander spread south of the Alps. He was therefore quick to take issue with Piccolomini's account of the Germans' alleged descent from Trojan ancestry, which he had come across while working on his speech for Maximilian I. While discounting it as one "among other trivial and vulgar slight histories," he was sufficiently irritated to address the genealogical question more fully, turning a mere section of the Innsbruck speech into a separate treatise.[22] "The Germans are indigenous" is its first sentence and title; published in 1509, it is basically a discourse on chapters 2 and 4 of the *Germania*. Bebel wrote it "not out of a desire to discredit Piccolomini or to advance [his] own reputation, but out of love for [his] country, to which [he owed] everything." Whatever its ultimate motivation, it would confirm not just indigenousness but also purity as central parts of the Germanic catechism.

For in addition to owing their beginnings to no one, the Germans, Bebel elaborated, had always remained "without the infiltration of [foreign] arrivals"; they had not been adulterated.[23] While waves of people had roiled over the Apennine peninsula, all that had passed over German lands was time. This guaranteed a direct link between the ancient past and Bebel's present and allowed him to declare: "We are of their blood [*sumus illorum sanguis*], we are their spitting image; in us shines the nobility and greatness of our ancestors." A full appreciation of this exceptional genealogy—few other people could pride themselves on such beginnings—required the recollection of the Romans' ordinary Trojan origin and their early development as a people. Bebel, on more than one occasion, made snide remarks about it. As his contemporaries knew, Rome's first king, Romulus, had declared the future capital of the world an "asylum" lest the newly founded city remain empty, and a good number of men from neighboring peoples quickly gathered there. This, an ancient Roman historian added, was the first foundation of future greatness. But when Bebel in his speech before Maximilian I, and then again later in his historical writing, alluded to the Roman foundation myth, he could hardly have chosen a more damning expression than "dregs of peoples"; associations with the Latin term *colluvies* vary, but they all share the notion of impurity (as emphasized by one of its earliest usages, in which it signifies the confluence of sewers).[24]

For more than one reason, it turned out, the Tacitean myth of the indigenous and pure German people was far superior to the previously dominant Trojan genealogy, which Maximilan's research staff had pursued. In consequence the latter met increasingly with ridicule, before it virtually vanished. A contemporary of Bebel's and the official court historian to the Bavarian dukes, Johannes Turmaier, better known by his humanistic name, Aventinus, vented his irritation at those who concocted Trojan beginnings for Germany, even though "the German kingdom had existed for 700 years before the kingdom of Troy"—founded seventy-one years after the Flood, to be precise.[25] Contrary to current opinion, the *Germanen* had come first. They were superior not only in origin but also in age.

THE BEGINNINGS of that primeval kingdom fell into the reign of Tuisto, the earthborn god whom ancient Germanic songs celebrated as primogenitor. He owed his prominence more to the counterfeiter Annius of Viterbo, who had identified him as a son of Noah's, than to Tacitus, who hardly mentioned more than the god's name. Bebel, who had a critical mind and should have been as skeptical of Annius's welcome testimony as he was elsewhere of negative reports on his ancestors, made ample use of it, allowing his patriotism to get the better of his judgment. He was far from alone. Aventinus, highly trained, well read, and tasked with the composition of the definitive German-Bavarian history, went further than most others. He faithfully repeated the narration spun from Annius's imagination and took particular pride in Noah's adoption of Tuisto's offspring, as it "reveal[ed] the Germans' superior virtue and fortitude over other peoples'."[26] But he found the German progenitor still to be lacking in personality: Even in Annius's allegedly reported account, he had, aside from his place within the Noachide genealogy, received no more than two or three desultory comments. For all that, he remained without a real face.

Aventinus, soon to be famed for "recounting at greater length . . . what Tacitus comprehended in briefest terms," dedicated dozens of pages to Tuisto in several of his works. Thanks to his pen the Germans obtained their "first king and lawgiver." His was the first in a chronologically organized series of portraits, that included Charlemagne.[27] Doubts about his existence were misplaced, Aventinus affirmed. Of course, given the king's antiquity, no one should be surprised by the slight variations in the spelling of his name (and Aventinus's own texts are not free of them either); and there was naturally also the occasional disagreement about his exact relationship to Noah—whether he was his biological or adopted son. But these trifles amounted to little compared with the evidence the Germans' founding father had left. Aventinus found vestiges of him in place-names: Tuitz, a village near the Rhine, and Teutoburg, the woods where Augustus's legions suffered defeat from German hands, both attested to his existence.[28] But his greatest legacy were his laws, by which for all times he shaped his subjects' virtuous character. For when Noah's cursed son, Ham, whose waywardness

6. Tuisco, the father of all Germans, in Aventinus's *Chronica*. *Houghton Library, Harvard University, Ger 9250.3.1.*

Aventinus stressed in his prehistoric account, arrived from Babylon, Tuisto feared for the morality of his people. He called a council (just as Tacitus's *Germanen* would later do). There he gave them their first laws, but only a few. For he was aware that too many laws might "incite rather than inhibit vice and villainy," wrote Aventinus, alluding to Tacitus, who had attributed to German mores greater force than to laws elsewhere.[29] The list of laws presented was for the most part likewise plucked from Tacitus's account; the law concerning "adultery and promiscuity," to give a slightly ironic example, would be so effective that it left "the Romans in particular" in wonder.

The foundations of the German nation laid, Tuisto died in the 236th year of his reign. He was succeeded by his son, the equally tacitean Mannus, "whom our ancestors also worshiped and for whom humankind is still called men [*mannen*]."[30] From Mannus's sons, in turn, originated a long coherent line of kings, which Aventinus followed to his own present. The royal lineage reflected the uninterrupted descent of the German people, who had never been driven out of their fatherland and never so much as budged before a foreign conqueror, let alone accepted an occupying force.

FREE, BRAVE, LOYAL, AND—FORGOTTEN

> An unconquered people . . . still lives where the earth, globe curved, slopes towards the North Pole, . . . neither sluggish nor afraid to die . . . in the struggle for fatherland and dear friends, and eager to kill if struck by offense.
>
> —Conrad Celtis, 1501

Enthusiastic humanists collected episodes and quotations from Greek and Roman sources for a collage of their ancestors' courage and accomplishments. They delighted in recounting how these "stalwarts of freedom" had time and again fought off intruders, defended their borders, and thrust out to foreign sites far and wide. Nature itself, it seemed, had destined this people for war. Hence the Tacitean physiognomic qualities, which they gladly enumerated: "bodies big and upright, faces bright in peace yet terrifying in war, and especially the eyes, threatening in battle and lit up, and a voice meant to inspire terror aplenty."[31] Many were the people whose yokes had broken on these warriors' necks.

Among the vanquished, the Romans had pride of place. For them, conquerors of most of the known world, crossing the Rhine had proved more pernicious than sailing far-flung seas. Even their mightiest general, Julius Caesar, "what," Heinrich Bebel wondered, "had he *actually* accomplished," once he had bridged the river?[32] With grim delight he, representative of many others, quoted Tacitus's damning and ultimately sarcastic reckoning of those approximately 210 years during which "Germany [had] been vanquished" by Rome—only to remain unconquered. Of all the defeats the Romans had suffered, the one inflicted by the young Cheruscan* nobleman Arminius in 9 CE was the greatest. In the woods of Teutoburg, a mountainous area dark with trees in today's North Rhine–Westphalia, he entrapped and eradicated three Roman legions, reportedly causing Emperor Augustus to cry out in despair: "Quinctilius Varus [the infelicitous Roman commander], return my legions!"[33] The victorious Germanic leader continued to harry Roman troops until he fell at the hands of his own, who suspected him to be desirous of royal rule. But he came back to life roughly at the time when the *Germania* profiled the Germanic warrior, more particularly after the first part of Tacitus's *Annals* resurfaced in 1515. They included an account of his skirmishes with Roman troops after the Varian defeat, which closed with what Tacitus might have intended for an epitaph: Arminius was the *liberator haud dubie Germaniae*, "unquestion-

---

* A Germanic tribe in what is now northwestern Germany.

ably Germany's liberator."[34] As such he rose to heroic prominence among sixteenth-century readers.

Hermann, as the reformer Martin Luther rendered Arminius's Latin name into German, had served the Romans in previous campaigns and risen to captain of their auxiliaries before he dealt his former employer the lethal blow.[35] As a Germanic mercenary fighting for Rome he was unexceptional. German humanists highlighted the fact that their bellicose ancestors had withstood foreign incursions but had been happy to lend their fighting force to Roman leaders and secure their victories. Had not Julius Caesar relied on Germanic cavalry in his conquest of Gaul? Even Piccolomini and Campano had granted this! And had it not been "with their help that [Caesar] overcame [his rival] Pompeius and his Roman troops [in the civil war]?"[36] Later on Germanic soldiers were even entrusted with the emperors' lives, serving as their bodyguards. The evidence was clear: Their necks had refused Rome's yoke, but their shoulders had carried its leaders.

Romans had trusted Germans more than Romans: Humanists interpreted this as proof of the exceptional "loyalty and integrity" that characterized their forebears (Arminius/Hermann's treachery was mostly overlooked, sometimes defended). They drew on Tacitus's account of German steadfastness, which he expounded in his colorful description of a leader's circle of "choice young men, [whose service was] an honor in times of peace, a protection in times of war." These followers, Tacitus appended, believed that "to return from battle surviving one's leader . . . was shameful."[37] Only death freed them. He also observed, most remarkably to his eyes, the steadfastness of gamblers who stood by their word, having wagered their freedom before the last cast of the die. No matter how easily the loser could extricate himself, he still endured being bound and sold. Tacitus allowed himself an expression of bewilderment, considering it "obstinacy what they [the *Germanen*] call faithfulness." He was quickly corrected by Franciscus Irenicus, who assigned a whole section of his 1518 history of Germany to the discussion of loyalty, insisting that this episode showed "proper perseverance."[38] This now national characteristic enjoyed greater popularity among Irenicus and others for its favorable contrast with their southern European rivals. Fickleness was one of the three stereotypical accusations volleyed at the Italians (and increasingly the French). Masters of fraud and deceit who changed loyalties lightly, they were portrayed as diametrically opposed to the Germanic character, which "guard[ed] loyalty with a pious and unwavering heart."[39]

Germanic men revealed another aspect of their unwavering hearts when they left home to fight for glory, as Tacitus reported to the delight of German humanists, who liked to add that their forefathers had descended upon Roman provinces at will. Heinrich Bebel confidently claimed that the *Germanen* had maintained their own empire even while the Romans were still flourishing. He was untroubled by the absence of evidence, given the "lack of [native] writers" and Roman bias. Germanic fortitude had won victories: "Few were the people in the wide world whom our name had not at least made tremble at one time."[40] Long lists of conquests circulated, made even longer by the inclusion of other peoples' achievements. For the tableau of Germanic tribes in the *Germania's* second part, and the varying ethnic notions of northern Europe, left "Germanic" sufficiently vague to include tribes in the west, east, and north. The massive migrations complicated the picture even further, tempting chauvinists to claim other peoples' triumphs for their own. (The Swedes, to cite one example, had originally belonged to the Germanic tribe of the Swabians, who were, the fanciful argument continued, the first to occupy Scandinavia.[41]) More critical minds ridiculed these paper conquests, believing them to be unnecessary given the great number of actual Germanic victories.

In the course of these conquests, Giannantonio Campano had suggested in his Regensburg speech, the *Germanen* had "brought forth such a multitude of glorious men that by founding colonies of nobility . . . everywhere, they spread the noblest and regal families all over the world."[42] His German readers leaped at this description. Some, like Aventinus, added the late-antique notion of the North as the "cradle of humanity" to Campano's description and termed Germany "the erstwhile mother of the noblest and bravest peoples, their factory."[43] Others, like Jacob Wimpfeling, drew on the etymological interpretation of *Germania* as deriving from "to sprout" (*germinare*) and rendered the meaning of "German" as "the seed of nobility." In fact, those who believed that Germany had received its culture and ruling class from the Romans were mistaken: "Rather, it was Germany that imbued the Romans with it." Most grandiose was the exclamation that Germans had contributed magnificently "not just in Europe but Asia and Africa even before the birth of Christ."[44] The late-nineteenth-century movement known as pan-Germanism would make surprisingly similar claims.

A HALLMARK since ancient times, German freedom was seen facing serious threats at the turn of the sixteenth century: Turkish forces battled at the gates of Vienna in 1529; the Curia tightened its grasp on German holdings; and the Roman legal code supplanted time-honored local laws. To German humanists these times called for Arminius's bellicose and freedom-loving spirit. None was more outspoken in this call than Ulrich von Hutten (1488–1523), author of the seminal dialogue *Arminius*, which started the warrior's idolization, and one of the most prolific pamphleteers in the years leading up to the Reformation.[45] Unrivaled by any of his German contemporaries in Latin diction, and—once he started writing in the vernacular—challenged only by Martin Luther, he enjoyed the respect of the leading humanists of his time, Erasmus of Rotterdam and Thomas More. Of knightly stock (traceable to the tenth century), he flung down the gauntlet like his medieval ancestors and generally wrote with the same passion that compelled him to fight French soldiers (at least once leading to manslaughter). "Let us liberate the fatherland, so long oppressed."[46] In this fight his weapon of choice was the pen, and his enemies the Roman law and the Roman church.

Law was a contested issue in the German-speaking territories of Hutten's time. From Rome came the legal code that, after humble beginnings, had accumulated into the *corpus iuris civilis* (body of civil law). Now, at the turn of the sixteenth century, it had ousted customary German law. An imperial decree passed at the Diet of Worms in 1495 specified that Roman law be applied within the boundaries of the empire, and the judges at the newly founded Imperial Chamber Court proceeded accordingly. German lawyers usually obtained their legal training in Italy, with centers in Bologna and Padua. Hutten himself had studied law at Pavia, Bologna, and Rome, only to realize the full scale of his dislike both of the code and of its "arrogant dispensers."[47] He did not obtain a degree. In a letter to a friend in 1516 he reminisced with the help of Tacitus about the former days of justice, when there were no lawyers and "good habits carried more weight here than written laws elsewhere." In replacing the adjective "good" (*bonae*) of the Tacitean original with "written" (*scriptae*), he pointedly implied that the Roman laws lacked that quality.

German litigation that affected the church's interest had to be adjudicated at the courts in Rome, a practice widely criticized as being conducive to curial abuse. Almost six decades after Martin Mayer's admonitory letter to Piccolomini, the grounds for complaint were the same but had hardened. Foremost among these "encumbrances on the German nation," as they came to be known, were the disproportionate financial contributions to Rome and the numerous church holdings along the Rhine. "One could truthfully say," Hutten quipped, "that more than half of Germany is in the possession of Holy Joes."[48] It seemed as though the Roman clergy succeeded where the Roman army fifteen hundred years before had failed. Hutten declared a feud against the Romanists, as members of the Roman church were snidely called, whose pompous lifestyle not only consumed German resources but also conflicted with true Christian spirit. The deep simplicity and purity of spirit, wanting in the present, had pervaded the Germanic religiosity that Tacitus described. Aventinus, who in his early days turned to the Bible and Tacitus as his constant companions, included Germanic piety among Tuisto's regulations. Germany's first king and lawgiver (once again going by the *Germania*) ordained that "God could only be sought and worshiped in one's heart; for he cannot be confined nor compared to any human or other corporal figure ... so he consecrated woods ... that all could worship one God under the free and common sky."[49] Worship should be simple, authentic, and pure—again; or rather, life as a whole should be.

A SIMPLE PEOPLE'S BETTER LIFE

They guard loyalty with a pious and unwavering heart, in loving awe of religion and the gods, as upholders of honesty; and their mind—clinging to what is true and just—is in harmony with their lips, as it shuns fabricated lies of a duplicitous tongue.

—Conrad Celtis, 1501

Even more than origin and freedom, ancestral morality excited enthusiastic praise. "Therein," Heinrich Bebel exclaimed, "we obviously outdo all other people."[50] He and his fellow humanists reinterpreted their ancestors' lack of laws, which Piccolomini had malignly attributed to cultural retardation, as a consequence of their superior morals. Soon joined by reformers, they campaigned to set up ancestral morality as a value on a par with Roman arts.

In the end they would base the greatness of their past on character instead of culture.

This new paradigm arose out of a predicament. For no matter how diligently one scrutinized the past, Germanic arts remained in the dark, and it was clear that the German ancestors could not compete culturally with the Romans. An ambiguous remark in the *Germania* suggested even that the "secret of letters" was unknown north of the Alps at a time when the Greeks and Romans had churned out world-class literature for several centuries.[51] Some humanists tried to argue in favor of a lost high culture: They fancied an intellectual caste of secretive druids, who, originally from Gaul, had bequeathed their doctrine orally to the next generation; or they collected proverbs as testimony to an elaborate Germanic philosophy. Serendipitously Tacitus reported on poetic songs of historical tales, which lent the promoted notion of a highly developed oral culture a veneer of possibility. Medieval texts as well as the latest German inventions—especially the printing press—were also put forth as proof of an inborn ingenuity, which, of course, characterized the ancient Germans too. But these efforts to stylize warriors as ingenious inventors ultimately failed. (This Promethean warrior would, however, make a remarkable comeback in the nineteenth century in the Aryan persona.) Another strategy to vindicate the past proved more successful: to concede weakness on artistic grounds while emphasizing other strengths in its stead—none more than moral integrity. With its panorama of Germanic life, the *Germania* provided suddenly less despondent humanists once more with what they needed. It was a gift so opportune that in time its authenticity would be questioned.

The extent to which Tacitus lay behind the humanists' flattering portrait of their ancestors' character can be gleaned from one of the most chauvinistic literary enterprises of the time: Jacob Wimpfeling's above-mentioned *Short German History* (*Epitome rerum Germanicarum*). Wimpfeling ended by summarizing the qualities that had become apparent in the course of his narrative. He emphasized that Germans had always excelled "by the multitude of their men, the modesty of their women, the excellence of their first men and leaders, and their pure and unblemished nobility, the fortitude and stature of their soldiers, their common liberty, loyalty, integrity, generosity, steadfastness, and a particular talent for the arts."[52] Tacitus furnished Wimpfeling and many other sixteenth-century writers with all but one of these characteristics, and for the most part even the particular words, some rather choice. Casting an anatomist's eye on young men and women, the author of the *Germania* had noted that they both were of "slender tallness (*proceritas*)."[53] The author of the *Epitome*, in turn, used this same word—of which there are no more than about thirty instances in all of classical Latin literature—to describe the stature of German soldiers. (Racists in the twentieth century would consider *proceritas* a primary trait of the Aryan-Germanic race and render it as a "slender and lofty figure".) It was Tacitus's Germanic character that Wimpfeling's generation embraced and celebrated as the German character.

Moving forward in the campaign against Italian lordliness, Hutten called upon this virtuousness in order to redefine barbarism. To Italian eyes, he complained, all outside Italy were barbarians. But if due attention and appreciation were given to good mores, amiable conduct, constancy, and integrity, then "Germany was the civilized nation, whereas the Romans lived in the most outrageous barbarism."[54] As much as the Romans excelled in the arts, they lacked morals, as Tacitus had intimated. Lists of their moral shortcomings were compiled. Bebel sneered that "their carefully cultivated mores paled in comparison with [the ancient Germans'] uncultivated barbarity."[55] Their ancestors were superior, and not just morally: for if one had to choose between the Germanic life of simple decency and the Romans' amoral artistry, had one not better choose the former? Several humanists suggested this, allowing their patriotic hearts to win over their humanistic minds (albeit only briefly and for rhetorical posturing).

But times had changed, for better and worse. The welcome recent spread and flourishing of the arts north of the Alps had, it seemed, come with a threat to the ancestral ways. From Rome, decried as "once a place of arms, now an amatory place," decadence and related vices infiltrated Germany; even drunkenness, along with sloth and ire a stereotypical German fault, was ultimately blamed on Italian influence.[56] Celtis, in his role as pedagogue, repeatedly warned German youth of leaving their forefathers' solid ground for the Italians' slippery ways. He urged them to study history for their own benefit: It would teach them not only what had happened but also what to do. Ever since ancient times, Clio—the classical Muse overseeing historical writing—had worked as an archivist as well as a governess. She not only preserved the past but also offered to instruct the present. For German humanists of the early sixteenth century, it meant that they looked to their ancestors for moral guidance but to the literary monuments of Greek and Roman antiquity for aesthetical directions. Their historical vision was split.

THE DEPLORED DECADENCE was among the vices that humanists and reformers alike associated with the Roman church in particular. Of the ninety-five theses that Martin Luther published in Wittenberg in 1517—tacked to the church doors but then carried in all the winds' directions—one referred scathingly to the pope as wealthier than Rome's richest man, Crassus. Why, then, would he turn to poor believers to finance Saint Peter? Because of greed, was the implied answer. More generally the clerical lifestyle appeared to be just what one would expect from those in charge of indulgences. The spread of these Roman practices in Germany caused Luther concern. Commenting on papist bribes, he fell back on a sarcastic quotation from Tacitus: The Romans have indeed "taught us Germans to accept money."[57] During one of his many journeys with Philipp Melanchthon, the man who stood shoulder to shoulder with him in leading the Reformation, he readily concurred that the Germanic values of steadfastness, loyalty, and fidelity that Tacitus had praised were now bygones. He hastened to express his hope that at least "Italian marriages"—one of his circumlocutions for homosexual relationships—would fail to gain ground on German territory. Illicit sex, corruption, avarice, and decadence: This standard catalog of vice, Luther, along with many of his contemporaries, asserted, had come from Rome. One could only pray, as a Lutheran commentator on the *Germania* soon would, that "God [would] see to it that Germany in good time returns to its former state of temperance, integrity, modesty, and uprightness."[58]

Reformation and humanism shared in the national sentiment: Luther was called "the father of the fatherland" (*pater patriae*). For the religious and moral betterment of their Christian compatriots, Lutherans turned to the *Germania*. They produced their own Latin editions, the first German translation, and an extensive commentary, thus increasing the text's circulation. Melanchthon (1497–1560), whose work helped transform the disaffection with the Roman church into the Protestant doctrine, played a role in all three endeavors. A professor of Greek at the University of Wittenberg whose assumed name was the Greek translation of his family's vernacular Schwartzerdt ("black soil"), he earned the honorary title of "teacher of Germany" (*praeceptor Germaniae*) for his efforts to refashion the educational system. It was as pedagogue and patriot that he published an edition of the *Germania* along with a few remarks and a minimal commentary in 1538 and again in 1557. He supplemented it with two of Hutten's dialogues, the *Arminius* and the antipapist satire *The Dialogue Called Julius*, and with Celtis's *Germania generalis*. In the epistolary preface to this telltale collection he expressed his hope that German youth would learn from the "honorable examples of their forefathers," not just from their bravery and skill in military matters but also their impervious chastity.[59] The comparison of past and present, facilitated by his commentary on name changes, would also teach them Christian humility:

> Reading this text, we will receive the greatest benefit if, in contemplating not only the strength and virtuousness of ancient Germany but also the ruin and various changes, we realize: the mutability in human life is such that one must bear changes of fortune with equanimity and strive for the heavenly country, while nonetheless each one must adorn his Sparta.

Melanchthon fulfilled his obligation by his edition—the ornament he bestowed on his Sparta.

A student both of Melanchthon and Luther and later a preacher, Johann Eberlin von Günzburg took it upon himself to make the *Germania* readable to a wider, non-Latinate audience. He produced its first German translation in 1526 (which would, however, not be published until much later). Intending it as a contribution to his patria, he did not hesitate to insert a "beware" here and there in his text to point out the contemporaneous relevance; and he purged by omission or paraphrase what might have lowered the text's reformist credentials: Human sacrifices once again were not practiced among Germanic tribes in his translation.[60] While Eberlin was working on his translation, another Lutheran, Andreas Althamer, sent drafts of his voluminous commentary on the *Germania* to Melanchthon—who kept encouraging him to revise it some more. The work, which its author wished to be considered as an expression of his love for "Germany, our common fatherland," finally came out in 1529. It attests to the maturity of the *Germanen*. Some of Althamer's comments on particular Tacitean passages contain related quotations from recent humanistic texts which had drawn on the *Germania*.⁶¹ The Germans, "a people neither clever nor treacherous," according to Tacitus, are with reference to Celtis's *Germania generalis* further characterized as being of a "mind [that] cling[s] to what is true and just." Three decades into the sixteenth century, in a circle of reference, the text that started the tradition is supported by the tradition. The *Germanen*, fully profiled, were becoming quite independent of their original source.

WITHIN LESS than ten years of the publication of Piccolomini's incendiary *Account of Germany*, Celtis's generation—buoyed by "their Cornelius"—defined and refined their ancestors' profile. By 1505 the mythical *Germanen* had become the exemplary Germans: pure and noble; long limbed, fair, and flaxen haired; free spirited, stouthearted, and straightforward. These ancestors provided a sense of national belonging and moral guidance toward a better future. They would have to fulfill these two roles for many centuries, during which Tacitus's readers would for the most part continue what the humanists had begun, merely modifying aspects of the Germanic portrait to make it fit their current needs. In most if not all respects the National Socialist vision of the *Germanen* would be a mirror image of the humanists', only slightly twisted through time.

5
Heroes' Songs

According to Tacitus's testimony . . . the old Germans took
great care of their untainted mores . . . and preserved their old
mother tongue unmixed and unadulterated.

—Justus Georg Schottelius, 1663

ARMINIUS FOUND himself on the fields of battle once again
when he was reborn in the middle of the seventeenth
century. In the play *The Victory of Peace*, which debuted
in 1642 at the Dankwarderode Castle near Brunswick in Lower
Saxony, he served as the dead hero commenting on the living; he
was joined, for that purpose, by another champion of the past:
the tenth-century Henry I the Fowler, the duke of Saxony and
first German king. The playwright and leading German linguist
Justus Georg Schottelius (1612–76) employed this rhetorical con-
trivance to make his audience see through their ancestors' eyes the
ugly face of war that pillaging, famine, and disease had imprinted
on the German landscape. After more than twenty years the fields
were scattered with bones, farms and town houses scorched by
fire, and city walls battered into ruins. "Is this country supposed
to be Germany, really?" wonders Arminius in conversation with
his companion.[1]

On the stage, Bolderian, a contemporaneous German, enters and
promises elucidation. Neat and groomed (with two plumes to his

hat, puffy sleeves, knee-high boots, and a sword for ornament), he speaks the language of the day. German, it seems, is the syntax, but French, mostly, the words. Arminius, hardly able to comprehend, sighs disheartenedly. How the "majestic, proper, pure, and abundant mother tongue" has been subjected to the slavish existence of a "bastard"—bastardized not only by French but also Italian and Latin words! Had he fought the Romans in vain after all? Even more enraging, Bolderian dared to mock him and his companion King Henry I for their rough appearance: beards, braids, sizable swords, horned helmets, and fur coats. The German heroes, meanwhile, failed to see the difference between their counterpart, who so readily explained the concept of the cavalier he prided himself to be, and the foreign soldiery. For "Spaniards, Hungarians, Croats, French, and Welsh" were everywhere in Germany, but Germans nowhere—at least none like those of Tacitus's unadulterated days when the mother tongue was as pure and honorable as its speakers.

When Schottelius's reborn heroes lamented the calamities of war, they expressed the sentiments of their weary audience. The Thirty Years' War, which had begun as a regional conflict (the Bohemian revolt, in today's Czech Republic), was now in its third decade, and at one point or another it involved all the dominant European powers. Gustavus II Adolph's Sweden, Cardinal Richelieu's France, and Hapsburg Spain had moved their mercenary forces across German fields, where the activity of war was centered. The greatest toll was on the peasantry. Famine and disease—plague, typhus, syphilis, scurvy—were the rearguard of the marauding troops. Within a few years Germany regressed by many decades: Württemberg, a state in the south, had counted 450,000 inhabitants when the war broke out. Twenty years later its population had been decimated to a mere 100,000. It would take 130 years to reach prewar numbers again. "Cry, companions!" are the opening words of the poem *Lamentation by an Observer of the Devastation of Germany*, published a year after *The Victory of Peace* was staged.[2]

During the lengthy war the "German question" was asked once again on battlefields and writers' desks. There was no room for the state of Germany, it seemed, amid the more than three hundred German states, independent cities, and free imperial villages that quarreled over the issues of liberty, independence, and power in the loose fold of the Holy Roman Empire of the German Nation. The emperor, a contemporary observer anonymously sneered, "had next to nothing except for his vain name."[3] Regional leaders, divided by faith, were tossed by the surges of the Reformation and the Counter-Reformation; Lutherans were at odds not only with Catholics but also with Calvinists. One German prince, Maximilian of Bavaria, suffered a conflict of loyalties, when he, a Catholic and patriot, dreaded a Catholic victory owed to Spanish forces as much as a Protestant German win. All struggled individually and pettily for their parcel of power to the detriment of the whole. By their ever-changing alliances they invited adjacent countries to enter and conquer. Paul Fleming, one of the finest lyric poets of his day, personified Germany bewailing her fate: "Woe is me! What I used to be! And now?"[4] Surveying the scene, he was reminded of Tacitus's prayer for German discord to continue, since it benefited Rome. But who, one wondered, benefited now?

Gone, too, were the days of military glory, when "the short Roman man ran back to the Tiber."[5] German troops, contemporaries complained, receded rather than resisted, as their ancestors famously had back in Arminius's days, and home territory, once free and impenetrable, was now overrun by foreigners. In the midst of economical, political, and military ruin, forlorn patriots continued to build Germany as a cultural nation. Since the days of Aventinus and Hutten, the focus of nationalistic interest had shifted: During the early phase of German Baroque, work in and on the German language (*Spracharbeit*) stood at the center of patriotic efforts, a space previously occupied by the writing of historical accounts. Like the humanists, intellectuals of the seventeenth century were proud of their Tacitean forefathers, "men brave and unbeaten," conquerors of near and far, and so virtuous and candid "that what others achieved only subsequent to a long and burdensome education with them seemed inborn and implanted by nature."[6] But the touchstone of pride was not German resistance to Roman legionaries anymore. Rather it was the age, originality, and purity of their mother tongue. "I write," one of the language enthusiasts professed, "because I love the language . . . because I love my country."[7] Heinrich Bebel had written history for the same reason. The conservatives of the German Baroque stood on the shoulders of their humanistic predecessors.

The humanists had already formulated thoughts on the German language. Celtis had heard in his mother tongue the speakers' rough and tough Germanic mindset: Their words bespoke their character. Elsewhere, however, he had expressed embarrassment about the "murmurings in that unlearned language," revealing an ambivalence not unusual among the *literati* of his time (who had initially neglected their vernacular entirely).[8] His student Aventinus, much read among Baroque writers, had reflected on how German entwined with foreign words ended up corrupted and incomprehensible. But, these scattered reflections notwithstanding, it was the seventeenth century that in spite—or, perhaps, because—of the war witnessed the emergence of self-conscious groups of authors who concertedly tried to codify and advance their mother tongue: its grammar, orthography, and poetry. Many of them congregated in so-called language societies (*Sprachgesellschaften*), founded specifically for the purpose of linguistic care.

Such care seemed necessary. Bustling cities, such as Hamburg in the north and Augsburg in the south of the German-speaking territories, functioned (often even during the war) as huge marketplaces where international goods including Asian spices and West Indian sugar were traded and distributed to other corners of Europe. German roads served as thoroughfares of commerce.

With foreign goods arrived foreign cultures. But more than what came from afar, it was what came from nearby that was perceived as a threat. For much of Schottelius's century, before and after the war, Germany was overawed by France and Spain in questions of fashion. At the courts the music came from Italy, the paintings from the Netherlands, and literature was consumed in many languages but hardly in German. Quotation marks hovered when German "culture" was discussed abroad. It was usually seen as represented by those princes who considered themselves witty when boxing their dwarfs' ears, or who tried to impress visitors with their endurance in gorging, swilling, and carousing, and who fittingly concluded their letters with "Farewell and get drunk."[9] In order to be cultured one assumed foreign airs. The Romance cultures and languages in particular dominated and subverted the allegedly pure "heroic language" and "untainted mores" of ancient times. Conservative observers perceived this "greed for anything foreign" (*Frömdgierigkeit*) to be so widespread and penetrating that if one were to dissect the heart of a man like Bolderian, it would be found to be one-eighth German—at best.[10] "If Tacitus should be restored to life, he would have to write the Germans a completely different little book about their manners and mores."[11] German humanists had worked in the shadow of their Italian counterparts; now the French were perceived as a challenge and a threat: The rival changed, the rivalry continued.

When Arminius and his companion complained in *The Victory of Peace* about the cultural changes—how what was genuine and German and alive in their days was now (in the metaphorical language of the day) *diluted*—they expressed the conservative leanings harbored by many men of letters across the German-speaking lands. Scornful of a present inundated by foreign-language imports, they wrote dreamily about their pristine past. "The splendid Roman C. Corn. Tacitus" was their primary witness.[12] He had such authority that in order to fulfill patriotic needs he was repeatedly forced to say what in fact he had not. Some of the greatest and most influential minds of their times interpreted his *Germania* with suspicious eagerness: Next to Schottelius were Philipp Clüver, the towering historian and geographer, and Martin Opitz, the "father of German poetry." Joined by numerous lesser-known intellectuals, they theorized about their mother tongue: its biblical age, Babylonian origin, and eponymous originator Teuto, previously and "mistakenly" known as Tuisto (or Tuysco). They conjured up German's long tradition as a poetic language that had been used skillfully since the days of the bards, who were now made to appear in Tacitus's text. And they emphasized how it intersected with its speakers' national character, considering its original purity an asset to be vaunted as much as the purity of its original people.

German superiority, as contended by Baroque patriots, continued to be associated with fortitude and virtue but was now also grounded in the German language, so old, so poetic, so pure that it was undoubtedly "the richest in words and the best."[13] Rather than the past, it was now the language that provided forlorn patriots with a fatherland.

TEUTO—RESTORED

It is because of a scribe's lapse or negligence that in Tacitus "Tuisto" is written instead of the name "Tuito" or "Teuto."
—Philipp Clüver, 1616

The origin of the German people, in which humanists had taken great pride, now attracted the interest of those studying the beginnings of the German language. Theories, as diverse as fanciful, soon circulated. Some proposed that German rather than Hebrew was the primary language and that "Adam was a German man."[14] Others speculated that paradise had been polyglot and that "the German thunder" had served to pronounce expulsion. The majority, however, left the eminence of Hebrew untouched and dated the emergence of German to right after the confusion at the Tower of Babel. A typical chronology specified that about a hundred years after the Flood, a time when "the people were one, and they all had one language," Noah ordered his three sons—Shem, Ham, and Japheth—to oversee the earth's repopulation. Yet before their divergent departures, they participated in the erection of the tower "whose top should reach unto heaven."[15] It fell because of human hubris, and one common language gave way to seventy-two.

No sooner were the languages divided and the peoples dispersed than Ashkenaz, a grandson of Japheth and great-grandson of Noah, led his people to the part of Europe later to be called Celtic and comprising the Balkans, France, Spain, Germany, and the British Isles. Ashkenaz was the "father of all Celts," of whom the primeval Germans were believed to have formed the largest faction.[16] Arriving at the Rhine, they already spoke an original version of German, venerable because of its temporal proximity to the holy single language. As with people, so with language: Age conferred prestige. Modern German was said to be older than French, since its core had remained the same as in Ashkenaz's day, whereas French developed later and under the influence of Latin. (One early-seventeenth-century author after careful calculation declared it to be 3,822 years old.)

Trying to peer into these prehistoric times, linguists relied on etymology, the science of the origin and meaning of words. If properly understood, names, they believed, could bring to light their since-obscured beginnings. The city name of Nuremberg, for example, revealed to them that it had been founded by the Roman general Nero Claudius Drusus, who had camped on a hill (*Berg*, in German) the peasants came to refer to as "Nero's *Berg.*" In time it became Nürnberg, and its name its history. As often as not etymologists cut and carved words so as to yield a desired origin. Practicing such word masonry, they elucidated how Ashkenaz was related to Tuisto.

The integration of the Tacitean myth into biblical genealogy had remained an issue ever since the fraudulent Annius of Viterbo had identified Tuisto as a previously unknown son of Noah. German writers, discontented with this son's obscurity, looked for a better-known and biblically attested founding father. Many settled for Ashkenaz: For his name, as a commentator on the *Germania* pointed out, was a Hebrew word for German.[17] Said Ashkenaz, the argument went, was also known as "Ascanes," whose sons had been called *thi Ascanes*. An elision of the article (a variant of today's German *die*), by which the ending *-i* was lost, followed by a change of the offspring's initial vowel from *a* to *u*, resulted in *Th-uisc*. This form was obviously related to "Tuysco," as Tacitus's god was spelled in one manuscript (and Annius's fabrication). Many of these dizzying linguistic maneuvers—elision, mutation, and crisscrossing between dialects and even languages—were common. But in this particular instance they met the ridicule of Clüver, a historian and "leading geographer of his time," who advocated a different interpretation.[18] It involved a novel reading of Tacitus, which appeared as part of his *Germania antiqua*, published in 1616.

PHILIPPUS CLUVERIUS—his name's Latinized version—was born in 1580 to a blue-blooded family in Gdańsk (formerly Danzio). Growing up in this international marketplace by the Baltic Sea and the mouth of the Motława River must have awakened his desire to travel the world. After stays at the courts in Warsaw and Prague, he left for the Netherlands to study at the University of Leiden, where Joseph Justus Scaliger, the leading scholar of classical studies at the time, taught. Clüver's father, a mintmaster, had chosen law for his son. But the son—handsome, of amicable manners, and with a tongue as quick as his wit—spent the little time he had for study on history, geography, and philology. Disowned by his father and at best secretly (and barely) supported by his mother, he lived a peripatetic life, traveling to Norway, Scotland, England, France,

Germany, and Italy. When he finally returned to Leiden with his wife, he published the *Germania antiqua*. It earned him the title *Geographus Academicus* and, more important, an appended salary. But he soon fell ill and died at age forty-two in 1622, too soon to see his fame.

The *Germania antiqua* provided, in the opinion of its author, "by and large an extended commentary to Tacitus's book."[19] Leafing through this four-hundred-year-old three-volume text, the reader quickly realizes that it provides a pictorial commentary too. For it is adorned with a set of twenty-six woodcuts of Germanic life, the settings as well as the details of which were culled from Tacitus. They present the life of a primitive people: A battle, a sacrifice in a grove, and funerary games all visualize parts of the Tacitean narra-

7. A Germanic feast, depicted in Clüver's *Germania antiqua*.
Houghton Library, Harvard University, GC6 C6275 616g.

tive, as does the image of a feasting party. Framed within a wooden structure are *Germanen* gorging on meat, gulping from a jug ("to continue drinking day and night carries no stigma," Tacitus writes), leisurely reclining on hides, most of them naked except for a cloak. Here the "clothing [appears to be] the same for men as for women." The men are shown carrying weapons, whose frequency reminds the viewer of the Germans' bellicose nature. The women appear to share in their men's endeavors or to take care of the children. The boy in the front is one among many who, in the pages of Clüver's book, play about as "naked and dirty" as Tacitus claims, soon "to grow such limbs, such bodies as [the Romans] admired." Indeed, the people populating this tableau (and many others) all look tall and muscular: The mesomorph in the lower right corner may well represent the lot.[20]

These woodcuts would soon take on a life of their own, serving to inspire and illustrate the stereotypical *Germanen* who stomped across the stage in Brunswick. One playwright, contemporaneous with Schottelius, specifically referred to these cuts to help readers visualize the heroes of his play. As rough but righteous warriors, they were cast standing tall in the midst of debonair types like Bolderian. Gruff and genuine, they soon figured in historical novels too. Fusing with the emerging Grobianism, a satirical genre that centered on bluntness and other loutish behavior, they helped introduce uncouth simplicity and coarse integrity to a wider audience. They would eventually meet indignation from twentieth-century writers who thought that these *Theatergermanen* damaged the reputation of their historical Germanic ancestors.[21]

The dependence of the images on the *Germania* is the more apparent as Clüver included it in its entirety in his own work—not once but twice. For he considered the standard edition by the great Dutch philologist Justus Lipsius to be flawed in places and therefore printed his own version too in side-by-side columns so as to facilitate comparison. Yet in spite of Tacitus's monumental importance, Clüver granted sole and single truth only to the Bible. As a consequence the pagan belief in indigenousness stood in need of correction. Like many others, Clüver believed the Germans to have come forth from the Babylonian dust speaking their own language and following Ashkenaz toward the north as part of the Celtic ur-people. But he presented his own interpretation of Tuisto's role therein.[22]

The Latin *Germani*, Clüver pointed out, was not the original name of the German ancestors. Taking the etymologist's approach, he believed that name to be hidden in the current vernacular of *Teutsch*, *Tuitsch*, and *Deutsch*, all of which regional variations meant "German." "Teutsch," he continued, is an adjective that, in line with established linguistic rules, derives from the noun *Teut*. He suspected that the name of the god as spelled in Tacitus was slightly off: For if the Germans' vernacular name was derived from Tuisto, they should be *Tuistische*, not *Teutsche*. Clüver gleaned evidence from Tacitus and elsewhere to support his claim that what the Roman historian should have written was *Teuto* or *Tuito* but not *Tuisto*. Since this mistake, probably made by an inadvertent scribe, was easy enough to explain, he adjusted the spelling and proceeded with his argument as if the critical passage read: *celebrant carminibus antiquis . . .* Teutonem *deum terra editum*.[23] German humanists had interfered with the transmitted text to make barbaric human sacrifices disappear; now Tuisto had to make room for Teuto. The *Germania* repeatedly fell victim to its readers' wishes and ideologies.

More than a name correction, this proposal pronounced death for the pagan god. Clüver went on to illuminate the relation between the name *Teut* and the Greek and Latin words *theos* and *deus*, both of which may signify "god" as well as "God." It was obvious, he proclaimed, that when ancient Germans sang of Teuto, they simply if unwittingly praised the Christian God. This interpretation allowed Clüver to dispense with the problem of how to connect Tacitus's earth-born god to the biblical Ashkenaz. His name corrected and its true meaning expounded, Tuisto simply disappeared into God. Clüver then moved on to reinterpret the next generation within the Tacitean genealogy accordingly: Mannus, now Teuto's son, is revealed to be none other than the first offspring of God: Adam. Etymology comes to Clüver's aid once more. Both names—Mannus and Adam—mean "human" in their respective languages.

Ingeniousness faced one final intransigence. The Germanic songs, according to Tacitus, attributed three sons to Mannus/Adam. Clüver concedes that they could not be Adam's but had to be Noah's, since his family was the only one to survive the flood that swept over the sinful land. As Noah's sons (mistakenly attributed to Adam), Shem, Ham, and Japheth also found their place in the *Germania*. Clüver concludes happily that aside from the misspelling and the filial confusion, there was only one genuine mistake in Tacitus's otherwise luminous account: God was not himself earth-born, as Germanic songs related. Perhaps, Clüver speculated, the ancient Germans themselves had mixed up these details, quite understandably given their age, or maybe the mistake was Tacitus's, who "misunderstood the German song?"[24] In any case Clüver could adhere to the authority of the holy book while embracing the content of the "golden booklet." All that was required was the right reading.

Pages bound in a book, books aligned on a shelf not only symbolize the continuous history of a set of ideas; they make it. Clüver's work contains not only his version of the *Germania* but also numerous references to humanistic writers who had themselves made heavy use of Tacitus. Within a few decades the fame of the historiogeographer from Leiden, a "highly meritorious and experienced" scholar, spread; his influence would extend far beyond the Baroque age.[25] He would carry the humanistic heritage from the sixteenth to the nineteenth century, adorning the desks of the poet Friedrich Gottlieb Klopstock and the polymath Jacob Grimm. Just as the widely read Aventinus helped lead the Tacitean *Germanen* from the humanistic to the Baroque age, Clüver contributed to their continuing presence for eighteenth-century writers. "Because of your [Clüver's] merits," wrote Martin Opitz on March 31, 1631, in a poetic epitaph, "the entire fatherland will owe you gratitude for all time."

LET THE BARDS SING

The Germans' poetry, their bards' heroic songs, reanimated Mannus's spirit and Tuiscon's ashes.

—Daniel Casper von Lohenstein, 1689

The "restorer of the German language," Martin Opitz (1597–1639), enjoyed the appreciation of his contemporaries, some of whom even celebrated him as the father of German poetry.[26] When he put his first verse down on paper, Latin was still the language of the literate: at higher schools and universities, in the correspondence and often the conversations of the learned, not to mention most of the literature in Germany. While England had beheld the genius of William Shakespeare, Italy Torquato Tasso, and France Pierre de Ronsard, there was no author of such standing in the German vernacular. Opitz himself, when succumbing to the Muses' charm, composed in Neo-Latin at first, as was the order of the day. But he soon set out to lead the Muses into his fatherland and remedy the fact that they "never knew how to speak German."[27] Never? Except, of course, in Tacitus's time, when bards led warriors into battle, and actually, it would soon turn out, already all the way back in Tuisto's days.

The nine daughters of Zeus and the goddess of memory, Mnemosyne, had been escorted from one national abode to another before. Celtis, along with other northern humanists, had prided himself upon their transfer from Mount Helicon to the Rhine River. But neither he nor any of his contemporaries conceived of teaching them to sing in German; quite the contrary, when Heinrich Bebel had treated the deplorable linguistic misuses among his compatriots, the language both of his writing and of his concern had been Latin. Opitz's generation now insisted that the Muses learn German. There should soon be a vernacular literature superior to lowly folksongs and chants and at least equal to the refined works in French or Italian. Lifting German literature to such a higher level should come easy: After all, groves had resounded with German poetry before. Did not Tacitus attest to age-old songs, *carmina antiqua*? And surely, those had been composed "in the style of their very own language," as an enthusiast asserted around the middle of the century (even though Tacitus had said no such thing).[28] One of the oldest languages, German also looked back on one of the longest poetic traditions. Opitz could be cast both as the restorer and as the father of German poetry at the same time: While he merely resumed an ancestral art, it had been neglected for so long that the resumption amounted to reinvention. A new generation of German writers agreed: "The heroes' language should become courtly again."[29] They strove to compose poetry with the sophistication and skill that characterized Greek and especially Latin verbal artistry. Cicero and Virgil's standards should remain; but as models for German literature they should finally retire. For their language, Opitz had claimed when he was hardly twenty years old, was dead—its hollow words echoing the sentiments of men long gone.

WHEN OPITZ delivered his obituary on the Latin language in the fall of 1617, less than a year before the Thirty Years' War began, he spoke decorously and solemnly in Latin. Some probably thought it ironic, if not wayward, that a student of the gymnasium of Schönaich in Upper Silesia (in today's western Poland) argued vividly in Latin that Latin was dead. After all, one of the school's foremost aims was to train well-versed and well-spoken Latinists. But Opitz disagreed. The son of a butcher in a long line of butchers, he had shown intellectual interests and promise quite out of line with the family tradition. Upon early admittance to school, he moved from Bolesławiec (Bunzlau), his birthplace in southern Silesia, north of Bytom (Beuthen), on the Oder. He stayed in the house of Tobias Scultetus, a well-connected dignitary who was admired for his erudition, linguistic competence, and judgment. The musty smell of books mingled with the breeze of the wider world, and the young Opitz inhaled both with relish, a happy experience as formative as his participation in the circle of Caspar Dornau. A professor at the newly founded Schönaich gymnasium, Dornau took a particular interest in his students' rhetorical training and encouraged them to argue the two sides of a selected topic: Should, he queried, elegance be aimed for in speaking German? To many ears "German elegance" sounded like an oxymoron. Neither elegant nor poetic, it should only be spoken with an enemy, since it sounded so terrible. Spanish, Italian, and French, on the other hand—majestic, dignified, and graceful, respectively—were to be used in conversation with God, princes, and women, according to the predominant linguistic stereotypes of the time. But Dornau's circle believed that there was poetry in German and favored other national traits in conjunction with the mother tongue: purity, heroism, and originality. Which is what Opitz suggested in his scandalous address, published later that same year as *Aristarchus, or: On the Contempt for the German Language*.[30] It would soon be recognized as an early manifesto of German poetics, but only after it seems to have caused the budding poet's hastened departure from town. The establishment in all likelihood did not like what the young man had said.

Jotted down in slightly more than two days, the *Aristarchus* probably responded to the question of German elegance bandied about in Dornau's circle, and it might have been delivered in front of fellow students and teachers (both assumptions are speculative but plausible).

The title alluded to the Homeric critic Aristarchus of Samothrace, who flourished in the second century BCE and applied his outstanding philological acumen to the production of the standard editions of *The Iliad* and *The Odyssey*. The Greek's name signaled Opitz's revolutionary direction: to strive for Aristarchean accuracy and diligence in speaking and, even more so, in writing German, which was unfairly held in contempt. For historical perspective he dexterously sketched the virtuous German past with its glorious deeds—a mere copy of the standard Tacitean picture—but then quickly turned to the theme of his ancestors' language, which had not been "unequal to their deeds."[31] (Not to be able to match the greatness of his countrymen's deeds with his words was the famous fear of Sallust, one of the outstanding Roman historians; Opitz pointedly combines a witticism and praise for his own ancestors with a slight to Rome.) The German ancestors had expressed their thoughts freely and forthrightly, "admonished one another to battle, . . . and often merely with their mother tongue turned away their enemies' threats, as if by lightning." They had handed down the vernacular to later generations, fully preserved in its original form. In contrast Opitz pondered Latin: decayed, decrepit, dead. Under the numerous bad Roman emperors the Roman mores had deteriorated along with the language, which "cannot be better than the rulers of the times."

How few, he complained, even tried to cultivate this "graceful, decorous, and solemn language which was most worthy of its fatherland?"[32] On the contrary, many pretended not to comprehend German, embarrassed by fatherland and mother tongue alike. This neglect, or rather contempt, he claimed, impeded the development of a vernacular literature. Yet Germans had no reason to shy away from comparison with any other vernacular literature. After all, there had been poetry in Germany ever since Tacitus's time, if not before. To continue this tradition and enhance German-language poetry, Opitz specified rules and provided examples. His address ended on a familiar but modulated note: "See to it that you, superior in fortitude and faithfulness over all other people, do not cede in excellence of language."

Opitz, whose youthful essay resonated with most of the time's major literary topics, would return to the early history of German poetry shortly after in another work. Confronted with the absence of any artistic products, he conceded that "neither men nor women applied themselves to the arts [in Tacitus's time]; nevertheless, they put in verse and poems whatever they wanted to remember."[33] Further inspection of Tacitus and other sources revealed to him also that his ancestors had venerated poetry in as much as they assigned poets to a guild (the appeal of which was further enhanced by the fact that many Baroque writers were organized in societies). Along with the druids, who performed as teachers and censors, and the *vates*, who were priests and soothsayers, they formed one of the three groups that enjoyed particular honors, and their sole duty consisted in "singing laudatory poetry." Tacitus's Germans had been heroes before, but now they also listened to bards' heroic songs.

THE ROMAN HISTORIAN reports twice on poetry—in its broadest definition. First, as has been mentioned, on olden songs, in which the *Germanen* celebrated their divine progenitors. The second—crucial—passage, at the beginning of chapter 3, revolves around Hercules, the Greco-Roman demigod whose cult moved across Western Europe along with the Roman Empire:

They relate that Hercules once visited them, too; and they sing of him first of all their heroes, when they go to battle. They have other songs also. Their recital is called *barditus*, whereby they rouse their spirits; and from the mere tone of it they predict the result of the battle soon to unfold. For they spread or feel fear, just as their line sounds. And rather than voices, it seems like a general cry of valor.

This seemingly unexceptional passage proved crucial for the relationship suggested between valor and voices (which carried associations of "words," as the Latin *vox* may signify both) and the mention of *barditus* (of which *barditum*, as quoted earlier, is the accusative case; some manuscripts of the *Germania*—to complicate the picture even further—read "baritum," but that most likely resulted from a scribal error). Given the frequency with which this passage is quoted or alluded to in historical, linguistic, and poetic treatises of the time, one could almost overlook the obvious: Bards themselves are not mentioned at all.

The three cultural castes of teachers, priests, and singers, which Opitz did much to promote, had been reported in ancient times—but for the Gauls only. Some German intellectuals of the sixteenth century, looking for kindred spirits in their past but finding no obvious traces, had mustered all their imaginative talent to explain why and how they crossed the Rhine to establish themselves in Germany. Seventeenth-century writers could locate bards in Germany, once they had found them in the *Germania*. Opitz himself had merely insinuated that Tacitus attested to bards; others proceeded to pin them down between the Roman's lines. Even though there is no relation between the Tacitean *barditus*, a term that occurs nowhere else in classical Latin literature, and the Celtic word "bard," a professional poet in service of a nobleman, numerous generations of writers, starting with Opitz's, inferred happily from the recital to the reciter, from *barditus* to "bard." This is particularly obvious from a text composed around the middle of the seventeenth century, where the bards are defined as "the old versifiers or poets among the Germans," who had a particular way "of moving the spirits with vehemence."[34] The bards were simply inserted into Tacitus's passage concerning the *barditus*; the epigraph to this section tells the same story. This reading was too arousing for readers to worry about accuracy.

The ancient Germans appreciated and even institutionalized

poetry, because, some suggested, Tuisto/Teuto himself had so ordained it in the form of a law: "Great deeds [should be] commemorated in songs so that posterity could strive to be equally virtuous."[35] The progenitor, first king, lawgiver, and primal speaker of German thus also became the primary patron of vernacular songs—those songs in which he would be praised by later generations, as Tacitus reported.

LIKE CHARACTER, LIKE LANGUAGE

> Our ancestors handed this language—so noble, so distinguished, and full of the spirit of its fatherland—to us pure and unspoiled by any influx from outside.
>
> —Martin Opitz, 1617

Befuddled by the parley of the cavalier Bolderian, Arminius scorns "[those] words which you seized from abroad and now use, babbling and aping your enemies; [because of them] virtue and vice—I see that clearly—have often become indistinguishable from one another."[36] Outside of *The Victory of Peace*, on the larger stage of the world many agreed with him and King Henry I that alterations in one's language concurred with alterations in one's manners and mores. Employing French locutions and walking in French boots on German territory had not only tainted the inherited purity of the German language but ultimately also, they believed, caused and compounded the Thirty Years' War. In neglecting the heroic language, Arminius's scions forfeited their heroism. Worse, such linguistic carelessness would eventually result in the loss of national identity.

The assumption that foreign terms bring foreign customs and—more generally—that a people's words are inextricably linked with its ways, had great currency among the writers of the day: "Who heartily speaks German, the best German he will be."[37] It also stood at the programmatic center of the numerous language societies, which, providing institutional homes for like-minded intellectuals, framed the linguistic discourse and formed cultural life in the seventeenth century. In spite of their name and a few more radically minded members, they were little concerned with a linguistic purism that insisted on the replacement of familiar foreign words with neologisms, which, however creative, were palpably inconvenient: Thus Venus gratefully escaped names like *Lustinne* or *Liebinne*, amalgamations of "lust" and "love" with a feminine ending. Rather, and less specifically, they aimed at restoring ethical as well as verbal rectitude. For the ancient Germans moral qualities were now predicated on the health of the venerable mother tongue. Because of these ramifications, the production of a German dictionary—an urgent need of the time—was seen as both a moral contribution and a war effort. As such, it was one of the explicit targets of the preeminent language organization, founded in 1617, the same year that Martin Optiz delivered his *Aristarchus*, when two calls to German words were sounded.

THE FRUCHTBRINGENDE GESELLSCHAFT originated in Weimar (in today's Thuringia) under less than auspicious circumstances. Passing time in conversation, guests at a funeral discussed the literary societies already flourishing in France, Italy, and Britain. There was, however, no German one at the time, and they determined that redress was necessary. Inspired by the Italian model, the Accademia della Crusca in Florence, the "Fruit-bearing Society" was founded under the aegis of Duke Ludwig of Anhalt-Köthen, who, among other qualifications, brought experience as the first German member ever admitted to the Florentine academy. (Despite being the only person in a German-language society to choose a Latin motto, he remained its able head until his death in 1650; his society would continue for thirty more years under two further leaders.) Typical in its orientation and stipulations, it granted membership to men who were "lovers of their inborn German language, German mores, German integrity and virtue."[38] One of its members, the gifted epigrammatist Friedrich von Logau, extended the moral imperative to reject everything foreign and embrace all that was German even to vices. Faced with the sophisticated cultures of France or Italy and their various temptations, it seemed better to him to fall for drink: "Keep swilling! Keep swilling! Swill, you Germans, as you like. Let the fashion, let the fashion go to the devil."[39] It is no coincidence that the penchant for drinking had already been mentioned in the *Germania*, which enjoyed great popularity among the society's members, one of whom produced a translation.

The society's pursuit of the "conservation and propagation of German virtue, mores, and language" did not culminate in the production of the long-coveted dictionary.[40] Its significance lay elsewhere. Lasting for more than sixty years and with its registry counting almost one thousand, it facilitated extensive correspondence and precirculation of writings among its members and spurred promising writers to polish their contributions to the nascent German literature. Membership meant recognition: Martin Opitz was admitted only after he had followed up on his outline of poetics in the *Aristarchus* with the wider-ranging *Book on German Poetry*, including a collection of his avant-garde verse. It had, in fact, taken several nominations, a circumstance that makes it seem fitting that as an alias upon entry—the standard procedure within a society that mingled nobility and bourgeoisie—he received "the Crowned." It speaks to their sense of accomplishment that members, and Opitz was no exception, would often sign with their alias.

"The Seeker," another member, chose his pseudonym to let others know that he sought what lay hidden in the German language.[41]

What he had found in the course of his studies appeared in 1663. The most influential of the many works published in connection with the Fruchtbringende Gesellschaft, it carried the unassuming (and here, for the sake of readability, shortened) title: *Extensive Work Concerning German*. A compendium of its age, it contained the major linguistic themes and theories and would still be read and consulted in the eighteenth century. No less famed was its author, hailed as the father of German grammar and the German Varro.[42]

Justus Georg Schottelius, the devout son of a pastor born in Einbeck in Lower Saxony, had run off upon his father's death, leaving behind a merchant's career; his mind did not crave numbers but words. After years as an itinerant student, he fled Swedish troops advancing on Wittenberg, Luther's town, in 1638. Brunswick provided him with shelter. There he made the acquaintance of Duke August the Younger of Brunswick-Wolfenbüttel—a fortunate happenstance, for the duke, intellectually inclined and passionate about manuscripts and books, was using significant parts of his inheritance to turn his library, the Bibliotheca Augusta, into one of Europe's finest. When August, a member of the society since 1632, hired Schottelius to instruct his second-oldest son, he placed him within reach of many rare works that would leave traces in his writing. Schottelius was only twenty-six at the time of the appointment and without a degree. But he was rumored to be an artist of words, a *Sprachkünstler*, a qualification unobtainable at a university, since there was no institutionalized German philology at the time. The rumors about his talents and proclivities proved true in the end: Most of his work would concern language. Rewarded for his early efforts like *The Art of the German Language* (*Teutsche Sprachkunst*) by the head of the fruit-bearing society in 1642—the same year that he staged *The Victory of Peace* at the residence of his bibliophile employer—he continued to pursue his linguistic interests with singular passion. Some would suggest he suffered from "word-obsession," and looked to his *Extensive Work* as proof.[43]

Its complete title covers half a page in smallish print. It is as suggestive of the thoroughness of the fifteen-hundred-page-long work as it is expressive of those aspects commonly attributed to German in the theoretical debates to justify its excellence and superior status: As a capital language (*HaubtSprache*) it was characterized by its "ur-arrival, ur-age, and purity." Schottelius argued that German was a capital language like Hebrew, Greek, Latin, and Slavic, insofar as it did not spring from any other tongue; on the contrary, others, such as Danish, derived from it. One of Philipp Clüver's many diligent readers, he regarded modern German to be basically identical with Ashkenaz's original Celtic tongue, to the extent that he uses the adjectives "Celtic" and "German" interchangeably. In words like "teutsch" and "babble" he still heard this ur-language. These words not only pointed back to the progenitor and the language confusion at the Tower of Babel but also bespoke unbroken linguistic continuity. "The free Germans' age-old tongue" had remained the same at its core, because its speakers "had remained unbeaten in arms and tenacious of [their] original language from ancient times" (a tenacity about which there is no word in Tacitus, but many by his seventeenth-century readers).[44] Unlike the Romance languages with their dependence on Latin, German had remained "pure," a contrast also captured allegorically inside and outside the society: here "the pure and chaste virgin," there French, "the child of a whore."[45] The linguistic variant of chauvinism then claimed that just as Germanic warriors had protected their territory but descended on others' at will, the German vernacular, while impenetrable, had penetrated into other languages.

Schottelius crystallized the widely shared notion that a language was indissolubly fused with its speakers' moral character into the expression "the nature of the German language" (*Sprachnatur*). Heroes naturally spoke, as a contemporary phrased it, a "heroic language." The warriors' traditional virtues were also attributed to their tongue, which was not only pure but also upright, pious, and brave.[46] One among many, Schottelius trusted that "an explanation of the pious brave German words [would] simultaneously bring to light the age-old Germans' rightfulness and strenuous and serious bravery."[47] His work should help his nation's youth to learn this "upright (*redlich*) German language" and to develop—simultaneously—the desire for the corresponding virtues. Only a full embrace of the pure German tongue could resuscitate those virtuous men and women of Tacitean times, whom German humanists had recommended to their youth in the sixteenth century, and Arminius sought but could not find on the stage in the seventeenth.

Written "in the German fashion," Schottelius's *The Victory of Peace* attempted "to grace the mother tongue with its delicate language," thus resuming the long poetic tradition Opitz had fancied embodied by ancestral bards.[48] It hosted the old German heroes, reborn from Philipp Clüver's *Germania antiqua*, who bemoaned the impurity of the language and the decay of values on a stage framed by an artificial vine, another symbol of the Fruchtbringende Gesellschaft. More than to its audience, the play spoke to the cultural concerns of its day.

6

The Volk *of Free-Spirited Northerners*

Although today Germany [*l'Allemagne*] is in a state very different from that in which it was when Tacitus described it, although it is full of cities where there were only villages in ancient *Germanien* [*l'ancienne Germanie*], . . . and although, finally, the way of life and dress of the *Germanen* [*les Germains*] is, for this reason, in many respects different from the way of life and dress of the Germans, one nevertheless recognizes the genius and the characteristic spirit of the ancient *Germanen* in the Germans of today.

—Jean-Baptiste Dubos, 1719

FREDERICK THE Great, the monarch of Prussia's military might and eighteenth-century absolutism personified, was in the habit of conversing over dinner with his guests, on topics ranging from prehistory to the present-day economy. It was no different when in the winter of 1779 he stayed in Breslau. The occasion was in keeping with the king's character: a war. The chief city in Lower Silesia (today Wrocław in western Poland) hosted him and his diplomatic entourage during peace negotiations with his Austrian opponent, the empress Maria Theresa, in the War of the Bavarian Succession. Europe had seen young Prussia soar, many amazed more than amused, not the least the house of Hapsburg, which was headed by the empress. As Austria had failed to clip the Prussian eagle's wings during the Seven Years' War (1757–63), the two powers continued to battle for dominance within the loose confines of the Holy Roman Empire of the German Nation—a clumsy body of territories still. Now, fifteen years later, the scales of absolute power needed adjusting once more within Europe as well as within the empire.

One evening the king turned to Ewald Friedrich von Hertzberg (1725–95), his cabinet minister of foreign affairs, trusted for his competence and esteemed for his enjoyment of culture. They were on familiar terms: The count had served his king for thirty-five years, ever since Frederick II had spotted promise in the twenty-year-old graduate from the University of Halle. Now the francophone king—known for his disdain of German, which he considered unsuitable for any conversation except with one's dog—claimed in an impish tone that a German translation of Tacitus's Latin would fall short of the French in accuracy and pith. He followed up by asserting that the east Germanic tribe of the Goths had actually come from Sweden, and that the Parthian people—or, as he called them in recognition of the respective Tacitean passage: the Arsacid dynasty—had at the height of the Roman Empire been more redoubtable than their Germanic counterparts. The king, a friend of Voltaire's and the finest representative of the two principal movements of his age—absolutism and enlightenment— relished controversy; dull were the dinners lacking that condiment.

Hertzberg had learned to defer and yet to differ. A quicksilver worker and skillful writer ever since his high-school days in Stettin, he sent his king on the following day two passages from "Tacitus's famous work about ancient Germany": chapter 37, in which the Roman recounts the long history of Rome's shortfalls in Germany, along with excerpts from chapters 41 to 44, including the section concerning the Goths. A note in French accompanied this exercise:

I take liberty to present to your Majesty a chapter from Tacitus's *Germania*, which I have translated into German and French. It would seem to me that the German translation does not fall short of the French one in precision or clarity [*pureté*]. That chapter demonstrates at the same time how far Tacitus ranked the ancient Germans [*les Germains*] above the Parthians and the Arsacids; furthermore, Tacitus's text proves that the Goths, the Swedes or Vandals . . . , & other great nations, which later toppled the Roman Empire, had their ancient habitats between the Elbe and the Vistula—in those countries that are presently subjected to your Majesty's rule. I hope that your Majesty will not take badly the liberty that I took in presenting this little essay.[1]

The king sent a handwritten response about half an hour later:

I read that translation essay of Tacitus that you sent me, against which I have nothing to say. But it's his description of the mores of the ancient Germans—that's not difficult to translate; it's his sententious and vigorous style [in the *Annals* that is difficult], with which in so few words he draws the characters and vices of the Roman emperors. . . . quot verba tot pondera [his every word is a heavy blow]. I beg your pardon for my ignorance daring to cite Latin to a learned man like you, but I hope it's a presumption that you will excuse.

He added no kingly word, however, on Tacitus's appraisal of Germanic military power or the origin of the Goths, nor any acknowledgment of the flattering fact that he now ruled over a territory with people of such splendid history.

This was not the end of the matter. Hertzberg, taking his majesty's reservation as a congenial provocation, soon sent him another translation of a passage of the *Annals*, Tacitus's pathology of the Roman Empire under its tyrannical leaders. The king, apparently untroubled by the historian's reputation as the first hater of tyrants, praised its quality ("Voilà du bon Allemand"), but niggled about Hertzberg's use of the German word for "example" ("Beyspiel"); here the French *exemple* was indispensable. And yet, if men like Hertzberg were to take on the case of their mother tongue, Frederick the Great concluded, it soon would be in better standing.

His talented cabinet minister would indeed stand up for the German language; but first he turned to history. Less than a year after this incident, on January 27, 1780, as a member (and later curator) of the Prussian Academy of Sciences, he chose its annual meeting to expound on the self-same issues in more detail. In Berlin, the Prussian capital, in celebration of his king, the minister offered a belated dessert to that dinner in Breslau. With this first of eight speeches at the academy, Hertzberg addressed an interest of his since high school.

His speech for the most part plucked commonplaces from the inventory of the Germanic myth, but it also reflected its most recent, eighteenth-century additions. The *Germanen*—moral and brave—had been superior to the Romans. They stemmed from the north of Germany—which, Hertzberg emphasized, coincided with Prussian territory—migrated at will, and terminated Roman rule over most of Europe. Out of these ruins they initiated the major European monarchies. To verify these claims the minister mustered Roman authors, who testified to the Germanic people as "the most dangerous and the most redoubtable."[2] No one had expressed that fear more "elegantly, tensely, and truthfully" than Tacitus, from whom he cited passages, using his own royally approved rendering. He then interlaced his ancestors' insuperability with indigenousness and intertwined a few thoughts familiar from Philipp Clüver's *Germania antiqua* (which enjoyed unabated popularity): "Germania, as the Romans called it, and which, considering its origin and name in its original language, should be called Teutonia, is the only country in Europe and maybe the universe that was never subjugated. . . . It is still the same aboriginal and indigenous nation which has preserved its independence, its name, and its language from its origin to this day."

The long list of Germanic peoples and their conquests of Roman provinces led Hertzberg to affirm that not Scandinavia but the north of Germany was the cradle of the European people. In conclusion he raised doubts but only to quash them swiftly (a rhetorical scheme known as *occupatio*): How could disorganized nomadic bands have accomplished so much? First, he retorted, they had not been entirely nomadic; Tacitus himself attested "that they also cultivated the soil." Next, was there anybody unfamiliar with the Roman's glorious portrait of the original, moral, and simple warrior? Those among his audience who questioned the Germans' exceptional *esprit général* should, he recommended, remember the recent demonstration of the superiority of the northern climate and character.

A mere reminder sufficed. His audience was sure to have studied Montesquieu's famous *The Spirit of the Laws*, one of the most influential texts of eighteenth-century Europe.

THE NATIONAL SPIRIT

> If one wants to read the admirable work by Tacitus, *On the Mores of the Germans*, one will see that the English have taken their idea of political government from the Germans. This fine system was found in the forests.
>
> —Montesquieu, 1748

The Germans' national spirit awoke in the south of France in the middle of the eighteenth century. Others, such as Jean-Baptiste Dubos, quoted at the beginning of this chapter, had stirred it before; but it fell to Montesquieu to arouse and present it to German readers. They would gladly welcome it and, in continuation of the patriotic language enthusiasts of the previous century, eventually decide on the vernacular and folklore as its clearest expressions.

Charles-Louis de Secondat, baron de La Brède et de Montesquieu (1689–1755), showed an early preference to speak of himself simply as Montesquieu.[3] He was born about ten miles south of Bordeaux in the Château de la Brède, a castle built in the Gothic style and surrounded by a moat too broad to jump. When in 1734 he finally decided to write his chef-d'oeuvre, he would work in the muffled quiet of this fortress for almost two decades. To the more than three thousand books that lined the walls of its guardroom he brought wide learning, years of travel, and a conversational style honed in the salons of Paris—those like the circle of Madame de Tencin, in which the lack of morals was more readily condoned than the lack of wit and finesse.

These salons hosted intellectuals, such as the philosophes, leaders of the Enlightenment, to whom the baron was loosely linked. This movement aimed at freeing men's minds from prejudice—to adapt the words of one of its most prominent members, the philosopher and critic Denis Diderot. Regarding reason the sole source of authority, it advocated freedom in religious, intellectual, and political matters. Its aim was also the stated purpose of the *Encyclopédie*, a thirty-five-volume conquest of knowledge, emblematic of its time and trends and composed by many leading minds. It contained an article on "Germanie," in which Tacitus's book is referred to as being "in everybody's hands."[4] French readers turned those pages as they continued to look for the possible Germanic origin of the French people. The Franci, a Germanic tribe populating the eastern area of the lower Rhine, were assumed to have crossed the river seeking settlement in Gaul. The protracted controversy, which dated back to the late Middle Ages, posed the French as descendants of either these free and frank conquistadors—as Montesquieu did—or the Gaulish dwellers. The position in this controversy determined the view held of the *Germania*: To those favoring the Germanic origin of the French people it was a "gospel of honor and of all the human virtues."[5] Those, however, with no vested interest in the elevation of Germanic times found in it "savages who emerged from the swamps and forests of ancient Germany."

In the salons, where such questions were entertained, Montesquieu moved with the ease of success. The publication of the *Lettres Persanes*—a satirical collection of fictive letters by two Persian noblemen traveling in France—had made him famous. He was a member of the Academy of Bordeaux, an *immortel* at the Académie française, and a fellow of the Royal Society even before he wrote *The Spirit of the Laws*. But it was this work that would secure him a place in the hall of fame of political philosophers. Today it stands for the damnation of despotism and the advocacy of the separation of powers as well as legal limitations on government (commonly referred to as constitutionalism). But in its entirety it is a multifaceted reflection on laws—natural and social as well as political—focused on their relation to "[the] many things [that] govern men": geographical and climatic conditions, the regional mores and manners, and political and religious institutions.[6] They all formed and—to a certain extent—conformed to the character of the people, or, in Montesquieu's words, the *esprit général*.

The *esprit général* haunted the writings of French theorists and philosophers under various names, such as the "caractère de la nation." This character resulted, at least in part, from its country's environment; just as if, to oversimplify the idea (as many of its contemporaneous critics did), the degree of morality stood in inverse proportion to degrees Fahrenheit. This anthropogeographical theory experienced a renaissance in Montesquieu's age. It can be traced back to the Greek treatise "On Airs, Waters, Lands," said to be written by the Greek father of medicine, Hippocrates. (Tacitus might have been familiar with this treatise; he certainly embraced the theory.) Montesquieu, whose library at La Brède included a copy, spoke of "the empire of climate [as] the first of all empires."[7]

While it was the first, it was not the only empire, as there were other circumstances that would affect a people, as Montesquieu knew well (although occasionally he overstates climatic determinism). How, otherwise, could the differences between the Germans and the Russians be explained, considering, as a contemporary quipped, that "the climate does not contradict itself."[8]

Based on his experiments on the impact of freezing on a sheep's tongue, Montesquieu asserted that the cold air of the Northern Hemisphere caused higher blood circulation and greater, albeit impulsive, strength. The climate-conditioned temperament induced courage and sincerity, while reducing treachery and vindictiveness. The northerners, while large of frame, lived languidly and with scant pleasure: Hunting, raiding, and warring, they tried to overcome their torpidity. Overall, vices were few and virtues determinative of their life. This northern, more specifically German, character was widely believed to be captured in Tacitus's pages, from which Montesquieu also drew his inspiration. He knew the Roman well enough to rely on his memory for more than fifty (sometimes revealingly slipshod) quotations: "A short book," he opined, but by an author "who summarized everything because he saw everything."[9] He abridged it even further and helped establish the idiom "German spirit" as the shorthand for Tacitus's portrait.

IT WAS this spirit that lay behind the British constitution. Montesquieu had spent almost two years traveling in England, where he studied the checks and balances of its constitutional monarchy. His enthusiasm for this diversification of power carried over into his book, in which he gave an account of its workings (subsequently considered authoritative even in England despite inaccuracies). Its origins, he suggested, could be found mentioned in the *Germania*, a study of which revealed that "this fine system was found in the forests."[10] To speak of free ancient Germany prior to

Montesquieu meant to speak of its freedom from Roman tyranny: German humanists took great and oft-repeated pride that the Germanic people had always been free from any outside rule, and patriotic linguists congratulated their forebears on having fought off military forces *and* foreign words. Few commented on constitutional freedom, on how nothing happened without "the people's vote, cognizance, and volition," as one German humanist of rather exceptional interest had phrased it.[11] After the Peace of Westphalia in 1648 guaranteed German princes and electors independence, they became even fewer.

Montesquieu changed that. He cited in a footnote the Tacitean passage that to him contained the seed of this balance of power: "On lesser matters the leaders consult; on bigger ones all, yet in such a way that even what the people decide about is preconsidered by the leaders."[12] Montesquieu forwent elaboration. Yet it seems obvious that he regarded the role of the assembly in decision making as a check on the leaders' rulings. Elsewhere in his book he interpreted Tacitus's comments on the limited freedom of kings, the election of leaders for proven virtue rather than pedigree, and the necessity to decide about death penalties in the presence of the people similarly as hallmarks of the Germanic idea of government. In an age of failed freedom, when absolute rulers maintained their power, Montesquieu read the *Germania* as the blueprint of a free society. His protestations notwithstanding, these philosophical thoughts on self-governing were most certainly "injurious" to the political status quo, as a contemporaneous reader was quick to remark.

By locating this "beautiful system" in the north, Montesquieu not only redefined freedom from foreign rule as freedom from absolute rulers, but also modified the traditional semantics of geography: Politically, the formerly wild and bristling north, which contrasted unfavorably with the cultured and civil more temperate climes, became the cradle of freedom. Many cheered; others disagreed angrily. In particular Voltaire (1694–1778), a dominant figure of the Enlightenment and a pen pal of Frederick the Great, sarcastically queried whether the House of Lords and the House of Commons had come from the Black Forest as well? Maybe even the English cotton factories, even though Tacitus reported that ancient Germans used to raid rather than work for a living? Voltaire did not share Monstequieu's belief in the Germanic origin of the French either: Who were those Franks whom the author of *The Spirit of the Laws* called "our fathers"? he wondered.[13] Like the other barbarians from the north, they were ferocious beasts seeking pasture. Yet when Voltaire's commentary appeared in 1777, his criticism was hardly heard: Europe had been speaking the language of Montesquieu for almost thirty years.

PUBLISHED IN 1748 in Geneva to circumvent French censorship, *L'esprit des lois* was received in Germany as "a masterpiece of its kind" that deserved "not merely to be read through, but to be thought through."[14] Less than five years after the French original, Abraham Gotthelf Kästner, a literarily inclined mathematician, published the first German translation under a title notable for its omission as well as creative spelling: "Mister Montesquiou's work on laws, or . . . " (the ellipsis stands for the subtitle, which amounted to a brief summary). Kästner shirked the crucial term *esprit*, citing the complexity of the French term (unmatched, he felt—in kinship with Frederick the Great—by any single German word). But then, in 1760, a disquisition on German legislation came out, whose title used *Geist* to render the French notion of *esprit*; it was the initial appearance of an enduring term.

A spirited debate followed, centering around an essay by Friedrich Carl von Moser (1723–98). A nobleman in rank equal to a baron, he worked as a lawyer and public servant but was more widely known for his penmanship. In the imperial city of Frankfurt he composed his treatise *About the German National Spirit* in

1765. Its opening lines trumpeted: "We are One people, One in name and language."[15] Despite several unifying features, however, Germans lacked a common "national attitude." Contrasting past and present, he frowned (and the frown was printed in larger letters than the regular text): "we don't know ourselves anymore; we have lost touch with one another. Our spirit has left us." The rulers and aristocrats of the German states cared more for themselves than for their "fatherland," which was "but a dead name." Moser concluded his depiction of the German situation with an impassioned vision: "How happy, how peaceful Germany could be if a man from Berlin would learn to respect, love, and honor as his fatherland Vienna, the man from Vienna [would learn to respect] Hannover, and a man from Hesse [would learn to respect] Mainz." The dream of an imperial patriot who identified Germany with the empire, it would remain a dream for now.

Moser's essay swiftly met with criticism. For four years, reviews, letters, and rejoinders discussed and defined the national spirit. He had failed to specify this central idea, critics complained, and he had mistaken the German aristocracy for the nation, as if they were the spirit's trustees. One reader carped that he had paid to learn from Moser's work about the national spirit but would have better spent his time reading Tacitus. He also dismissed it as preposterous to write about the Germans' national spirit without proper attention to their origin and old mores. Otherwise, how could one compare and claim that it had vanished?[16] In the ingenuously titled *More on the German National Spirit*, a later author delineated that spirit as "the particular quality, or rather the quintessence of all such particular qualities, by which one people is different from another," appending that "these special qualities belong either to the soul or the body."[17] In its profile the author cited so much of the *Germania* that he wearied and straightforwardly referred his readers to the original. By the end of the debate, the national spirit was definitively pinned down in Tacitus's pages.

A contemporary in 1767 noted that no other works were as

widely known as those that addressed the question of the German national spirit. "In Frankfurt and [its] vicinity," he writes, "upon entering a half-decent inn, the convivial host is bound to strike up an edifying conversation about the much-vaunted controversy."[18] The anonymously conducted debate helped spread Montesquieu's ideas and above all to specify the notion (and establish the traits) of the national spirit. The contestants' mutual questioning of its definition and location (among the elite or the people?) brought new attention to the long-lived "German question."

THE REPUBLIC OF FARMERS

> On the National Assembly of the Ancient Germans: the nobles and . . . commoners were thus two coexisting and independent estates. The latter were the true constituents of the body of the nation, and everything hinged on their consent.
>
> —Justus Möser, 1768

Germany wavered between the lure of an empire already past and the allure of a nation-state still out of reach. One could assert that "the finest heads in Germany regardless of their remoteness [from one another] form[ed] a small republic of sorts," and yet wonder where in the midst "of so many small parts and contending factions [the German] fatherland [was] to be found."[19] The Seven Years' War (1757–63)—the first global war, with its two front lines in Europe and North America—threw these two Germanys into sharper relief. While smaller German states, allied with either Prussia or Austria, fought against one another on battlefields within the Holy Roman Empire, a supraregional "German movement" came into being, wherein publishers and pamphleteers concertedly embraced the dubitable nation in journals such as the *German Mercury* and the *German General Library*. Goethe and Schiller summarized the paradoxical situation in one sentence: "Germany begins for the learned where it ends for the politicians." Another tetrarch of Weimar classicism, Johann Gottfried Herder, reflecting on the same disparity, declared the most natural state to be the one that enclosed one people of one national character.[20] Another century would have to pass, however, before this nation-state actually appeared on a map.

For the time being the past still had to compensate for the present. It continued to attract nationalistic speculations, but now of the kind that focused on the government, constitutional makeup, and electorate. Montesquieu had stressed the interdependence of a people's spirit with its political and legal framework—tyrannies engendered slavish spirits—and in discussing the northern spirit repeatedly referred to the so-called laws of the barbarians, legal codes of the Germanic peoples dating back to the early Middle Ages. For they expressed "an admirable simplicity," which to him seemed to "breathe an original coarseness and a spirit that no change or corruption of manners had weakened."[21] He pointed to parallels between a specific law or, rather, custom in the *Germania* and a particular decree in the laws of the barbarians: In his view the Tacitean description—subtly sharpened to meet his ends—of how the *Germanen* did not live in towns but in houses that were surrounded by free space agreed with Germanic decrees against trespassing and housebreaking. Both the Roman's treatise and the Germanic laws bespoke the same spirit of freedom and independence.

German lawyers were predictably quick to follow up with their own studies, even though the states and cities—some so small that Montesquieu could quip they had fewer subjects than a sultan had wives—each relied on their own legislation.[22] Like a broken kaleidoscope, these disparate legal systems failed to form a coherent whole. Johann Heumann von Teutschenbrunn (1711–60) struggled with this discrepancy between the unitary German spirit and the multitude of laws in his *The Spirit of the Germans' Laws*. The past, at least, offered the desired unifying vision to the professor of law at the University of Altdorff near Nuremberg, who praised German lawgivers in the old days for specifying legal elements, like the age of maturity, in accordance with the people's characteristics, like the comparatively late coming-of-age.[23] It was only when Roman law subverted indigenous practices that a much earlier and unsuitable age of majority was imposed, which necessitated exceptions.

With his long-standing interest in Tacitus, Heumann belonged to a growing number of legal historians who, in spite of an authoritative disavowal of the *Germania* as a legal source, eagerly thumped its pages.[24] They took a particular interest in the political system it described, not least since Montesquieu had identified it as the precursor of the English constitutional monarchy. One particular collection of legal essays totaling 1,015 pages (not including the table of contents and the index), published in 1766, unfolded on dozens of pages the greater significance of Tacitus's brief remark that kings were elected.[25] Two years later, in the empire's northwestern city of Osnabrück, a twofold review appeared that also took a closer look at the Germanic idea of government. Discussing Moser's incendiary treatise *About the German National Spirit* and the long-winded latest reaction that had offered *More*, its author joined others in finding the German nation elusive and in refusing to look for it among the aristocracy. But musing where and what the nation might be, he added a surprising assumption: "Back in the days during which a Frank or Saxon worked his ancestors' lands and defended it in person, when from his farm he went to the common assembly—that time could have shown us the nation; but the present cannot."[26] A golden Germanic past of freedom, surely, but one steered by an assembly of farmers?

JUSTUS MÖSER (1720–94) had seemed an unlikely bet to emerge as the commanding figure in Osnabrück's politics between the Seven Years' War and the French Revolution. Returning from his listless studies at the Universities of Jena and Göttingen with trepidation instead of a degree, he was admitted to the legal profession only because of his father, a lawyer and member of the board of admissions. But Möser Junior soon collected offices and titles, and—sloughing off the slacker he acknowledged himself to have been—established himself as a member of the influential class of administrators in a society structured by estates. Osnabrück, a city in (modern-day) Lower Saxony that had long outgrown any ox bridge that might have inspired its name, served as the capital of the eponymous bishopric, an ecclesiastical state measuring a mere fifty square miles. Leaderless because of the underage and absent prince-bishop in the 1760s, it was de facto run by Möser. He would ultimately guide the state's fortunes for almost thirty years. While thus "living in the real world and attempting to have an impact," as a friend and biographer wrote, he kept an inquisitive eye on the past.[27] Ever since his student days, his interests had tended beyond the rigor of law to belles lettres and history; and, in the midst of his administrative duties, he made time to work on his *History of Osnabrück*. Even though it announced its regionalism in its title, it would quickly be recognized as "the first German history with a German head and heart."[28]

The introduction to the *History of Osnabrück* promised an iconoclasm of sorts. Contrary to current practice, this historical narrative would focus on "Saxons working their ancestors' lands" instead of on kaisers, kings, and princes. Only these landowning farmers embodied the national spirit.[29] Unfortunately it would be a history of decline and depreciation. At first free peasants governed themselves, farmed their properties, and fought for their communities. This original state of freedom and autarchy subsequently degraded to autocracy and the miseries of serfdom. But Möser's work, though meant to trace the descent from farmer-soldiers (a suspiciously Roman-sounding ideal) to famished serfs, never descended further than the thirteenth century: Contemporary censorship kept it safely situated in the past.

This golden period, Möser argued, was aptly captured in the *Germania*, or so, at least, he would make it appear. His enthusiasm for the Roman historian went back to his school days, when long excerpts and comments filled his adolescent notebooks. Now, in the *History of Osnabrück* he called upon Tacitus to detail the political structure of the Germanic state. In a prologue to the main historical narrative Möser provided a "short introduction" of seventy pages to the Germans' oldest political system. It centered on the general assembly: No laws were passed without the landowning commoners' explicit approval; under a priest's guidance, speakers stood up in order of achievement and rhetorical talent; and during war a leader was elected from among the bravest, whose rule, if not his role, terminated once peace was secured. The ancient Germans had certainly been artists in protecting their freedom, Möser concluded. Even if nothing else were known of their life than that their homes were independent and scattered, one could still fathom the greatness of their constitutional idea. But thankfully much more was known, and Möser cited excerpts from the *Germania* in his footnotes to substantiate the finer points of this alleged constitution. But—a contemporaneous reviewer was quick to spot—one such Tacitean snippet, in fact a most crucial one, could not possibly carry the weight placed on it. The quotation *ex plebe consilium et auctoritas* could mean: "from the people came counsel and power," which is how Möser wanted it to be understood so as to support his claim that the people had wielded political power. Yet Tacitus had actually written: "a hundred associates are selected from the people, from whom the legal authorities derive counsel and power."[30] Möser knew Latin well enough to know better. Overall he uses Tacitus fairly, but here the temptation to discover the republic he desired proved too strong.

Möser's second historical assumption equally rested on shaky Tacitean grounds. His ancestors, he claimed, had farmed their own farms and only as property owners qualified for full political participation. Such qualification, by either service or property, was generally held to be necessary at the time. But Möser gave landowning particular emphasis, as he had witnessed the misery of destitute peasants in his bishopric, especially during the Seven Years' War (when much work on the *History of Osnabrück* was done). It is unfortunate, therefore, that the *Germania* contains statements to the contrary: The ancient Germans "change[d] their fields yearly and farmland [was] left over and [lay] fallow."[31] Tacitus elaborated further on how they could more easily be persuaded to challenge the enemy than "to work the field and await the yield," and how they generally preferred to leave the farming to their wives, neither of which tallied with Möser's portrait of the peasants. Möser, however, disagreed with those who referred to Tacitus and Caesar, arguing (as Montesquieu had) that the *Germanen* had cultivated the land but little. Caesar was simply wrong when he denied that Germanic tribes practiced agriculture. Tacitus, on the other hand, did report on farming, despite a few statements to the contrary. For he related how everyone surrounded his house with free space. How could that be said of a people who did not own property? To those who knew how to read Tacitus—a talent a contemporaneous commentator in favor of Germanic agriculture quite understandably emphasized as necessary—the Roman writer attested to such a peasantry. But in spite of such hermeneutical ingenuity, attempts to find evidence of farming in the *Germania* would remain controversial.

A woodcut adorns the *History of Osnabrück*. Traditional and Tacitean, it looks back to the prints included in Philipp Clüver's *Germania antiqua* (a copy of which was in Möser's library). But it also contains elements alluding to the peasant and his property (the spear in the right corner should probably symbolize Möser's "defense"—when farmers turned soldiers to fight for their community). In the first edition of his *History*, as quoted in this section's epigraph, the landowning commoners overruled the nobles. In a

8. A Germanic farmer in Justus Möser's *History of Osnabrück.*
Widener Library, Harvard College Library, 47528.1.10.

concurrent letter Möser, who had himself refused nobility, bluntly stated that "the nobles in Germany did not really belong to the nation."[32] Although he softened that declaration in the second edition to include both the people and the nobility, the commoners— the simple *Volk,* as they are specified in a footnote with reference to Tacitus—remained the backbone of "the body of the nation."[33]

No hardworking commoner himself, Möser increased the people's clout in politics. He thus helped bring about the change in meaning that would lead Jacob Grimm a few decades later to reflect on how the noun "folk" and its adjective "folklike" now were associated with the free.[34] Outside the Holy Roman Empire others advanced the voice of the people in poetics. They, too, had little of the common folk experience.

NORDIC FOLKLORE

> Now look about you in Germany for the character of the nation, for their particular sound of thought, for the true mood of their language; where are they? Read Tacitus; there you will find their character.
>
> —Johann Gottfried Herder, 1767

For a few years the authoritative workshop of Nordic mythmaking was Copenhagen, where Germany met Scandinavia, and the past met the present. The Danish king, Frederick V, upon his succession to power in 1746 aspired to change the austere image of his kingdom by making its capital a center of the arts. In the 1750s and 1760s he invited many famous literati, one of whom, Paul Henri Mallet (1730–1807), was appointed Professeur Royal de belles lettres françaises in 1752. With knowledge of French either lacking or rudimentary among the royal court's audience, the professor found himself with time to spare. "Yet," an early biographer continues, "he put his leisure to most profitable use."[35] In 1755 Mallet published an oversize *Introduction to the History of Denmark, Which Deals with Religion, Laws, Mores, and Habits of the Ancient Danish.*[36] A second volume—and further prolegomenon—in the following year presented *Monuments of the Celts' Mythology and Poetry, and in Particular of the Ancient Scandinavians* (in which the Celts are once again taken to be of the same stock as the Germanic people). Irony ruled that a francophone Swiss would advance the Nordic Renaissance.

Mallet wrote in the wake of Montesquieu's thoughts. The preface speaks of the northern spirit, its ties to the climate and—its major contribution—the liberty that Europe possessed (a fact well known, Mallet added). He did not differ from Montesquieu either in his frequent recurrence to the *Germania* as a paramount source. But unlike the author of *The Spirit of the Laws*, he promoted the Scandinavians as the embodiment of the Nordic: They received credit for what the Germans more usually laid claim to. The Danish king delightedly read how Scandinavia had been the cradle of the European people, derided and destroyed the Roman power, and founded modern monarchies. In praising these as specifically Scandinavian feats, Mallet took advantage of the fact that the "North" embraced Germans and Scandinavians alike. The Cimbri, a famous Germanic tribe, in his *Introduction* entered Danish territory to settle there as future founding fathers. Vagueness is a generous host, and for Mallet, Tacitus is "the excellent historian of ancient Germany" whom he can call upon to bring to light the Scandinavian past.[37] While most—such as Hertzberg in Breslau and Berlin—disagreed and continued to claim the cradle and past greatness for Germany, the recognition of the Scandinavians (along with the Icelanders and sometimes the British and the French) as the Germans' "true brothers" in one big Nordic family stood mostly uncontested.[38]

The second major difference with Montesquieu was Mallet's expanded interest in religion. The German ancestors' religiosity had been celebrated ever since the humanistic age, but interpretations of their religion had ranged from barbaric and pagan to truly Christian. With religion now considered a "faithful mirror wherein [a people's] spirit may be seen," as Mallet wrote, it received further scrutiny. In his view the excellent mores Tacitus witnessed ultimately resulted from Germanic piety. But who were the Nordic gods they had piously worshiped?[39] Tacitus provided preciously little information on this question. It was a different text that brought Odin, "the founder of a new religion," and with him the Nordic pantheon, into Mallet's pages and thence to Europe's attention.

The *Edda*, a collection of Old Norse texts in poetry and prose, was written down in Iceland in the thirteenth century (some texts are even older). It brims with Nordic myths about gods led by Odin, ruler over Asgard, and heroes like Sigurd, the dragon slayer. Mallet, with the help of a Norse-versed Icelandic scholar also living in Copenhagen, included a partial French translation of it in his *Monuments*. It caused a sensation among francophone readers throughout Europe. The primitive and primordial had repeatedly been proclaimed as an aesthetic alternative to the subtle and sophisticated. Most recently the work of Jean-Jacques Rousseau had advocated the original state of man and its natural, primitive culture as a paradigm preferable to urban artificiality. An anticlassical poetics was the order of the day. The *Edda*, its earthy songs delivered in alliterative verse, fitted the bill.

A few of its multifarious myths had also provided the subject matter for rune stones (like the Ramsund carving, found near the southeastern coast of Sweden, which depicts Sigurd). Along with other inscriptions, they made for an abundance of tangible relics of the past, much missed by Germans rarely fully satisfied by their heavy reliance on their single Tacitean source. The runic letters—one of which, stitched and printed on millions of lapels and documents, would come to symbolize the terror spread in the Third Reich—also told of the high level of culture: Resting his case on them, Mallet reinterpreted the Tacitean remark widely taken to signify Germanic illiteracy.[40] Adding one more detail to his account of the north's flourishing cultural landscape, he mentioned bards, recently come to fresh prominence in the songs circulating under the name of the Celtic poet Ossian. These bards used to glorify not

9. SS runes. Cover of Photo Album B in the Himmler collection. *Hoover Institution Archives.*

only gods and heroes but also leaders desirous of commemoration. Poems, Mallet reminded his readers, had served as annals, just as Tacitus reported.

Upon the appearance of Mallet's work, Heinrich Wilhelm von Gerstenberg, a member of Copenhagen's German circle, rejoiced: "We are an original people, we have an original language, what we see in history, mythology, and mores is ours and original."[41] Sixteenth-century historians had celebrated their original people, seventeenth-century linguists their original language; now, at a time when the Romantics emphasized the genius's originality above all else, Gerstenberg and like-minded writers included an original mythology in their heritage. Its source lay in the north, as the title of Gerstenberg's *A Skald's Poem* highlights: The prominent reference to the Scandinavian bard (the Skald) hints at the agenda, which the first verse proceeds to enact: "Braga's song in astral sound . . . ." Braga, as Gerstenberg's notes "on the language of the *Edda* and the allusions contained in the poem" explain, was the Nordic god of poetry. He had finally retired Apollo, the Greek and Roman leader of the Muses, to whom humanists had appealed for inspiration. More than a change of name, this reflected a change of paradigm. Now German poets should shun classical mythology just as they had the Latin language; they should sing of original myths, and "original" meant "Nordic." The alleged kinship between Scandinavians and Germans facilitated Scandinavian claims on the German past; it also prompted the filling of gaps in the German tradition with Nordic material.

A friend of Gerstenberg's and a contemporary of Mallet's at the Danish court, Friedrich Gottlieb Klopstock (1724–1803) seized upon the Nordic as German heritage with equal enthusiasm. "I had used Greek mythology in some of my earlier odes," he told a similarly inclined friend in 1767, specifically referring to one composed two decades before.[42] "I removed it and inserted the mythology of our ancestors, in those odes as well as some more recent ones." Odin had battled Zeus and conquered Klopstock's poetry. But more than mere replacement was necessary: German poetry should express German culture and customs. In the same year that he changed his ode, Klopstock composed the first of three plays centering around Hermann, the scourge of Roman legions. The Germanic leader was called to arms once again. When he had first appeared in the sixteenth century, he spoke Latin. Since then he had sloughed off many Roman attributes; now, Klopstock wished, he should be animated by the German spirit.

The most celebrated author before Weimar classicism, Klopstock owed his invitation to Copenhagen to the impression the first part of his *Messiah* had made on Frederick V. As an "expression of [the king's] esteem" for this poem of sacred history, a royal stipend was tendered, neither stingy nor generous but more than Klopstock could have hoped for anywhere else.[43] Born near the Hartz Mountains in the medieval town of Quedlinburg, Klopstock, the eldest of seventeen children, had gone to Schulpforta, a boarding school by the river Saale. It retained the discipline characteristic of the erstwhile monastery, and the budding poet, like others on its list of famous graduates before and after (including the philosophers Fichte and Nietzsche), received a solid grounding in the classics.

Studies in theology followed and, upon completion, the common (but in his case brief) stint as a tutor. Taking up an itinerant's life, he moved where lodging and living beckoned. When he settled in the Danish capital, he could not foresee that he would stay for nearly twenty years. But this "Danish end of Germany" was very accommodating: His mother tongue was spoken at court, and all but six aristocratic families were in fact German—not to mention the group of German expatriates, including Gerstenberg.[44] In their midst he would not only complete his *Messiah* but also work on German history to become the "poet of religion and his fatherland." The history of his fatherland should become poetry again; Klopstock only had to resume the tradition of the *Bardiet*.

A neologism would seem proper to signal something new. Yet Klopstock, ever eager to creolize the present and the past, insinuated that the term *Bardiet* had merely fallen out of usage. "Bard" had survived in German, and Tacitus, the "meritorious friend," attested to *barditus*; so why not reintroduce *Bardiet?*[45] He defined this genre as primarily concerned with historic characters and events of consequence, faithful to detail, and partly sung. His three *Bardiets* centering on Hermann followed this poetics. For historical accuracy the poet depended on Tacitus, as the annotations reveal. Where the chorus reminds the Germanic warriors: "You descend from Mana," the notes explain that Mana was the German ancestors' name for the divine hero mentioned by Tacitus.[46] The historical characters on the stage are equally pastiched from the Tacitean textbook: brave and loyal to the defiance of death, outspoken, and trusting in honor and piety. "I'd almost presume that you haven't read Tacitus as carefully as I have," Klopstock playfully suggested in a letter to an acquaintance, adding specific examples of where his plays followed Tacitus's account. To a certain extent the *Bardiet* is the *Germania* in verse.

The clearest acknowledgment of his debt to Tacitus was a passage excerpted from the *Germania* and tacked onto the play, which "must warm the heart of any German in the old and stout mold." What Klopstock hoped for the snippet he also hoped for his plays (and thematically related poems): to inspire patriotism. Whoever wrote in German, he opined, should be considered a German; history and common culture would teach them to think as Germans. With his consuming passion for "the language of Thuiscon," he stood so firmly in the tradition of the seventeenth-century linguists that he reminded contemporaries of a more-extreme-leaning member of the Fruchtbringende Gesellschaft from a century before.[47] One of his poems described *Our Language* as "what we once were in years gone gray, when Tacitus looked at us: separate and pure, like no one but itself." Klopstock, who prided himself on being of "pure Cheruscan blood," dreamed of writing in it the accomplishments of his prince, whom—back in the old days—he would have accompanied into battle.[48] "I hope you know," he added for the recipient of his historical fantasies, "that it was the bard's duty to be close [to events]."

THE BARD attracted followers, most famously the poets who formed the Union of the Glade in Göttingen (the *Göttinger Hainbund*). Like Klopstock, they cast themselves as bards, even choosing dubious bardic names for pseudonyms, and emphasized the Nordic and national elements in their poetry. But their songs did not carry very far; and soon they were forgotten. Anonymity is a blessing, however, if the alternative is notoriety.

Johann Gottfried Herder (1744–1803) also found himself one day sitting "in the Bards' old German glade."[49] Born in East Prussia, in Mohrungen (now Morag in northern Poland), he had revealed his poetical inclinations when at the age of eleven he wrote a poem about the recent death of his younger brother, "the dearest thing that he had lost in this world."[50] With more talents and interests than his hometown of two thousand inhabitants could accommodate, he left for Königsberg and never saw his birthplace or parents again. He studied theology and, among many other subjects, philosophy with Immanuel Kant. Though concomitantly teaching to make a living, he found time to write his first major study, *On Diligence in Several Learned Languages*, in 1764. It contained the ideas he would stand by for the rest of his life: Nations differ in their spirits, which, partly shaped by climate and environment, are most clearly emanated by each in its vernacular and indigenous culture, its folklore. Much of this would have met with the approval of Montesquieu, on whose work Herder penned *Thoughts While Reading Montesquieu*. But his thoughts would eventually take him further, conceiving of a nation as an organic whole, imbuing its spirit with a mythical quality, and declaring the people's lower art forms alone to be genuine.

The original Nordic mythology, which Herder celebrated in a review of Mallet, could legitimately be claimed as German, since it came, as he would later express it, from a "neighboring German tribe."[51] For a people to adhere to its own culture was existential. His *Fragments on Recent German Literature*, written around 1767, asserted categorically: "No greater injury can be inflicted on a nation than to be robbed of her national character, the particularity of her spirit and her language." This was particularly true for a nation lacking a state, and as his study of German literature in its historical development revealed, the common language and literature were still *all* the German nation had in common. A nurturing interest in both was once again a patriotic duty. To Herder's distress, too few of his contemporaries were heeding the call:

> Look about you in Germany for the character of the nation, for their particular sound of thought, for the true mood of their language; where are they? Read Tacitus; there you will find their character: "The tribes of Germany, who never disgraced [*entadelt*] themselves by mingling with others, form a peculiar, unadulterated, original nation, which is its own archetype

[*Urbild*]. Even their physical development is identical, considering the large numbers of the people: and so forth." Now look
about you, and say: "The peoples of Germany have been dis-
graced by mingling with others; because of a long-lasting servi-
tude they have lost their nature completely; since for a long time
more than others they imitated a tyrannical archetype, they are
among all European nations least like themselves."[52]

In translating Tacitus, Herder used terms that carried his own aesthetic theories. The purity of his ancestors was primarily cultural
and linguistic; they were "original" as opposed to pettily imitative;
they constituted their own "archetype." Whereas Tacitus had written that the Germanic tribes were "a people like none but themselves," Herder pointedly concluded that the Germans of his day
were like all others but themselves. But all was not lost: They had
the template of themselves presented to them by Tacitus, whose
insight had "penetrated the spirit of things."

The German cultural nation was in such a sorry state as it still,
more than one hundred years after the Fruchtbringende Gesellschaft, ached to appear French in style, literature, and conversation.
This zealous appreciation of a foreign culture overlooked that just
as nations differed in character, they also each carried their own
criteria for cultural development and accomplishments. To Herder,
who emphasized a people's entitlement to self-determination, all
languages sounded beautiful. But in a rare instance of patriotic
exuberance—and directly contrary to Frederick the Great, for
whose bellicose and Francophile reign he, born a Prussian subject,
bore little sympathy—he elaborated on the particular beauty of
German and its poetry in its rough simplicity:

Let us assume that a Roman describes our language as Tacitus
our land: *its country wild, its climate rough, in manners and looks
sullen*—if he knew the language better, he would recognize it

as the bards' song, which with its throaty tone, with its muffled sound, with its full and heavy resonation deserves praise: *It is not speech as much as the consonance of virtue.* And why should we be embarrassed by our consonants, since they are a consonance of fortitude to acclaim the gods and founding fathers of our people, and the heroes and saviors of the nation, to sing battle- and victory-songs, as never sung again, . . . ?[53]

Wielding this consonantal language, the old poets, "our fathers," had composed "unrefined songs," which carried the German spirit. Luckily, then, their songs had been preserved in the folk songs of Herder's day.

The age-old national spirit could still be resuscitated, and not just from the Tacitean pages; for there was folklore. While Francophiles were numerous among the elite, they could hardly be found among "the big venerable part of the public that is called the people," who spoke, sang, and thought in their vernacular tongue.[54] Like Justus Möser—whose introduction to the *History of Osnabrück* he included in an influential volume that would precipitate the Sturm und Drang—but more concerned with poetics than politics, Herder believed the common people to be the true carriers of the spirit: The spirit of the German people was in its people. In Herder's work, the change of *Volk* from a predominantly sociopolitical to an ideological term had well advanced. He used *Volk* and "nation" interchangeably out of conviction—not lack of attention.

HERDER'S THOUGHTS reinforced those previously formulated by Klopstock—tellingly praised as "the first poet of our [German] *Volk*"—the mythologer Paul Henri Mallet, the historian Justus Möser, and the political philosopher Montesquieu.[55] Just like them he fell back on Tacitus when he defined the German nation culturally, its mystical spirit alive in the past and in the present still preserved in the language and traditions of the *Volk*. Herder's nationalism was not chauvinistic: The demands he specified for the Germans—the vigorous embrace of its own words, myths, and poetry and the right to self-determination—applied to all peoples, united in his hopeful notion of humanity. Herder never spoke of bloodlines and explicitly rejected the term "race" for its vagueness.[56] But the *Volk* and its spirit would take on a life of their own, leaving their author to watch in wonder like the sorcerer's apprentice.

7
White Blood

The Romans justly considered the German people as an
ancient, pure, and unmixed original people. It resembled only
itself; and like identical field plants that spring from a pure
seed . . . do not differ one from another through degeneration,
so also, among the thousands stemming from the simple German race, there was but one firm and identical form of body.

—Friedrich Kohlrausch, 1816

FROM THE summit of his years the view was good. At eighty-
three in 1863, Friedrich Kohlrausch sat down at his desk to
write a life of domestic happiness and plenty. The teacher,
influential administrator, and widely read author recalled personal
details—his many friends, his flourishing family—as well as some
unfortunate public events like the German humiliation under
Napoleon at Jena in 1806 and the dashed hopes of the Frankfurt
parliament in 1848, when the Prussian king refused the offered German crown. His had been one of the many nationalistic voices that
grew steadily louder during the nineteenth century, lamenting the
"unnaturally split fatherland," as his contemporary Jacob Grimm
would phrase it.[1] One *Volk* deserved one *Reich*. The proclamation of
the German Empire in Versailles in 1871 arrived too late for Kohlrausch by four years. But had he not died in 1867, he would have
welcomed the state with the passion that inspired him to address

the nation, when he delivered his well-received speeches on "The Future of Germany," or when he wrote two of the most-read schoolbooks on German history.[2] With them he introduced the *Germanen* to the broader public and considerably expanded and enlarged Tacitus's readership. It was in this age that the *Germania* and its derivative Germanic myth reached beyond scholars and intellectuals and entered the living rooms of the growing German middle class.

Kohlrausch admonished generations of students to learn to be German from their virtuous past—above all from the Tacitean "mirror of honor and pride."[3] While much of it looks familiar from previous centuries, that mirror reflects an aspect heretofore unseen; it can be glimpsed in the epigraph to this chapter. In Kohlrausch's adaptation Tacitus's paragraph on Germanic purity and physiognomy received a racial taint and a vivid biological simile; both reflect anthropological and (para)scientific views that, developed at that time, would last for 150 years. From the turn of the nineteenth century, the Roman historian was twisted to testify to the purity not only of the mores and the language but also and increasingly of the racial constitution of the Germanic ancestors as members of the Caucasian, then Aryan, and finally Nordic race. Racially pure the Germans had been; racially pure they should be again.

NATIONALISM IN THE ABSENCE OF A NATION

> Where does the *Germane* begin? Where does he end? May a German smoke tobacco? The majority rules no. . . . But a German may drink beer; indeed, he should drink it as a true son of *Germania*, since Tacitus mentions specifically German *cerevisia*.
> —Heinrich Heine, 1840

The Prussian eagle was straitjacketed by the tricolor, and Berlin under French occupation, when Johann Gottlieb Fichte, a leading figure of philosophical idealism and Kohlrausch's mentor, delivered the first of his fourteen *Addresses to the German Nation* in the round hall of the Academy of the Sciences in December 1807. The mood was bad, the attendance good; his notoriety promised entertainment.

Some in the audience might have wondered what German nation the famous philosopher intended to address. Prussia had genuflected before the "nameless one" (as Fichte called Napoleon) after the Battle of Jena. With Rhine provinces annexed to France, the Holy Roman Empire swept from the map, and Prussia reduced to a subsidiary kingdom, the German nation more than ever seemed a political vacancy. The situation might well have caused a patriot's hair to turn gray overnight, as one of them—Friedrich Ludwig Jahn—famously claimed had happened to him. In the absence of a political nation, nationalists retreated even further into the cultural realm, fortifying language, law, and above all history as bastions of Germanness.

Fichte's primary demand in his *Addresses* was for a national (re)education. He defined "the whole German nation" as "everyone in the domain of the German language."[4] Other patriots had used and continued to use the same criterion. "What else," Jacob Grimm would wonder, "have we [Germans] in common but our language and literature?"[5] Fichte himself—like many itinerant compatriots—had experienced Germany rather than lived in it before he settled in Prussia's embattled capital. Born in a village in the Duchy of Saxony where fortune rarely visited, he graduated from nearby Schulpforta, moved on to Thuringia's Jena to study theology, then to Königsberg, the German cultural center in East Prussia (now Russian Kaliningrad) and hometown of the critical philosopher Immanuel Kant. Fichte's anonymously written *Critique of All Revelation* brought fame and appointment to a chair of philosophy at his alma mater. Returning to Jena, he published his *Contributions to the Correction of the Public's Judgment concerning the*

French Revolution, wherein he—a staunch believer in freedom—
defended the Revolution even when current opinion had grown cold
in the long shadow of the guillotine. Reputed to be a Jacobin and a
proven hothead, he ultimately lost his professorship. (The episode
did little to dampen his quick-tempered spirit; he continued vitriolic
exchanges with his enemies—all of them "shitheads" and *canailles*—
whom he collected the way some men collect tin soldiers.[6] By the
end of his short life, after years of turbulences, both public and private, his "display cabinet" contained a fine collection.) He found a
new home in Prussian Berlin, where he announced his "usual lectures . . . for a mixed public of both sexes . . . at the usual hour, Sundays from noon to 1" for the winter of 1807.[7] The national spirit,
Fichte decided, needed a wake-up call.

With the French occupying German territories, their culture
seemed to threaten "Germanness" more than ever. Fichte saw present times offering little "that [was] German among the Germans
themselves."[8] Though most celebratory in his remarks about medieval greatness, whose mailed armor titillated Romantics' fantasies,
he saw "the original stock of the new culture" rooted in the Tacitean past. The Roman writer was his main source of inspiration
while he was working on his *Addresses*. The national characteristics, which he wanted to be embraced again (and which he traced
through history in his sixth lecture), comprised the Tacitean canon
that humanists had already evoked: an "earnestness of soul" that
expressed itself as "loyalty, uprightness, honor, and simplicity."
Germans with those virtues had fought for freedom from Rome
under Arminius's lead and more than a millennium later from the
Roman church led by reformers. Now freedom required fighting once more, the more so as shaking off the French yoke would
advance all of humanity.

The philosopher believed the fate of humanity to hinge on the
fate of the German nation: "If you perish . . . , then there perishes
together with you every hope of the whole human race for salva-

tion."[9] This idea of a German(ic) mission gained ground rapidly. In an earlier lecture series, Fichte had divided the history of mankind into five epochs ending in the reign of reason. Within this boldly sweeping world plan he now read the Prussian defeat as the unmistakable symptom of the "age of completed sinfulness."[10] Germans sinned and suffered for humanity. But the nadir was a turning point; if they could rally to their traditional mores, they could rise and raise humanity towards the next level. As history revealed, they were a special people. For unlike other Germanic peoples—whom Fichte set apart from "neo-European nations" such as the Slavs— the Germans alone "remained in the original dwelling places of the ancestral stock."[11] Fichte soberly conceded that all Germanic tribes had mingled with other peoples and none could claim purity. It was therefore of even greater importance that the German people had "retained and developed the original language of the ancestral stock, whereas the [other Germanic peoples] adopted a foreign language and gradually reshaped it in a way of their own." Autochthony and originality—of the people as well as of its language— were motifs so worn by use that Tacitus could be discerned behind them even where he was not explicitly mentioned.

THE *ADDRESSES* "had a great effect on the minds of the cultivated class," according to the Prussian statesman Karl vom und zum Stein.[12] They expressed commonplaces of the nationalistic discourse: the imperative return to the purity of German language and culture, history as panacea, and German predestination. Friedrich Ludwig Jahn, a restless nationalistic agitator, shared most of these ideas but with a vehemence that made a contemporary think of him as a "cute bloodhound."[13] Having left secondary schools and numerous universities with ill repute and no degree, he published *The German People's Essence (Das deutsche Volkstum)*. Drafted in 1808 (when the Napoleonic shock was still fresh) and published in 1810, it became an immediate success. Jahn sifted Germanness and pleaded for a return to the traditions of the Germans of old. "We can be rescued still," he proclaimed, "but only by ourselves."[14] The road to salvation started with a national education program that targeted what he called the *Volkstum*: all "that a people has in common, its inherent character, its stirring and living, its regenerative force, its generative ability." The neologism, hardly more than what was previously known as the spirit of the people, quickly became a well-worn coin in nationalistic currency.

Jahn opined that the resuscitation of the *Volkstum* necessitated not only caring for the national culture, but also for physical training. Far too little was left of the vigor his ancestors had displayed in hunting and wrestling with bears. Even Romans had admired their physical fitness, how "their infantry . . . is so speedy that it fights among the cavalry."[15] As good as his word, in 1811 Jahn opened the first gymnastics field outside the southern wall of Berlin. The Father of Gymnastics (*Turnvater*), as he came to be known, founded a national movement. In referring to the sets of exercises, he chose another neologism, *turnen* (to do gymnastics), in remembrance of medieval tournaments with their chivalrous striving for valor.

Other populists embraced Jahn's ideas. Their interest in the *Volkstum* intersected with the efforts of those trying to systematize the inquiry into the German past, which resulted in major collections and editions of texts, like the series called the *Monumenta Germaniae historica* (Germany's Historical Monuments). These scholarly interests and pursuits, meant to "energize the love of one's fatherland through knowledge of its history," would eventually be institutionalized at universities in the new academic discipline of German Studies.[16] Nobody contributed more to this new discipline than Jacob Grimm. He was brought up a patriot—first for his particular region of birth in Hesse, soon for all of Germany—and his manifold works would all pertain to "our common fatherland and nurture love for it."[17] Bereaved of his father as a boy and still haunted as a middle-aged man by the image of the black coffin, he translated longing into labor. Partly in collaboration with his younger brother Wilhelm, he collected fairy tales, legends, and myriad information about German mythology, law, and language. He believed, in the tradition of Montesquieu, that they all expressed a people's spirit. Language was this spirit's "full breath," and its poetry and law were its particular utterances.

Grimm had been immersed in legal studies at the University of Marburg when he accompanied his teacher, Professor Friedrich Carl von Savigny, to Paris; he would return to the history of German law repeatedly throughout his variegated career. When he left for Paris at the time that Fichte gave his *Addresses*, German law and its study were in a state of transformation. The perspective had changed away from the fixed law of God, nature, or reason toward law as an expression of a specific people's will at a specific time. To scholars of a certain bent the acceptance and adaptation of Roman laws instead of Germanic customary law therefore seemed a national misfortune (but many others realized that even the distinction between native and foreign laws was elusive). The Napoleonic Wars focused scholarly attention on domestic law even further; for the French law code had been introduced into the occupied territories, putting German law at risk—again. Karl Friedrich Eichhorn, who along with Savigny promoted the new historical perspective on law, declared in the preface of his epochal 1808 *History of German Law and Constitution* that in the current situation of fundamental changes it seemed "more important than ever to turn one's eye to the past and acquaint oneself with the spirit of our foregone circumstances."[18] Those interested in such acquaintance read Tacitus. He continued to be a sometimes more, sometimes less, popular read throughout the nineteenth century among those intent on the rediscovery (and sometimes reinstitution) of Germanic laws, even though the *Germania* provides scarce information on fundamental Germanic legal concepts like the "clan" and "outlawry."[19] Jacob Grimm himself in his legal research considered the *Germania* merely as one source among many, but given his holistic view of the nation's past, he made ample use of it throughout his work and even produced his own Latin edition. For it was this "Roman's immortal writing [that] brought the light of dawn into the German past, which makes other peoples envy us."[20]

THE GERMANS THEMSELVES, many intellectuals felt, were not sufficiently aware of their glorious past; they lacked proper historical instruction. Fichte had urgently requested that a German history be written that would serve as a "national and popular book, just like the Bible," and "raise the national spirit."[21] Newly graduated, Friedrich Kohlrausch, serving as tutor to the two elder sons of a Danish envoy, attended the lectures of the well-known philosopher, whose incisive thoughts and crisp presentations did not disappoint. Kohlrausch met Fichte when he joined a group that dissected arguments on Sundays at the philosoper's house. Mutual esteem led to repeated encounters. A few years later Kohlrausch, now employed at the lyceum in Düsseldorf in North Rhine–Westphalia, heeded Fichte's plea for a work of an accessible national history.

During the nineteenth century the German states finally assumed responsibility for the education of their young. Kohlrausch not only reformed the schools in the kingdoms of Hannover and Prussia and shaped the history curriculum, he also wrote *German History for School and Home*, whose first volume appeared in 1816, when the pall over European battlefields had recently cleared after Napoleon's defeat. It fulfilled a "deeply felt need," one reader wrote, joined by Baron vom Stein, Field Marshal Gneisenau, "most recently victorious at Waterloo," Prussian privy councillors, and professors of history, who all sent "laudatory notes."[22] The appreciation lasted: The sixteenth edition appeared almost sixty years later in 1875. There were even an English translation and an abridged

version of the German original, which, published in 1822, reached
its fifteenth edition more than seventy years later. From the southwest of Germany, in Bavaria, to the northeast, in Prussia, Kohlrausch's work was considered *the* German history nonpareil. Even
after it was superseded in the 1870s, it enjoyed the recommenda-
tion "for study at home," by directors of higher schools.[23] It was
as popular a book as Fichte could have hoped for, and in spite of
inaccuracies and shortcomings it shaped the public view of German history.

The preface dates to April 1816: Ten years after the dissolution
of the Holy Roman Empire of the German Nation and one year
after the Battle of Waterloo, it advocates reflection, redirection,
and a future built on past German values. Kohlrausch believed that
no discipline save religion could provide better guidance than history. He acknowledged that patriotic incitement at least occasionally took precedence over accuracy, which had led him to include
questionable historical details. Before he turned to the first period
in German history, "from the most ancient times to the conquests
of the Franks under Clovis, 486 A.D.," he reproduced what "the
Romans" (well, one) had left behind: "an inspiring image . . . which
for all millennia that our tribe is to last will serve as a mirror of
honor and pride as well as imitation (*Nacheiferung*)."[24] This section
of approximately thirty pages is based on the *Germania*, which is
mostly paraphrased, but occasionally translated. Tacitus himself, with his "deep feeling for simplicity of manners," had gifted
them this "invaluable book, . . . a temple of honor to the German
nation."[25] Generations of pupils and their parents entered this
nationalistic sanctuary through Kohlrausch's pages—worshiped,
meditated, and returned fortified.

In Kohlrausch's history the "ancient Germans" live as simply,
bravely, and honestly as they had ever since the earliest reception
of the *Germania* among Italian and German humanists. The following historical backward glance may at first appear similarly

narrowed by tradition: "Our fatherland owes its freedom to this great victory in the Teutoburger Forest, and we, the descendants of those races, are indebted to it for the *unmixed German blood* which flows in our veins, and for the pure German sounds pronounced by our tongue."[26] But a closer look reveals the embedded novelty: Like Heinrich Bebel in the sixteenth century, Kohlrausch feels his Germanic ancestors' blood pulsing in his veins; like Justus Georg Schottelius in the age of the Baroque, he credits his forefathers with the protection of the pure German tongue. But unlike either he emphasizes the blood's purity. Elsewhere in his *History* he describes the *Germanen* "as an ancient, pure, and unmixed original race," likening them to "identical plants springing from a pure seed," which are free from "degeneration." He planted racial notions in Tacitus's text. But where had he, a historian and teacher, obtained them?

THE FINEST OF THE ARYAN RACE

The Germanic people ... were a pure race ... and owed their overwhelming success and longest-lasting impact to this purity. . . . This has been emphasized since the days of Tacitus until today.

—Ludwig Schemann, 1910

Racism may be defined as a belief in inherent racial differences. These differences are thought to be visible in physical characteristics, which correlate with intellectual and cultural traits. The aggregate of racially specific characteristics determines the race's place within the racial hierarchy. Though racist thinking can be traced back to the Middle Ages, not until the mid- to late eighteenth century was "the scientific concept of race" advanced.[27] Botanists and zoologists tried "to read in nature's book," aiming to place each plant and animal within its particular chapter, section, and paragraph.[28]

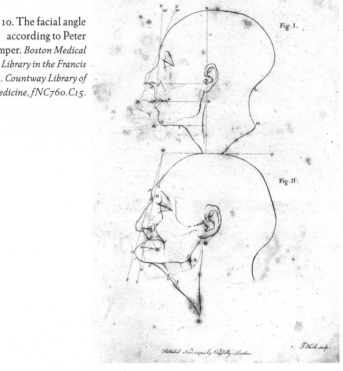

10. The facial angle
according to Peter
Camper. *Boston Medical
Library in the Francis
A. Countway Library of
Medicine, fNC760.C15.*

In the name of such classification, scientists soon cast a gauging eye on the human species in its variety. Human individuality was reduced to allegedly objective features, such as the proportions of the human skull or the color of the skin. The versatile Dutch artist and anatomist Pieter Camper in the 1760s had suggested as a criterion for beauty the angle between the line that runs from the jawbone to the forehead and the one that connects the nose with the ear. This "facial angle," originally meant as a guideline for sculptors and painters, was quickly misappropriated for racial purposes. A few decades later Anders Retzius, a Swedish anthropologist, calculated the ratio of the length and width of human skulls. This "cephalic index" soon served to differentiate between two types: The broad-

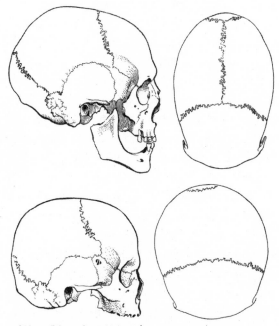

Abb. 8. Oben: Langſchädel ⎫
„   9. Unten: Kurzſchädel ⎭ in Seiten- und Scheitelanſicht.

11. Illustration of the cephalic index in Günther's *Rassenkunde.*
Widener Library, Harvard College Library, Ger 330.435.

skulled and the long-skulled, rendered in Greek respectively as "brachycephalic" and "dolichocephalic" (Heinrich Himmler, to give an example, was decidedly brachycephalic, much to his chagrin). Throughout the nineteenth century, scientists would scour far and wide *mis*measuring human anatomy. The more data was compiled, the less significant the results became. Where science failed, prejudice stepped in and observation yielded to opinion. From this farrago the white race emerged as dominant.

JOHANN FRIEDRICH BLUMENBACH (1752–1840) was a scientist of international repute at the University of Göttingen. A professor of medicine, he pursued his interest in anatomy with the passion that had caused him, as a little boy, to hide bones of domestic animals in his bedroom (the housekeeper was not amused). It was, a contemporary quipped, "the modest beginning of [his] famous collection" of skulls.[29] Blumenbach published craniometric studies about these 264 skulls which were as foundational to craniometry as his dissertation *On the Natural Variety of Mankind* was to modern anthropology. The latter helped establish the Caucasian race, which Blumenbach's colleague Christoph Meiners—today forgotten and fortunate in his fate—had introduced into the racist discourse. What is it, the doctoral candidate Blumenbach wondered, that "changes the course of generation, and now produces a worse and now a better progeny, at all events widely different from its original progenitors?"[30] Such degeneration, defined as deviation from the original type, resulted from changes of climate or lifestyle and the "intercourse of different varieties [i.e., "races"]." The German ancestors had not engaged in intercourse with outsiders and could therefore exemplify "the unadulterated countenance of nations unaffected by any union with any other nation." But since those days climatic conditions had changed, people had mingled, and degeneration was evidenced in the scarcity among Blumenbach's contemporaries of those "huge bodies of our ancestors, powerful only for attack, and their . . . fierce eyes." Germans were no longer *Germanen*. This oft-heard complaint was no longer about cultural and moral decline but physiological and ultimately racial degeneration: The "fierce blue eyes" had lost their spark.

Blumenbach was not a racist. A monogenist, he believed in the unity of human kind; a clearsighted scientist, he saw through allegedly impermeable lines between races and vociferously spoke out against the supposedly innate intellectual deficits of "Negroes." And yet he regarded the Caucasian race—eponymously named after Mount Caucasus, thought to be its original habitat—not only as the original form of humankind, but also as "the most handsome and becoming."[31] Elevating Caucasians to aesthetic superiority, Blumenbach implicitly suggested that degeneration was decline and difference deficiency. He thereby provoked the racist notions he rejected for himself in his famous feud about the human race with Christoph Meiners. Despite their dispute the two foes together established the Caucasian race as the ultimate human type, and Tacitus as a corroborating source.

Blumebach had taught Kohlrausch, who stayed interested in anthropology and anatomy even after his departure from Göttingen. In Berlin he attended not only Fichte's lectures but also those by Lothar Gall on phrenology—a theory that inferred intellectual capacities from surface features of the skull. Critics sneered at the mountebank, others granted him serious consideration, and Kohlrausch—ever curious—even secured a skull with borderlines demarcating the various powers of the intellect. Racial theories and platitudes flourished inside and outside academia, bandied about in pamphlets and popular philosophy: "The purer a people, the better; the more mixed, the more lowlife," *Turnvater* Jahn declared.[32] Ernst Moritz Arndt, another kindred spirit, joined with Jahn in visiting Kohlrausch in Düsseldorf during the summer of 1814 (they both contributed "stimulating suggestions" to his *German History*).[33] The racial interpreation of Tacitus that Kohlrausch inserted into his history had been amply prepared for.

Arndt, who came to be known as the Father of Germany, had previously traveled in Europe and had suffered. His German name "stank," so he passed himself off as a Swede.[34] During the final years of the Napoleonic Wars, he produced political pamphlets along with poems and songs that met Prussian state minister Baron vom Stein's request to "heighten and intensify [the patriotic] feeling of the [German] people." In his pamphlets Arndt rewrote Tacitus's chapter on the physiognomy and purity of the *Germanen* at least three times. Outlining a racial history wherein the decline of a people results from degeneration caused by miscegenation, he asserted that Rome had perished because of its bastardization. However,

> The Germans are not bastardized by alien peoples, . . . they have remained more than many other peoples in their original purity and have been able to develop slowly . . . the fortunate Germans are an original people. For our ancestors we have a great piece of evidence from one of the greatest men who ever lived, from the Roman Tacitus. This extraordinary man . . . clearly saw the worth of our fathers, and prophesied their splendid future; and so far history has not contradicted him. But of all things he saw most clearly how important it was for the future greatness and majesty of the German people that they were pure and resembled only themselves, that they were no mongrels; for he saw his Italy, which had once been the mistress of the world, a bastardized canaille, cursed and outcast.[35]

By using Tacitus's racially tinged account in his widely read political pamphlets, Arndt—like Kohlrausch—significantly widened his circle of readers. In linking decline to degeneration, Arndt conceived of a racial theory of history, of which the French writer Arthur de Gobineau, also influenced by Blumenbach, would a few decades later develop the gloomiest version.

When Alexis de Tocqueville, the author of *Democracy in America*, was appointed France's minister of foreign affairs in the wake of the February revolution of 1848, he recruited Gobineau (aged thirty-three) for his ministry. He had discerned talent in the young man, who was noble, impoverished—and rancorous. Even though this new position suited Gobineau's sense of his standing in life better than any he had previously held, he was still resentful, when, as the secretary of the French legation in Berne, he moved to Switzerland with his wife and daughter. It was a return of sorts, as he had lived there during his adolescence, when his mother's scandalous elopement with his tutor had caused him to study at a Swiss high school. Posted to Berne almost two decades later in 1849, he did not feel challenged by his work but by his environment. His frustration with his situation grew, and so did his *Essay on the Inequality of Human Races*, most of which he wrote during his Swiss stay.[36] The first two volumes appeared in 1853, the final two in 1855, in an edition of five hundred published at the author's expense. A second printing toward the end of the nineteenth century did little to increase the number of readers. It speaks to the limited availability of the *Essay* that Richard Wagner in the 1870s had to borrow a copy from an acquaintance from another town. The bulky work seemed destined for oblivion.

The world, according to the *Essay*, is inhabited by "three great and clearly marked types," discernible by hue of skin: the black, the yellow, and the white.[37] Within these basic races, there are minor groupings, like the Aryan, "that illustrious family," which is "the noblest within the white race." Other types of humankind over time resulted from miscegenation. The original three were intellectually unequal and their fate preordained: "No human race can . . . leave the path that has been marked out for it by God." With moral and intellectual talents stemming not from education but from disposition, the white race held "the monopoly on beauty, intelligence, and power." It propels or, rather, used to propel history. Skipping through history with major civilizations (he counted ten) as stepping-stones, Gobineau observed that the Aryan-Germanic part of the white race was responsible for all the highlights in human civilization. "Chaldea in its dotage was succeeded by the young and vigorous Persia, tottering Greece by virile Rome, and the degenerate rule of [the last Roman emperor] Augustulus by the kingdoms of the noble [Germanic] princes." Nations rose and fell according to their racial makeup; they reached glory following infusions of white blood, and slumped due to its diffusion. There were those among Gobineau's contemporaries who believed that the present chaos was transitory and an upswing imminent. But the disenfranchised French noble opined that there was no hope that "the races of modern times [would] regain their lost youth." White blood was thinning out in an ever more promiscuous world. Gobineau believed in doom but not in redemption.

The *Essay* effectively reduces human history to a racial epiphenomenon. Simple and sweeping, its naturalistic and fatalistic theory explains the current cultural lows with the diminished role played by Aryans and *Germanen*. Both were established terms in French intellectual salons. The term "Aryan" had appeared half a century prior to Gobineau's work. Originally the name by which certain Indo-Iranian tribes who roamed the central Asian steppe referred to themselves as early as 2,000 BCE, it came to prominence in the wake of Sir William Jones's publication of his discovery of striking linguistic parallels between Sanskrit, Greek, and Latin. "No philologer could examine them all three, without believing them to have sprung from some common source, which, perhaps, no longer exists."[38] "Philologers" and others continued Jones's work, and the term "Aryan" was soon used not only to signify the Indo-European ur-language (the common source that Jones did not want to speculate about) but also an Aryan ur-people. Ambiguities followed, and soon arguments. In a famous series of lectures delivered at the Royal Institution of Great Britain, the German-born orientalist Friedrich Max Müller suggested that "it would be best, perhaps . . . to use the name *Aryan* in a purely physiological sense, and to restrict it to the dolichocephalic people, with blue eyes and blond hair, regardless of the language they speak."[39] As a mythical race—rather than a linguistic group—Aryans were believed to have conquered, colonized, and acculturated the world.

But had they really descended from the heights of the Himalayas, as was commonly believed? The north of Europe was proposed and promoted as an alternative location for the cradle of the Aryan race. Linguists traced questionable etymologies to make Caesar's Germanic opponent Ariovistus the bearer of an Aryan name related to the German *Ehre* (honor). Just as the Aryans were considered the finest of the white race, so the Germanic people became the Aryans par excellence.[40] By the mid-1850s, according to a contemporaneous German reviewer of Gobineau, to speak of the ancient Germans as the noblest within the Aryan aristocracy was to state a truism.

Barring his gloomy pessimism, there is little new in Gobineau, in whose opinion "the Germanic race is provided with all the sap [*toute l'énergie*] of the Aryan variety."[41] He justifies his calling the original cultural force "Aryan," asserting that at least some of the tribes had referred to themselves in that way. They could not have chosen a more beautiful name, "as it signifies the honorable," and, he continued, "[they were] men worthy of esteem and respect and . . . knew to take their due when it was not given to them. This interpretation may not be based strictly on the word, but as we will see it can be justified by their deeds." How quickly his fancy took flight! As a disenchanted noble, Gobineau believed in the descent of the French nobility from the Germanic invaders. He was well familiar with the *Germania*, yet critical of it. For, he felt, Tacitus "does not want to see anything but estimable savages in the heroes of his booklet; therefore he falsifies his entire account of the degree of their civilization." Whatever the Roman historian asserted, the *Germanen* knew how to write. Gobineau also disputed that their housing bore resemblance to "the sordid dwellings, half concealed in the ground, which the author of the *Germania* took such great pleasure to describe in Stoic colors."

In his Aryan-Germanic profile, however, especially in discussing the "capacity of the original Germanic races," Gobineau followed Tacitus's description of their leadership, sense of honor, and even their passion for gambling at the risk of slavery.[42] He also drew on his account of the high esteem enjoyed by women and their impeccable chastity—which Gobineau may have emphasized in remembrance of his mother, whose behavior continued to embarrass him even after he had cut all ties. "The influence [*puissance*] of women within a society can serve as one of the most certain indicators of the persistence of the Aryan elements." If not culturally, then morally at least, the Tacitean Germanic tribes were the prime bearers of Aryan blood.

It would seem a small step from this characterization of Germanic society as particularly Aryan to asserting that Tacitus attested to the purity of Germanic "blood"—as numerous racist writers read chapter 4 of his little book. But Gobineau was not one of them. On the contrary he explicitly denies purity, dating its end to the time of Jesus Christ's birth. Current Germany fared even worse in his eyes, for "scraps" were all that was left of the Germanic heritage.[43] As if he had not been explicit enough, in a posthumously published article he discredited "the blood extolled by Tacitus [as being] neither as abundant nor as wide spread as has been willingly believed." This obituary on the Aryan-Germanic race, which was interspersed with notes mourning the state of Germany and lauding the Jewish people, is decidedly incongruous with what would become National Socialist ideology. But Gobineau visited with Germany's most controversial and influential composer of the time.

RICHARD WAGNER (1813–83) was pushing his plan to establish a permanent venue for the performance of his musical dramas when Germany albeit belatedly became a nation-state. Three consecutive wars against Denmark, Austria, and France in the 1860s and early 1870s had helped forge a stronger sense of unity in the Prussian-led coalitions. On January 18, 1871, the German Empire was proclaimed in the Palace of Versailles, and the Prussian king,

William I, was hailed as the first German emperor. A wave of enthusiasm swept over the newly unified territories of the former North German Federation and the southern German states of Bavaria and Baden, the kingdom of Württemberg, and the Grand Duchy of Hesse. The body politic salvaged, Wagner opined in a letter, the German soul was in need of "invigoration."[44] A political activist of nationalist stripe earlier in life, he continued politicizing in his music, essays, and other writings. For him, like many others since the eighteenth century, art came from the people, to the people, and for the benefit of the people. The genuine artist was a mere medium through which the people's spirit—the *Volksgeist* Herder had profiled with Tacitean help—expressed itself. Wagner believed himself to be such a genial bard, and his works, like the *Ring of the Nibelung*, with its thundering evocation of Nordic heroism and its celebration of Germanic virtues, was meant to regenerate the German people. All he needed was a suitable place.

Bayreuth at the time was a little town, about fifty miles northeast of Nuremberg, within the Kingdom of Bavaria. Centrally positioned in the new empire, it appealed to this musician who wanted to reach all of Germany. He selected it for his festival (the first of which would take place in 1876). In his stately Villa Wahnfried, which abutted the town's ornamental centerpiece, the Court Garden, he and his second wife, Cosima, entertained a string of friends and proselytes. They formed the so-called Bayreuth Circle, a quasi-religious sodality in which—especially after Wagner's death in 1883—the maestro's musical works and cultural ideas were discussed, interpreted, and elaborated upon. To facilitate discussion inside the circle and to communicate the doctrine to the members of the numerous Wagnerian societies spread across Europe, the *Notes from Bayreuth* (*Bayreuther Blätter*) were launched, appearing monthly from 1879 to 1937. Recurrent themes were the *Volk*, "Germanness" (*Deutschtum*), art's contributions to politics and society, and the need for regeneration: the rebirth of the German people first through Wagnerian art, later—when the discourse became ever more racial—through eugenics. Richard and Cosima introduced Arthur de Gobineau and his all-but-forgotten work to this circle of sympathizers, two of whom would redirect his Aryan-Germanic theory and channel it into the *völkisch* surge.

Wagner's first encounter with Gobineau, late in 1876 in Rome, was brief and inconsequential. But their second conversation four years later in Venice led to Wagner reading Gobineau's works and Gobineau visiting Wagner twice at Wahnfried. His death in 1882 prevented further visits, but not his works' expanding presence at Bayreuth. For when the maestro had introduced him to Ludwig Schemann, he added the exhortatory words: "Save him!"[45] And Schemann, a pliant, docile, and dutiful Wagnerite who usually worked as a librarian in Göttingen, obeyed. He would spend much of his life spreading Gobineau's name, founding an eponymous society, translating his works, and writing a biography, commentary, and his own treatise on race—all of which would in due time be recognized by the National Socialist Workers Party, which would award him the Goethe Medal for Art and Science. But Schemann yielded to his own racial convictions, rendering Gobineau anti-Semitic and less fatalistic. His first translation stayed true to the original; it stated—in accordance with its author's belief in the dispersal and disappearance of the Germanic heritage—that England was the place where "the scraps of Germanic practices were best preserved." However, in 1940 the German reader did not learn about England but about "those countries that have best preserved the Germanic customs."[46] Similarly, in 1910, when publishing an anthology of Gobineau's writings along with his own comments and defense against critics, Schemann reasserted the notion of an originally pure race, which is characterized as "a gift of nature" brought about "when a people in its primeval time [*Urzeit*] in a closed region . . . lives by itself."[47] These were obviously the conditions the Germanic tribes enjoyed in Tacitus's account, whose formative presence Schemann acknowledges soon after: "The Germanic people and the Arabs were a pure race ... and owed their overwhelming success and long lasting impact to this purity. As for the Germanic people in particular, this has been emphasized since the days of Tacitus." Gobineau's pessimism was too bitter for his spokesman.

Schemann was not alone in disagreeing with Gobineau's fatalistic assessment of the state of the Aryan-Germanic race. Another member of the Bayreuth circle who read and rewrote the *Essay* suggested that "we all immediately put a bullet through our heads."[48] For this would be the only dignified solution, Houston Stewart Chamberlain stated, if Gobineau were right about the original races, their intermingling, and their inevitable decline. But, Chamberlain countered, he was not; on the contrary, Tacitus's pure *Germanen* were possible again in the future. According to this *völkisch* prophet, they could be reborn.

THE *VÖLKISCH* MOVEMENT "BEFORE HITLER CAME"

> This edition of the *Germania*, while primarily intended for
> use at schools, ... is meant to serve all who ... have retained
> an interest in the ancient classics and particularly this most
> valuable document of our *Volkstum*.
> —Eduard Wolff, Tacitus's *Germania*, 1895

The founding of the German Empire in 1871 delighted and disappointed: Finally there was a German state, but it was felt to fall well short of including the whole nation. Too many German speakers lived outside the Empire's territory. Numerous voluntary political associations formed a "secondary system of social power," wherein *völkisch* men—the majority were middle-class and highly educated— played a loud and oftentimes loutish role.[49] Agitating with "beer-emphasis" (to borrow Thomas Mann's expression), they rallied behind national symbols for the sake of national causes, real and imagined. They joined major organizations like the Alldeutscher Verband (Pan-German League), founded in 1891, the Germanenorden (Germanic Order), founded in 1912, and countless other associations, gymnastic societies, shooting clubs, student corporations, and youth groups. "What are three Germans?" a witticism of the time wondered. "A *Verein* [association]" was the answer.

Decentralized, disjointed, and miscellaneous, the movement was held together by a common ideology. The adjective *völkisch*, introduced into German for the sake of linguistic purity as a substitute for "national" during the late nineteenth century, refers to the *Volk* as the ideological centerpiece (the particular adjectival ending *-isch* connotes "excess," and for some writers *völkisch* would always sound negative). The movement's ideological components were assembled from previous nationalistic endeavors and circulated in journals like *The Hammer* and *Heimdall* (its Old Norse prefix signifying "home" and its motto printed in runes) as well as pamphlets and books. The German *Volkstum*, one program specified in the spirit of *Turnvater* Friedrich Ludwig Jahn, was to be strengthened "by keeping the [German] race pure, by influencing the caretaking of the youth, the educational system, language, script and law, by cherishing German culture and spirit."[50] Being German to most meant being Germanic once more.

But at the turn of the century this romanticization of the past was suffused with a fear of modernity, which translated into a dislike of the city, a distrust of intellectuals, and a love of the peasant life. Parascience, with its pro-Germanic and anti-Semitic racism, flourished. *Völkisch* men fancied that the Aryan-Germanic superiority, as evidenced in history, could be proved anatomically as well. Aryan-looking Germans, descendants of the people whom Tacitus allegedly described as "fully racially pure," were measured, especially their skulls, in order to demonstrate the correlation between Germanic appearance and talents.[51] The research was carried out with plenty of fervor and few results. Nevertheless racial purity became a major concern of the *völkisch* movement. A recruitment flyer of the Germanic Order would warn apocalyptically of the imminent extinction of the "blond heroic race," wistfully evoking the times "in which the Roman Tacitus still spoke of the old Germans as racially pure."[52] In their message for *Germanen* they pleaded for a systematic "breeding to former heights" (*Wiederhochzüchtung*). The organization wanted to start it off by admitting only Nordic men and women, whose membership applications had to specify the color of their hair, eyes, and skin. It is in the same spirit as the lonely hearts' ads printed in *The Hammer*, in which a man of Nordic appearance would search for a woman of similar looks.

The concern for racial purity was complemented by efforts to purify German culture and language: "Our *Volk* must retain its Germanic character." A Germanic warrior calmly faced the surging sea in the masthead that the *Alldeutsche Blätter* (Pan-German Sheets) displayed beginning in 1900; in looks and character he

12. The Germanic warrior on the masthead of the *Alldeutsche Blätter*.
Center for Research Libraries, MF 10155.

hardly differed from his etched ancestor in Clüver's *Germania antiqua*. *Völkisch* propaganda overflowed with maritime metaphors—for example, German culture was "flooded" with foreign elements—and its adherents liked to cast themselves in the role of their Germanic forefathers. The General German Language Association, founded in 1885, proposed to "foster the genuine spirit and unique essence of the German language, . . . and [to] activate a sense of its purity, correctness, clarity and beauty."[53] (Its program could have been copied from those of the seventeenth-century language societies, which, however, were hardly concerned with the purging of foreign words.) In the name of such purity, *völkisch* vocabulary excluded loan words like *Archäologie* and used *Spatenwissenschaft* (science of the spade) instead.

This *Spatenwissenschaft* was also recruited for the *völkisch* endeavor. Gustaf Kossinna, the most productive and innovative archaeologist at the time and a professor at the University of Berlin, argued based on his research that the *Germanen* had had a period of technical accomplishment and cultural sophistication in the Bronze Age. They brought culture to the primitive and barren Mediterranean region, where the ruling elites would continue to be of Nordic race—a consequence of this "first" Indo-Germanic migration.[54] Kossinna found the charge of barbarism laughable: "Germanic blood had revitalized" the Roman empire, and from Germany culture continued to spread. What Tacitus, an admirer of the *Germanen*, wrote about their inebriety needed reconsideration, given that "a people of sots cannot persist as a people of heroes, [and there was no question that] the *Germanen* were heroes." A member of several *völkisch* organizations, Kossinna popularized the results of the newly established academic field of prehistory, which—as his most influential book, *German Prehistory*, declared in its title—should be considered "a pre-eminently national discipline." He contributed significantly to the ubiquitous presence of the *Germanen*, who had a firm grip on imperial public attention. They titillated the imagination in historical novels like Gustav Freytag's *The Ancestors*, in wall-size oil paintings like Carl Theodor von Piloty's *Thusnelda at the Triumph of Germanicus*, and in countless lectures, journals, and popular books on prehistory. They also played a lead in one of the most influential texts of the Wilhelmine era.

HOUSTON STEWART CHAMBERLAIN was the most prominent member of the Bayreuth Circle around the turn of the century and one of the intellectual leaders of the *völkisch* movement. It seems safe to assume that nobody predicted this outcome when he was born in September 1855 in England to a well-heeled, blue-blooded, and well-connected British family. He never felt at home in England or ever at ease with most of his relatives. Upon the death of his Scottish mother he was sent to finish the first decade of his life with relatives in Versailles. Then, complying with his father's wishes, he entered an English boarding school. It was a horrible experience. He, a young French snob, suffered under what he would later describe as "the rule of the fist"; it probably did not help that he liked to play by himself in a corner behind a wall of chairs.[55] Whatever sense of belonging young Chamberlain might have possessed was lost. Having always been so dependably sick that his brothers nicknamed him P.L.O. (Poor Little One), he had his first mental breakdown at the age of fourteen. Others would ensue, making a regular line of work impossible. When, after the first crisis, he spent a decade traveling in Europe, he visited Germany for the first time. It would furnish him with a home. "The decisive movement of my life was towards *Deutschtum*. I attached myself to the German system . . . and at its center stood Richard Wagner."[56] He would eventually marry Wagner's youngest daughter and move to Bayreuth.

Chamberlain's Munich-based publisher, Friedrich Bruckmann,

felt the public's desire for appraisal and reorientation when evening settled on the nineteenth century. He inquired of his author
whether he might want to write an epilogue on the outgoing century. Chamberlain was delighted by this proposal and quickly
drafted a project comprising three parts. The first was a tour de
force, rummaging through history from ancient times to 1800,
duly noting major cultural developments. Next he planned a *tour
d'horizon* of the nineteenth century, citing political, social, scientific, cultural, and other accomplishments worthy of note. A final
part would be an evaluation of the concluding century in light of
those preceding it. But the distances proved too great, and Chamberlain never made it past the first part, though he kept collecting
notes for the remainder of the project. He worked on what would
become *The Foundations of the Nineteenth Century* from February
1896 to the fall of 1898, with a frenzy befitting the work's scope,
for eight hours a day.[57] After an appeal for God's guidance in the
morning, some time was spent leafing through volumes of his well-
stocked library in search of suitable quotations (with little regard
for their contexts), which he then arranged in a sweeping argument
abounding in inconsistencies aided by inaccuracies. Throughout he
displayed the kind of logic he used in a letter to his aunt, in which
he suggested that having lost a fortune speculating, he now enjoyed
other investors' heightened confidence. The work grew to twelve
hundred pages. Rightly damned as "the crapulous eructations of
a drunken cobbler" by one lonely critic, it mostly met with great
acclaim. Published in 1899, it went through more than thirty editions by 1944, including complete translations into Czech, English,
and French, and partial ones into Hungarian, Russian, and Spanish.
Among the scores of readers, the emperor William II was so infatu-
ated with the book that it caused concern among sober observers
inside and outside the empire. But these were not sober times.

Chamberlain predicated historical significance on racial purity.
He explained that the Roman *limes* had crumbled because of the

"raceless and nationless chaos" that reigned within.[58] Fortunately Germanic tribes swept in from the north and took over. They were "the lawful heir of the Hellene and the Roman, blood of their blood and spirit of their spirit," as they all belonged to one Aryan-Germanic family. Had it not been for these northern "barbarians," the Indo-European race would have perished, for Asian and African "slaves" sat on the Roman throne (Chamberlain alluded to the Asian and African origin of later Roman emperors), and Jews had used their learning to infiltrate and contaminate the Greco-Roman culture. *Ex septentrione lux*: the light that brought hope to the ruins of Rome came from the north.

From the rubble the Indo-European man was reborn, like the phoenix from its ashes. The *Germanen* for Chamberlain were the "makers of the world's history" (and ultimately the masons of nineteenth-century Europe): They founded nations, advanced humanity by their technical inventions, and elevated the human spirit with their art, to the extent that a people's degree of civilization stood in direct proportion to its amount of Germanic blood.[59] Skillfully using established mystical language, Chamberlain stated flatly: The *Germane* "is the *soul* of our culture." He readily admitted that when the Germanic peoples entered history, they did not call themselves by a single name. It took a "foreigner" to see racial unity in the tribes' variety, the "strong trunk" under "the copious offshoots," and to call them by one name. Chamberlain added that Tacitus had realized that "the physical characteristics of all these men [were] the same;" and from this "correct empiric basis," he had reached another "intuitively correct insight," namely that "the various tribes of *Germanien*, unpolluted by marriage with alien peoples, have from time immemorial been a special, unmixed people, resembling itself alone." And even though his *Germanen* comprised the Celts and Slavs as well as Tacitus's *Germanen*, he decided to retain Tacitus's term to signify all of them. Chamberlain finally elaborated on the two qualities that distinguished the *Germanen* from all other peoples, which, since the fifteenth century, had been based on Tacitus's account: "Freedom and loyalty are the two roots of the Germanic nature, or, if you will, the two pinions that bear it heavenwards."

In the *Foundations* history happens on the battlefield of racial conflict. For Chamberlain the downfall of Rome signified the beginning of real history. All else had been an overture. For the drama of the Germanic-Jewish conflict began then, and "to this day these two powers—Jews and Germanic races—stand . . . , now as friendly, now as hostile, but always as alien forces face to face."[60] Jews, "in a way opposed to all European races," are characterized as the alien element within Europe. Chamberlain postulates that they had avoided ethnic confusion: "This one race has established as its guiding principle the purity of the blood." While protective of their own race, they had married their daughters into non-Jewish families and subverted Indo-European culture with their own. Now, at the turn of the twentieth century, the survival of the Germanic life and culture was at risk.

In the preface to the fourth edition, Chamberlain responded to critics, quite a few of whom had charged him with plagiarizing Gobineau. He had encountered Gobineau's work in the *Bayreuther Blätter*, but it was not until about 1893 that, at Cosima Wagner's suggestion, he turned a more studious eye to the *Essay*. Even though he found the charge of plagiarism laughable, his debt was profound: Like the Frenchman he believed in racial differences, that race determined talent, and that races were "the actual [*eigentlichen*] historical individuals."[61] Like Gobineau he elevated the Germanic people to supremacy, for the most part calling them *Germanen*, but also using Aryan, Indo-Germanic, and a few other names (precision was not his strength, neither in language nor in thought). Instead of differentiating between better and worse races, Chamberlain suggested simply contrasting "those who are physically and morally Germanic and those who are not." But he rejected Gobineau's assumption of inevitable decline. While the author of the *Essay* had looked for the origin of the Aryan-Germanic race, mourned its decline through time, and bewailed its inevitable doom, the author of the *Foundations* was more concerned with the future: "Though it were proved that there never was an Aryan race in the past, yet we desire that in the future there may be one. That is the decisive standpoint for men of action."[62] Chamberlain believed in evolution and strayed into botany and zoology—areas he had taken an interest in ever since his studies with his German tutor, Otto Kunze—to illustrate two general points. Using fruit trees for comparison, he asserted that a noble race was a gradual process that could begin at any given moment. And to specify his concept of "race" and justify his claim that it was intuitively grasped, he imagined dogs and horses: Who could not tell almost instinctively the thoroughbreds from the rest? "One single unbiased glance can illuminate the truth like a sunbeam." In the light of such truth Chamberlain could see *Germanen* as pure in the future as they had been in the Tacitean past.

CHAMBERLAIN'S TAKE on history resonated with all the major ideological themes of the *völkisch* movement: racist, anti-Semitic, pan-Germanic. In its use of the *Germania* it was typical too. The first among the "German foundational writings," Tacitus's text figured prominently on *völkisch* reading lists, and was called upon to substantiate most of the claims for the Aryan-Germanic race which had accumulated over the centuries: Its purity, physiognomy, its purported peasant lifestyle, customs, and especially character (*Gesittung*).[63] Dozens of translations, adaptations, and commentaries presented it to the German public in order "to illuminate the past, explain the present, and unveil the future," as Ludwig Wilser—a physician with a penchant for *völkisch* writing—put it in his popular, often reprinted version.[64] Full of praise for the Promethean warriors, who had excelled with "the weapons of war as much as of the mind" and with their blood "rejuvenated and reinvigorated" other peoples, he exemplifies the fervor with which the imaginary Germanic past was embraced. It caused some to yearn for a return to a Germanic religion, but found more pervasive expression in religious metaphors and comparisons. The editors of the *Bible for Germanen* recommended their work to their readers as a complement to "the Jewish and Christian Bible"; and the *Germania* was included in it as the primary "holy script."[65]

Critics of these wishful views fared badly. Eduard Norden—the "greatest Latinist in the world," according to Harvard's contemporaneous president James Conant—cautioned against reading the *Germania* as if it simply displayed the German past. In a hefty tome that won the Fondazione Vallauri prize* as one of the finest works on Latin literature, he traced many of the allegedly Germanic characteristics back to Greek and Roman descriptions of various other peoples like the Egyptians and the Scythians. These were "wandering motifs," which, it seemed, Tacitus attributed to the *Germanen* because they fitted what the Romans considered a barbarous people. Norden's discovery cast doubt on the *Germania's* historical authenticity—a result, as the author himself conceded, "not particularly pleasant" to those enthusiastic about German (pre)history. Readers of a certain bent were indeed displeased. *Völkisch* dilettantes incriminated a scholar who was encyclopedic in his learning and exemplary in his diligence, suggesting that he had manufactured some of those parallels. There erupted such a storm of protest that Norden felt compelled to seek cover in ambiguity in his second edition, reassuring his readers that Tacitus's text remained "a historical source of the first order."[66] He had realized that the faith of those who wanted to believe was not to be shaken.

Norden's book appeared in 1920 in the midst of German postwar anxieties. The shattering experience of World War I, which forced the Germans to decide whether they would be "strong enough to

---

* From the Turin Academy of Sciences.

be reborn," and the dissatisfaction with the Treaty of Versailles led to a resurgence of the *völkisch* movement in the newly established Weimar Republic.[67] In its wake the Thule Society was founded in Munich under the aegis of the nation-wide operating Germanic Order. It disappeared into oblivion after merely five years of political machinations; but no sooner had the Nazis attained power in 1933 than the society's former head, the protean Baron von Sebottendorff, published the book *Before Hitler Came*. Its preface claimed: "Thule members were the people to whom Hitler first turned."[68] There were some specific personal and programmatic links between the society and the NSDAP*—Hitler's final version of the swastika appears to be indebted to the society's logo—but the cradle of National Socialism was not any particular one of the myriad organizations as much as the *völkisch* ideology itself.

THE *GERMANE* had enjoyed prominence inside as well as outside Germany right from the start of the nineteenth century. Most of his characteristics and achievements were familiar from his appearances in preceding centuries, with the notable exception of racial purity. Capturing the ever-increasing public attention in the German Empire, he stood firmly at the center of the *völkisch* ideology, promising salvation. He was as much as ever evoked from Tacitus's pages, the first text of the Germanic bible. As the events surrounding Eduard Norden at the beginning of the Weimar Republic revealed, the *Germania* was sacrosanct. Among countless others, it inspired one who would reach the highest echelons in the National Socialist apparatus: the second most powerful man in the Third Reich, the Reichsführer SS, Heinrich Himmler.

---

* The acronym stands for Nationalsozialistische Deutsche Arbeiterpartei (National Socialist German Workers' Party).

8

A Bible for National Socialists

We believe with [Tacitus] in the indigenousness [of the Germanic race] as well as the race itself with all the anthropological characteristics that [Tacitus] assigns to it.

—Professor Hans Naumann, 1934

A FOREIGN CORRESPONDENT noted the "breathless silence in the mighty room."[1] When the cardinal-archbishop of Munich and Freising, Michael von Faulhaber, ascended the pulpit of Saint Michael's Church in Munich to deliver his New Year's address, he held the heightened attention not just of his audience, with its numerous journalists from around the world: The newly installed National Socialist regime also listened uneasily. It was December 31, 1933. The Weimar Republic was dead but its gravediggers not yet certain of their power, and the cardinal made them nervous. Saint Michael's, the largest Renaissance church north of the Alps, on the preceding Sundays of Advent had proved too small to host all who wanted to attend, so Faulhaber's sermons were transmitted by loudspeaker to two other churches, both filled to the last seat. With forthright eloquence "welded in the fiery forge of the . . . prophets of the Old Testament," Faulhaber had addressed inopportune issues.[2] While the National Socialist program contained an article (number 24) that decried the Old Testament as an offense against the "moral sense and the sense of decency of the Germanic race," he had spoken about its value. And although he was careful to qualify his statements, he "should" have foreseen, in the words of the Security Service (SD), that in praising the people of Israel for having "exhibited the noblest religious values," he would outrage some and comfort many others.[3] Julius Schulhoff, a German Jew, thanked the cardinal in a letter, expressing his hope that God would strengthen his "wonderful courage."[4] Michael von Faulhaber showed courage again in his fifth sermon that New Year's Eve; he would need more for many weeks after.

The telling topic on the last day of the year was "Christianity and Germanicness" (*Christentum und Germanentum*).* The archbishop worried that there was "a movement afoot to establish a Nordic or Germanic religion."[5] The merits of Christianity were being cast into doubt. But who could possibly take a look at the Germanic existence before Christianization and doubt them? To explain his surprise the cardinal proceeded to rouse a drowsy specter of the Germanic barbarian from 450 years of sleep: Wittingly or not, the picture he sketched was almost an exact replica of the barbaric *Germane* that Enea Silvio Piccolomini had brought to the fore in his influential treatise in the fifteenth century. Like his predecessor Faulhaber used "a small but valuable historical source," and with it painted for his congregation an abhorrent picture of polytheism, human sacrifices, and "savage superstition." He disapproved of the pre-Christians' warrior existence with its primitive "obligation of the vendetta" and denounced their "proverbial indolence, mania for drinking," carousals, and "passion for dice playing." The list of shortcomings was long, and all were substantiated using Tacitus's text. To Faulhaber's eyes the admirable and duly mentioned qualities—loyalty, hospitality, and marital fidelity—hardly lightened the overall impression that there was no "civiliza-

---

* "Germanicness" is used to translate "Germanentum," just as "Germanness" is used to translate "Deutschtum."

tion properly so called among the Germans of the pre-Christian era." It was Christianity that brought civilization to these heathen backwaters; more important, the many Germanic tribes—some fifty of which Tacitus listed—were joined as one nation first and only under its roof of faith. The German nation, the cardinal provocatively concluded, owed its civilization and very existence to Christianity. Doubts about its merits were simply groundless.

A secret SD memo reported that all five speeches met with an "enormous resonance," but none more than the New Year's address.[6] The national and international press—including the *Bayerische Staatszeitung*, the *New York Times*, *Le Temps* (Paris), and *Il Lavoro* (Geneva)—all covered it. National Socialists of all ages and ranks refuted, scorned, and attacked the address in journals like *Germanien*, *People and Race*, and the *Vanguard*. It was "a political crime," they said, and its speaker, "a categorical and determined enemy of the National Socialist state."[7] Alfred Rosenberg, the regime's chief ideologue, charged the cardinal with "severely disgracing the process of self-reflection which [was] under way in the Third Reich."[8] But the German people would not, he added threateningly, "quietly accept such utterances." Far from acquiescing, Nazi opposition took violent form during the night of January 27, when two shots were fired into the living room of the cardinal's home. No one was hurt. The book containing the sermons came under fire as well. Members of the Hitler Youth, "with the warrior passion of the ancient *Germanen*," tried to disrupt its distribution.[9] Just as in May 1933, when the Bebelplatz in Berlin had crackled, ablaze with a bonfire of books, they burned it in the course of a demonstration (to no avail: It sold at least 150,000 copies and was translated into eleven languages). A caricature ominously suggested that a similar fate might be in store for its author. Even though some critics occasionally ventured into the territory of rational argument, all in all the reactions "cast the contemporary cultural sophistication in a less than flattering light," as the archbishop wryly wrote.[10] When he uncovered the barbarian past, barbarity reared up in the present.

But to National Socialists such behavior represented a valid response to a bold challenge. The New Year's address had depicted the Germanic past disparagingly. It was therefore regarded as a "declaration of war," flying straight in the face of those who believed that the regime change in 1933 heralded "an understanding of German cultural and intellectual history that valued its Germanic element higher than ever before."[11] The Germanic race, with its alleged high culture in the Bronze Age, its "eternal values" grounded in a hard and simple peasant lifestyle, and its blood's purity mythically originating in the nourishing soil (*Blut und Boden*), formed an integral part of the National Socialists' Germanic revolution.[12] The new age promised a return to olden days: Followers would not be taken to "new unknown shores"; on the contrary, sailing closely on newly freshened Nordic winds they would be carried "home in the ultimate sense of the word," back to a timeless, placeless, utopian *Germanien*.[13] In the Third Reich the *Germania*, Roman fiction, served as a blueprint for Nazi German reality and inspired politics and laws, and "old Aryan peasant blood" was believed to have run through Tacitus's veins.[14] Faulhaber had committed a "cardinal" sin by attacking the revered past and its sacred text. The *Germania*, Nazis insisted, was a "bible that every thinking German should possess, as this booklet by the Roman patriot fills us with pride in our forefathers' superior character."[15] Racial purity and death-defying loyalty were its most important commandments.

THE GERMANIC REVOLUTION

A people will live happily in present and future times, as long
as it remembers its past and its ancestors' greatness.
—Heinrich Himmler, 1943

The National Socialist political machine was a system of envy and suspicion, fueled by a shared desire for power and maintained by the seemingly "weak dictator" Adolf Hitler.[16] It provided checks and balances between its leading individuals and proliferating offices, departments, and institutions, many of which drew up and distributed their own programs. Still, Hans Frank, a Nazi from the first hour and later to be known as the brutal "butcher of Poland," overstated the diversity when after World War II he testified that there were as many forms of National Socialism as National Socialists.[17] For even though the ideology behind the Nazi standard sometimes grew frayed, the ideological centerpieces—like the familiar emblem of the black swastika framed in white—remained clearly identifiable. There was an official National Socialist worldview beyond mere Hitlerism: It comprised extreme German nationalism and racism along with anti-Semitism and a crude form of social Darwinism.

"Germanic Revolution" appeared as the title of an early draft of the first volume of *Mein Kampf.*[18] The subsequent change indicates Hitler's ambivalent attitude toward the widespread devotion to the Germanic myth. He appeared sometimes critical, sometimes scornful, mostly aloof, when faced with enthusiasts like his acolyte Heinrich Himmler, who envisioned his SS as the vanguard of a Germanic era, whose arrival he anticipated by referring to his Führer as the "leader of the great Germanic empire."[19] Hitler had distanced himself in *Mein Kampf* from those "scholars . . . [who] rave about old Germanic heroism, about dim prehistory, stone axes, spear and shield"; and over dinner many years later, as the Führer, he soberly admitted that "at the time when our forefathers were producing stone troughs and clay pitchers . . . , the Greeks were building the Acropolis."[20] Alfred Rosenberg would not have been amused to hear the leader of the NSDAP repeat such sentiments—the same ones, in fact, that drew such vicious opposition when issued from the mouth of Faulhaber. For the ideologue revered his Führer as the successor to the Germanic warlord Hermann and the Saxon Widukind, chief opponent of Charlemagne, in the struggle for freedom and prosperity of the Germanic people.[21]

Fortunately, whatever Hitler's private thoughts about the hirsute barbarians who ate with their fingers while the smooth Greeks carved temples, his public persona remained largely in line. At political events "the greatest Germanic leader of all times," as he would be addressed from 1940 onward, knew what marching tune to play and how to stir Germanic sentiment.[22] At the funeral of Paul von Hindenburg, when the second president was buried along with the republic he had served, Hitler, his virtual successor, concluded his eulogy by wishing him safe passage to the hallowed palace in Germanic mythology: "Dead general, now enter Valhalla."[23] In the same year, at a rally in Karlsruhe, Hitler professed his failure to see why Germans should be "discomfited by [their] ancestors"; after all, he stated, they "had experienced a period of high culture one thousand years before Rome was even founded."[24] Even though Hitler was irritated by Himmler's mystical fits and ridiculed the ideology of the SS in the absence of its leader, the pair jointly envisioned in the future a "Germanic state of the German nation," whose capital was to be called Germania.

National Socialism in the opinion of its leader was to be "a movement of the people, not a cult."[25] Yet, Germanicness was practiced as a cult by a significant group inside the movement, and during the Nazis' early years its sacred text figured ubiquitously and prominently within National Socialist culture. The party convention in Nuremberg in 1936 featured a "Germanic room" decorated with Tacitean snippets. Above the entrance the visitor read a tenet ascribed to the Führer: "German youth shall know: Manly loyalty was the virtue of the old *Germanen*. The new state is erected upon that virtue."[26] This epigraph resonated with Tacitus's account of Germanic loyalty, which was most likely cited inside. Doctrinaire articles built around Tacitean passages abounded in ideological journals like the *Educational Letter*, the *Black Corps, National Socialist Education, Germanic Heritage, People and Race*, and the *National Socialist Monthly*—to name but a small fraction of the shelf-breaking output of the totalitarian regime. From the cozy warmth of their armchairs, numerous little-known Nazis conjured up Germanic hardship with its mortal combat and daily toil, each pen a sword, each study a battlefield. At the end of one such article about the Germanic clan and the familial role of women, heavily substantiated by excerpts from Tacitus's text, the editors printed a pronouncement of Hitler's to the effect that the family was "the most valuable unit in the buildup of the entire organization of the state."[27] Believing the German people's existence to be in danger, National Socialist doctrine specified that a woman's "natural and most important vocation" was to be "a spouse, a mother, and a housewife."[28] Women who had borne an exceptional number of children received the Honor Cross for the German Mother, or, in street parlance, "the rabbit award."[29] Propaganda recommended the Germanic woman as a female role model. One "commandment" ordered the German maiden to select a suitable husband in the spirit of her Germanic ancestor who refused a suitor "because his blood did not seem sufficiently high grade."[30] And since even a single act of sexual intercourse was said to suffice "to poison [a woman's] blood forever," Tacitus's description of the sanctity of marriage and embrace of chastity loomed large in ideological discussions of female virtues.[31] The Roman writer taught "today's German girl, tomorrow's German mother: purity of the youngster and the virgin, chastity, [and] restraint."[32] Joseph Goebbels, minister of propaganda and master of an acid wit, suffered temper tantrums when the words "Germanic" or "Nordic"—reiterated ad nauseam in print, on air, and on screen—were mentioned; but the movement he helped whip along with his rhetoric promised to make the Germanic past alive again in the future.[33] "Make way, you Old Ones," the movement warned; this future belonged to the young.[34]

FACED WITH the attentions of the party, many of the National Socialist youths were in turn "wooed and flattered beyond limits."[35] Yet to the coldly calculating eyes of the Nazi elite like Goebbels they merely presented the "raw human material" that through the "kneading process" of education could be transformed into "a coherent mass" in order to be "utilized and manipulated for the political aims of the state."[36] Education collapsed into propaganda. The new regime, which considered intellectual capability a disability, established new institutions, like the Adolf Hitler Schools and the Order Castles (*Ordensburgen*); traditional schools were radically changed and ideologically aligned. Hitler had made his pedagogical priorities plain: The new education would not aim at "stuffing" students with knowledge but at "breeding absolutely healthy bodies."[37] Physical education loomed large inside school and even larger within the Hitler Youth and the Union of German Girls. In athletic exercises, it was believed, the *Herrensinn* (master-spirit) revealed itself, and true *Germanen* had always had a penchant for sprinting, jumping, wrestling, and swimming, not to mention exercising with weapons. Tacitus's account of the sword dance—"those naked young men who leap and bound in the midst of swords and hostile spears"—was called upon in countless discussions of Germanic sports.[38] The training of the Nazi mind, meanwhile, was of secondary import and should primarily lead to strength of will and willingness to decide. (Elsewhere, and less publicly, Hitler confided that education was dangerous.) National Socialist pedagogues like Rudolf Benze, headmaster and National Socialist director of the Central Institute for Education and Teaching, expounded the Führer's ideas—happily applying their own intellectual skills in promoting a system meant to produce human beings like Arno Breker's sculptures: marble hard, muscular, mindless.

Teachers fought as "brave combatants" at the forefront of the revolution.[39] Organized in the National Socialist Teachers Association (NSLB), they received ideological guidance at conferences, through booklets like *Racial History—What Does a Teacher Need to Know?*, and in countless articles in journals like *NS Education*. This last publication, the teachers association's own periodical, contained in its first three issues four Germanic articles. "German Prehistory as a Formative Force," as one programmatic title read, was discussed in eleven articles in 1937, the year following its launch (afterward, the foundation laid, this topic would figure less prominently). The prefatory note to the first issue speaks with parroted conviction of the "rebirth" of the German people, accompanied, it continues, by "a radical change of unexpected dimension" in the field of education.[40] The shaping of students' nationalistic and racist conscience in the mold of the Nordic character now ranked as one of the highest priorities. Hitler himself thought it imperative that every boy and girl realize the "necessity and essence of blood purity."[41] They were to learn how on the battlefield of history the Aryan race excelled culturally. Rosenberg, at the third national conference for German prehistory, emphasized the new focus in historical research on the "eternity of *those* characteristics and *that* blood that remained the same throughout the centuries."[42] Those with an ideological bent all agreed that history should inspire. Once again history became History. The few critics expressing concern about the lack of "so-called" objectivity learned that "[one is] objective, when [one is] German."[43] Even-handed accounts of the *Germania* were undesirable and discounted as being "too historical."[44] In discussing the famous little book, teachers were to focus their students' attention on how to "fashion the German future in the ways of their forefathers," a task made difficult since instructors ran the risk of getting carried away "out of sheer joy about the subject at hand."[45]

Along similar lines, the *History Book for the Youth of the Third Reich* sanguinely assures "the dear German youth" that it will kindle their enthusiasm for their nation and its values.[46] It traverses the less inspiring phases of the Holocene cursorily—not, however, without developing fundamental racial genealogy and emphasizing that the ancient ancestors' living space is also "yours" and that their blood pulses in "your veins." The book then enters upon a discussion of the soil of the "German people 2,000 years ago"—Tacitus's textual terrain. The ministerial guidelines stipulated that the heroic spirit and the Germanic notion of leadership be illuminated. Accordingly the *History Book* paints the hostile Germanic landscape in Tacitean colors and demonstrates how under those harsh environmental conditions the Germanic people "braced up [and] showed endurance." The book's youthful readers are heirs of this hard people: "Show yourself worthy, and be always fearless and strong-willed." Its subsequent depiction of leadership expounds on the death-defying young men at arms, who are fully pledged to their leader. The contemporary political lesson follows suit: "Never will the German people perish as long as this manly loyalty persists. In the Third Reich, is not the Führer also surrounded by a loyal following? . . . These German compatriots embody Germanic loyalty and heroic spirit and are your shining examples."

Part hardy warriors, part handy farmers: Once more meeting the directives of the ministry to the letter, the *History Book* then visits a Germanic farm with all its sophisticated equipment and ornament in order to reject the slander that these ancestors had been barbarians. On the contrary, their creativity in innovation is presented as the equal of their bravery in fighting: These men were Promethean warriors. As the Faulhaber episode revealed, the suspicion of barbarism never lost its sting; in response the author of *Are the* Germanen *in* Tacitus Barbarians? not only illuminated Germanic qualities but also attempted to lighten some of the darker characteristics that Cardinal Faulhaber had evoked. Germanic fondness for drinking and the habit of arguing about important issues in a festive environment continued, the author opined in the spirit of German humanists, "even today"; for important issues were still weighed by eminent citizens and peasants in inns.[47] For those who knew how to read the *Germania*, it presented a "noble and uniform peasantry." The *History Book*, even though it chooses to reprimand—tongue in cheek—the inclination to inebriation (and subsequent sobering sleep on bears' hides), uses the *Germania* to this very effect. Partly quoted, partly paraphrased, sometimes acknowledged but mostly not, it serves here and elsewhere as "the guiding sign and admonition, [at a time] when we have come to realize that in blood and soil [*Blut und Boden*] we have the nourishing source of our *völkisch* existence."

Blood and soil are precisely the topic of *People and Race*, an educational booklet written by the professor of philology Martin Staemmler. As hideous as it is insidious, the work teaches the significance of race to German adolescents with jovial condescension: "Right, you all know, don't you, what you mean by saying: that's an able and spirited guy! He's got what it takes. He's got race."[48] Racy cars and purebred dogs are evoked to help them form a clearer notion of human races, for a full grasp of which the students are invited to travel the world. After pictorial visits to Africa and Asia, they reach Sweden, the land of "people tall and slim, with blond hair and blue eyes, beautiful figures that make us rejoice." They look like "we picture ancient Germans," Staemmler added, operating on the racist belief that the Germanic purity of the past was preserved in the people presently living in Scandinavia and Iceland—prime specimens of the Nordic race. "The ancient Roman author Tacitus in deep admiration describes the old Germans, . . . who were an almost purely Nordic race. He praises their courage, their loyalty, their purity . . . ; they were born soldiers. Today's German owes to his Nordic race what marks he has of heroism and the honest and loyal soldier." German youth learned that they owed the cultivation of their Nordic heritage to their past; racial health and purity were their imperatives.

As a people "like no one but itself," characterized by "fierce blue eyes, red-blond hair, and tall frame," Tacitus's *Germanen* populated the treatises of anthropologists and overt racists during the nineteenth century. Now, Nazis of all professions received this profile happily, except for the occasional regret that there was no mention of the elongated form of the Nordic skull, the Dolichokephalie. Moreover, they made chapter 4 into a law.

BLOOD AND SOIL

The purity of German blood is the prerequisite for the survival of the German people.

> —Law for the Protection of German Blood
> and German Honor, 1935

Provoked by one of Himmler's racist monologues on the superiority of the blond, willowy, and steely-eyed Aryan race, Mrs. Best,
the brunette wife of a high-ranking member of the SS, quipped
that it seemed a rather dangerous doctrine. Once instituted, the
party would forfeit its entire leadership, "the Führer, you, Herr
Himmler, Dr. Goebbels."[49] Herr Himmler, who shaved the sides of
his head to make his skull look elongated, kept his calm. His retort—
that a round skull like his could house the long brain of an Aryan—
reflected the Nazi movement's official belief in the racial specificity
of psyche as well as physiognomy, but it did nothing to cover the
blatant contradiction between the regime's doctrine and its leaders'
miens. This inconsistency was aptly exploited by a sardonic street
saying of the time that pronounced the typical Nazi to be as slim as
Göring, as athletic as Goebbels, and as blond as Hitler.

For his contributions to the party's doctrine, the professor of
racial studies Hans Friedrich Karl Günther received the first
NSDAP Prize for the Sciences during the 1935 National Party
Convention, dubbed the "Convention of Freedom" in the newspeak
of the day (the final one, the "Convention of Peace" in 1939, was
canceled by the war). The festive audience in the opera house in
Nuremberg was still dazzled by the self-aggrandizing of the carefully choreographed parades, when the eulogist, none other than
the party's chief ideologue Rosenberg, lauded Günther for his written work. With his *Racial Ethnology of the German People* in particular, the award-winning scientist had established "the spiritual basis

for the strife of our movement and the legislation of the National Socialist state."[50] Four days after the award ceremony the Nuremberg race laws were promulgated. One of them, the Law for the Protection of German Blood and German Honor, mandated two of Günther's central ideas. The racist visionary was hoping—and National Socialist legislators now determined—that through selection Germans would once again become a people "special and pure and like no one but itself."

"RACE GÜNTHER," as friends fondly called him, was a dabbler in many fields. He had received his doctorate in 1914, and on the day that he signed up for the obligatory oral exam, he also volunteered for the army, aspiring to "honor his university on the battlefields."[51] Yet a medical condition posed an insurmountable obstacle on his way to heroism. Like Himmler, who never saw combat either, he would long for the war experience he had missed and fantasize about the manliness he was never able to prove. In *Knight, Death, and Devil: The Notion of Heroism*, published in 1920, he vented his frustration with the effeminate and degenerate culture of his day—an ulcerous body in need of surgery—and vaunted the heroism and manliness of Germanic warriors. These true representatives of the Nordic race he found alive in Tacitus's book—a volume, he exclaimed, that revealed a "moral attitude . . . so elevated that in the face of it we should fall silent."[52] But he kept writing, which would eventually redound to his benefit in 1930, when Dr. Wilhelm Frick, the first National Socialist minister in the Weimar Reichstag, appointed him to a professorship at the University of Jena, variously for Philosophy, Prehistory, Race Science, and eventually for a new chair of Social Anthropology. At first the appointment encountered the opposition of the faculty, which failed to see how Günther's likability should compensate for his apparent lack of academic qualification. But scholars protested in vain.

Knight, Death, and Devil, the debut that already contained the main ideas Günther expounded in later works, moved Himmler: It expressed what he had "felt and thought ever since I've thought."[53] It so excited the publisher, Julius Friedrich Lehmann, that after testing Günther's scholarly credentials during a two-day stroll with him in the Alps, he commissioned the young author to embark on a project he had long mulled over: a *Racial Ethnology of the German People*. Their collaboration proved enormously successful: The *Racial Ethnology* sold 32,000 copies by 1932 and was later published as the abridged *Little Racial Ethnology*, the combined sales of which amounted to more than 300,000 copies. Günther became the aforementioned National Socialist–decorated scientist, Lehmann the "entrepreneur of ideology," and Tacitus the widely read reporter on the Nordic race.[54]

"A race," in Günther's oft-quoted definition, "manifests itself in a group of people that through a specific combination of characteristics of the body and the soul differs from any other group and produces always and only those like itself."[55] This definition echoes Tacitus. Günther, well read in the classics as well as in racist literature, quotes the Roman frequently: "There was all over *Germanien* this Nordic people," he writes, blending quotation with his own opinion, "born to be heroes, pure and like no one but itself." In his racial theory, a curious mix of observation, imagination, and selective summarization of scholarly work, it was this Nordic race—"glorified" by Tacitus—that towered above the other four European races. He considered the notion of "the Aryan" to be outdated, siding instead with the French-Russian anthropologist Joseph Deniker, who had introduced the Nordic race (although it should be noted that, in general, National Socialists used "Germanic," "Nordic," and "Aryan" interchangeably). Different from the other races in appearance as much as in attitude, the Nordic specimen carried itself high: tall, long-legged, and lean, with a longish head and a narrow face, fair skin, blond hair, and a Nordic eye with a "terrifying glance." Like the body, like the soul: If a painter wanted to portray a courageous, noble, and dignified heroic man or woman, Günther opined, the portrait would inevitably resemble someone of the Nordic race. Other admirable race-specific qualities—also more or less Tacitean—included: "the urge toward truthfulness, a knight's sense of justice, farsighted leadership [in politics]," and creativity in the arts and sciences.[56] The Nordic race held the monopoly on desirable traits of character (most of which Jacob Wimpfeling and his contemporaries had already claimed for their ancestors). It was this emphasis on its distinctive psyche that allowed Himmler to assert that the bravest Polish officers were of German blood, and that his own skull accommodated an "Aryan brain."[57] But even Himmler's sleight of mind did not change the fact that National Socialist policies set physiognomy as the prevalent criterion: In cases of doubt those individuals were to be deemed Jewish "who because of their appearance suggested a Jewish background."[58]

So bright the past, so bleak the present. Because of "crossbreeding" the Nordic race to Günther's strained eyes had virtually perished among contemporary Germans. "Re-nordification" (*Aufnordung*) was necessary to resuscitate it. He advocated the racial selection of Nordic men and women and the eradication of societal elements deemed "degenerate" in order to return to the former purity. He found Tacitus's *Germanen* to have anticipated such practices. They had embraced various eugenic measures, "hang[ing] or drown[ing] in the marshes those who were inferior or predisposed to perversion," among whom Günther lists traitors, turncoats, cowards, and morally indecent men, including those who were homosexually inclined (even though it is highly uncertain whether Tacitus or the *Germanen* indeed had this last group in mind).[59] This punitive practice guaranteed a continuous purification of the people, he explained, "since the genes of those people would not be passed on to future generations." The harsh punishment of an adulteress—first shorn and stripped, then flogged through the village, according to Tacitus—is similarly read through an ideological lens as another expression of a conscious "obligation to keep the chosen clan clean." A woman's infidelity carried the risk of a tribe's penetration by foreign elements, Günther supplied, pointing in conclusion to what he claimed was a Tacitean example of continuous "racial decline" resulting from miscegenation. The tribe of the Bastarnae had, in his translation, "because of cross-breeding degenerated to the looks of the Sarmatians." The Latin is quoted along with the German in seeming scrupulousness: But both are altered by the omission of qualifying or contradictory details. The Latin *nonnihil* (meaning "to some extent"), which had qualified the "degeneration," is expunged, and *connubium*, which signifies "intermarriage," is expressed as "cross-breeding." Even more cavalier is his quotation on Germanic "bodies that are born to fight," where the Latin for "only" is cut before "to fight," an act of prestidigitation by which Tacitus's restrictive and (at least partly) negative comment is changed into yet another laudable characteristic.

Though it waned as years went by, Günther's impact on National Socialist ideology was profound. His doctrine was outlined in handbooks like *The ABC of National Socialism* and summarily found its way into school curricula. It figured centrally and prominently in doctrinaire booklets authorized by Heinrich Himmler, and it left traces in the second part of *Mein Kampf* (Hitler's library contained many of Günther's writings).[60] Rosenberg, who may have initiated the conferral of the NSDAP prize, also noted in his Nuremberg speech the race expert's legal impact. The Law for the Protection of German Blood and German Honor was passed "out of the deep conviction that the purity of German blood is the prerequisite of the survival of the German people." On the strength of this creed, then, the Reichstag "unanimously decreed the following law . . . : Marriages between Jews and citizens of German or related blood are forbidden." Just as the *Germanen*, in Günther's interpretation, had discouraged mixed marriages in an effort to retain racial purity, National Socialist legislation prohibited mixed marriages between Jews and Germans.

It was hardly the only National Socialist law based on an alleged Germanic practice. Shortly after coming into power the Nazis dissolved unions and passed the Law for the Organization of National Labor, which framed the relationship between manager and employees as one of "leader" and "followers," the former answerable for the common good, the latter obliged to be loyal—just like Tacitus's *Germanen* in chapters 14 and 15.[61] Similarly, what the Nuremberg race laws chiseled into stone was ultimately an adaptation of the erratic ethnographical stereotype that the Roman historian had taken from Greek sources and applied to the *Germanen* in chapter 4. As a result ideologically aligned readers of the *Germania* considered the laws concerning the "Jewish question" as the "most recent effort" to restore the racial purity Tacitus mentioned.[62] But there had never been any such thing.

THE NATIONAL SOCIALIST concern with blood (synonymous with race) would come to naught, a propagandistic brochure authorized by Himmler asserted, if it were not grounded in the "conviction of the value and sanctity of the soil."[63] Contemporaries simply identified National Socialism with the ideology of "blood and soil," a phrase so catchy that Goebbels, his pen dripping another blot of cynicism onto his diary's page, considered it "ridden to death" by 1940.[64] Stripped of its mystical embroidery, it emphasized an opposition between city and countryside, elevating the latter as the seat of the Nordic race's health, morals, and authenticity. Within the party apparatus the ideology's promotion fell to Richard Walther Darré, a booster of the peasantry, who believed in breeding humans as if they were Hanoverian horses for the sake of the Nordic race. Born in Argentina, brought up in Germany and England, and fluent in four languages, he had quickly decided on a career in agriculture, which he felt to be his vocation. He devoured much *völkisch* literature, a corpus to which he added two books of his own—*Farming as the Life Source of the Nordic Race*, which appeared in 1928, and *New Nobility from Blood and Soil*, published in 1930— which established his reputation. When he met Hitler in 1930, he made such an impression that he was subsequently sent to Munich to help set up the Department of Agriculture and to work on winning German farmers over to the NSDAP. He rose rapidly, collecting titles: Reichsminister of Food and Agriculture, Reich Peasant Leader, and director of the Race and Settlement Office. The last office belonged to the SS, and in this capacity Darré, appointed by Himmler, answered for the preservation of the purity of the Aryan race and the augmentation of the Nordic element among the German people (*Aufnordung*). His responsibilities did not stop there: He also oversaw the acquisition of lebensraum (literally "living space"), which *Webster's Third International Dictionary* defines as the "territory that is held to be necessary for the . . . existence of a state," and its Germanization.

National Socialists tied the Nordic race's values to its alleged roots in the peasantry: The countryside sustained itself; cities were parasitic. This antiurbanism was joined to a cultural pessimism: Modernity had destroyed the farmer's life, which was built around the continuous care for crops and adjusted to the rhythm of the seasons. Seen in this golden light, farming represented a lifestyle characterized by endurance, seriousness, and responsibility, in contrast to the uprooted existence of the effete city dweller. The Germanic clan, the doctrine continued, considered their land a gift to be preserved for future generations. It would be handed over to the best among the sons, once he had proved himself by his sword. He then chose an equally excellent woman to marry. Other sons, however, were often forced to depart from their former home and support themselves as marauding warriors. Thus they gave the impression to outside observers, such as Tacitus, that the Germanic people were nomads rather than peasants. Unfortunately, Darré added, this misconception about the *Germanen* lingered on in popular belief. In order to increase the number of Germans farming the countryside—the "bloodstream of the people" and the source of rejuvenation of the Nordic race—Darré (until 1938 together with Himmler) elaborated schemes on how the acquired lebensraum in the conquered eastern regions outside Germany would be developed by farmers of German origin.[65]

TACITUS'S OWN characterization of Germanic farming was ambivalent, to say the least: The bravest fighters do nothing, delegating day-to-day duties, including agricultural work, to the weaker members of their family—women and the elderly. Günther elevated this inertia to heroic laziness, an inactive phase during which the hero focused on combats to come. The majority of National Socialist readers, like so many of their predecessors since the days of Justus Möser, preferred to ignore the critical passages and flatly declared: "According to Tacitus [the *Germanen*] were a noble homogeneous people of peasants."[66] It was on their farms, Darré elaborated, "that the body of the people penetrate[d] the home soil (*Heimatboden*) with its roots."[67] This and similar metaphorical language was amenable to fusion with the mythical indigenousness of the Germanic people, stemming ultimately from Tuisto, the earthborn god, whose son, Mannus, had fathered the three ur-fathers of the Germanic tribes. The Reich Peasant Leader, though intimately familiar with the Roman's book, shrank from embracing this myth about the Germanic origin. Many others did not: Drawing a direct line between the two thousand-year-old text and National Socialist politics, Max Schlossarek, the author of *Tacitus's 'Germania' as the Prophetess of an ur-German Heroism*, read the myth of Tuisto as evidence that "from the beginnings the German people drew its strength from the soil, and it is no wonder that in the new Germany, the Third Reich, the peasantry, lovers of the soil [*Scholle*], are the most important basis of the people."[68] He was joined in the

1930s by one of the many translators and editors of the *Germania*, Julius Weisweiler, who inserted National Socialist doctrine into the title: *Tacitus: Germania. Of Blood and Soil, Mores and Customs in the Germanic Sphere*, adding in the preface how "Tacitus recognized the source of our forefathers' strength and dominance to be the ancient rootedness in the home soil." And when Hans Naumann, the first Nazi rector of the University of Bonn (in 1934), made his widely noticed "profession of faith," he emphasized his belief in "the indigenous nativity of the Germanic race," as quoted in this chapter's epigraph.[69]

No one believed more fervently than Heinrich Himmler in the superiority of the farmers' existence; the supremacy of the Nordic-Germanic race and the dire need for "re-nordification"; and in a future greatness built on Germanic virtues. He also, more than any other leading Nazi, tried to institute what he had found in the *Germania* when he was a pale lost man of twenty-four.

MISSION(S) UNACCOMPLISHED: THE REICHSFÜHRER AND HIS SS

"Wenn alle untreu werden, so bleiben wir doch treu" [When all are faithless, we will still remain faithful].

"Treuelied der SS," originally composed by Max von Schenkendorf, 1814

Heinrich Luitpold Himmler read Tacitus in the course of a bumpy train ride in the fall of 1924, when, under the moderating influence of Gustav Stresemann—first as chancellor, then as foreign minister—the Weimar Republic had just entered its golden period. He still had a long way to go before he would become the head of the SS and one of the most powerful and pernicious men in the Third Reich. Living in Landshut, a city in the south of Germany, he worked as personal assistant to Gregor Strasser, leader of the National Socialist Freedom Movement and a deputy of the regional parliament. Hitler's failed coup d'état in Munich in November 1923, known as the Beer Hall Putsch, had changed the political land-scape. Strasser traveled frequently in his official capacity and asked Himmler to represent him back home in Landshut. The future Reichsführer, an unemployed "half-starved shrew," threw himself into his new duties, motivated more by the prospect of promoting his *völkisch* ideals than by the meager remuneration he received.[70] He zipped along on his motorbike from one farm to another. At night he rested above his employer's drugstore, at a chilly distance from family and former friends, who disapproved of his activities on the political fringes. He had little to comfort himself except his dreams of a great German future, built on the foundations of a great Germanic past.

The past had been a constant presence in Himmler's home. His father, Gebhard, was a teacher of classical languages, whose fawn-ing over members of the upper class incurred his students' unspo-ken ridicule. Like the aristocrat he wanted to be, Himmler senior fitted out an ancestor room (*Ahnenzimmer*). When in the midst of family possessions he spent his evenings studying history, his son often watched him—never happier than in the twilight of his historical fantasies. But Heinrich, the dreamer, was also a pedant: He kept a diary, filed his correspondence, and compiled a meticu-lously annotated book list of some 270 titles, covering his reading from September 1919 to February 1927. These autobiographical sources span most of his formative years and reveal the *Nazi in the Making.* In rapidly multiplying and increasingly hostile com-ments on Jews—"carnivorous vultures"—Himmler's hardening anti-Semitism came to the fore.[71] He loathed decadent city life and longed for the peasant's simple existence, confiding in a letter to a friend: "I am myself a farmer, even though I don't have a farm."[72] With enthusiasm he read about the Nordic race and the Germanic past. His feelings are particularly evident in his comments on Tacitus's text, number 218 on his booklist.

Himmler had borrowed a copy from friends. When his train left Landshut on September 24, 1924, he lost himself in "the glorious image of the loftiness, purity, and nobleness of our ancestors."[73] He held in his hands a sourcebook of the *völkisch* movement in which he had grown up, and it confirmed what he believed in so far as it had formed those very beliefs. His leaden face still flushed with rare excitement, he penned on his book list his vow: "Thus shall we be again, or at least some among us." A decade hence his SS would represent those "some."

HITLER APPOINTED Himmler as Reichsführer SS on January 6, 1929. Under his auspices the organization burgeoned from 270 loosely linked louts to a fine-tuned machinery of terror numbering fifty thousand in 1933. He ushered in a new era, as the official propaganda put it, and suddenly wielded the power to shape reality. Part of Himmler had never left his father's ancestor room: He liked to speak of himself as a *Germane* and envisioned his SS, originally founded by Hitler to serve as his personal bodyguard, as the vanguard of the great Germanic empire. Himmler's rivals for power, the commander of the Luftwaffe, Hermann Göring, and the propaganda minister, Joseph Goebbels, were little enthused with Nordic ideology, and the Führer himself felt compelled to rein in the Germanic sentiment, as the title change of *Mein Kampf* indicated. Among the National Socialist leadership of power-eager opportunists, Himmler was the genuine believer, joined only by his intermittent rival Rosenberg, who made his way to prominence rather than power. Unperturbed, the Reichsführer walked his ideological path slowly and steadily: His SS should form "the basis on which the next generation can make history."[74] In its Fascist uniforms, produced by the Hugo Boss company, it presented itself as an elite.

13. Photograph of Heinrich Himmler
(1900–45), from 1931–32.
Hoover Institution Archives.

SS aspirants had to be racially pure and sworn to loyalty, cama-raderie, honor, will for freedom, and obedience—all but the last celebrated by Tacitus and claimed for German ancestors ever since the time of Jacob Wimpfeling's *Epitome.*

Himmler's organization pursued the selection and breeding of a pure Nordic race as its "irremovable overall aim."[75] Since the "tall frame" that Tacitus particularized was a Nordic characteris-tic, SS members were required to measure at a minimum five feet nine inches. Their Nordic origin should also show in their fair and flaxen-haired appearance. With characteristic detachment the Reichsführer likened himself to the nation's foremost seed-grower, whose "task consist[ed] of bringing *back* a good *old* kind, *now mixed* and decayed, by careful breeding [emphasis added]." In the name of such purity he founded, as early as 1936, Lebensborn (Wellspring of Life). It granted pregnant women shelter and facilities regardless of their personal situation. They had to meet the elite criteria of the SS, however, as their children were meant to populate its future ranks. Eager to advance the Nordic race, Himmler spread word sotto voce that single women hoping to conceive could in all confidentiality count on being set up with suitable fathers. In like manner he later intended to institute bigamy as a special decoration for outstanding SS men and war heroes (just as Tacitus reported that Germanic tribes exempted men of elevated social position from monogamy: Power rather than passion was the rationale).[76] For blond-haired blue-eyed beauties of considerable intellectual talents the Reichsführer also envisioned a special decoration: They should be trained in several languages, as well as the arts of conversation, debating, and chess, at a "Women's College for Wisdom and Culture." Subsequently married to high-ranking members of the SS, these "sublime women" (*Hohe Frauen*) would serve as counselors in national affairs and diplomats on the international stage. In conversation with an incredulous Dr. Felix Kersten, Himmler's physiotherapist and confidant, he added that the ideal he had in mind was—aside from Roman Vestals—the sage Germanic women. For "sacred was the Germanic woman," he mumbled on another occasion, repeating a statement often underpinned with Tacitean help in texts of National Socialist color.[77]

Margarete Boden—Himmler's motherly wife, with whom he had a daughter—had attracted the attention of her "wicked darling" by her blond hair and blue eyes.[78] The "little bunny," as he and others affectionately called his longtime mistress, Hedwig Potthast (who bore him two children), was also of Nordic appearance, but leaner. The Reichsführer himself to his unspoken chagrin was less fortunate. At five feet eleven inches he met the self-imposed SS criterion of height; but dark haired, near-sighted, and flat chested, he embodied the counterexample of his Nordic ideal. "If I looked like Himmler," Albert Forster, governor of the province of Danzig-Westpreußen, spit out during an internal investigation in 1943, "I wouldn't even mention the word race."[79] To the contrary, the Reichsführer vaunted not just the Germanic look but also the allegedly Germanic virtues, the more so as he secretly knew that he possessed neither.

As the Nordic soul loomed large in Günther's doctrine, Himmler prescribed that it animate his men's Nordic bodies. They wore a belt as part of their gothic attire, its buckle engraved "My honor is called loyalty" (*Meine Ehre heißt Treue*). According to a decree of November 9, 1935, SS troopers were to embark on their careers at age eighteen. Until then they should have been members of the Hitler Youth, where they were indoctrinated by such propagandistic manuals as *Following—The Germanic Combat Unit*. This particular collection of excerpts from various writers was intended to "convey an impression of the Germanic forebears' lifestyle and moral integrity," and carried a Tacitean epigraph: "It is the greatest honor, the greatest power to be at all times surrounded by a huge band of chosen young men."[80]

Toward the manual's end, adolescent readers learned about "the following's honor in combat and courage" with the help of two paragraphs of Tacitus's most dangerous book, rendered in Nazi jargon and darkly resonant with the cult of the Führer. Once, the excerpt relates, the Germanic youngster was seen "fit for military service" by his elders, he received a shield and a spear from them during a solemn ceremony, thus joining the "body politic" as a full member. Two thousand years later the juvenile Nazi would enter the SS upon the ceremonial acceptance of a dagger. Though this rite of passage derived from the medieval culture of knighthood, the Hitler Youth certainly perceived its time-honored Germanic tradition. And the parallels extended further. Newly armed, the Germanic forebear fell in with the following of the "Gaufürst," as the excerpt translated the neutral Latin *princeps* (*Gau* being the Nazi term for an administrative district). With his peers he competed for the place of honor at the side of "his Führer" (as *princeps* is now translated), to whom the choice crowd of young men lent power and prestige in times of war as well as

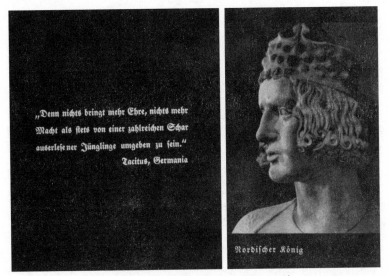

„Denn nichts bringt mehr Ehre, nichts mehr
Macht als stets von einer zahlreichen Schar
auserlesener Jünglinge umgeben zu sein."
Tacitus, Germania

Nordischer König

14. Tacitean motto of a Hitler Youth manual.
Widener Library, Harvard College Library, KD41701.

peace (which takes the reader back to the epigraph). While this Germanic Führer fought for victory, his followers fought for him. To survive him entailed shame and ignominy. In the belief that their voices echoed through time and were amplified by those of their forefathers, future SS men pledged by these lines upon entering Himmler's SS: "We swear by you, Adolf Hitler, loyalty and fortitude. We vow to obey you and the superior appointed by you until death. So help us God."[81]

Just as their Germanic forefathers had practiced physical dexterity—as displayed in sword dances and the infantry's habit of running along with the cavalry—so "battle games and physical exercise [would] guarantee eradication and selection within the order of the SS for all times."[82] SS men should strive to match such strength and endurance, also ensuring maintenance of two further Germanic qualities: the will for freedom, and combative spirit.[83] They had to earn a performance badge each year. The Reichsführer himself lacked physical prowess. Pictures show a sportively dressed Himmler, pale, puffy, and overweight, surrounded by athletes, like a chubby dwarf in the midst of men. Undaunted, he exercised privately, encouraged more than supervised by his personal assistant, Karl Wolff. For months he trained an hour a day, chased by the taunting memory of his physical education teacher Karl Haggenmüller. When he finally dared to be tested, his underling Wolff held the stopwatch; Himmler, the *Germane*, passed.[84]

The Germanic will for freedom, which Himmler and his men thus exercised on the tracks, was mostly praised by National Socialist writers with a backup reference to Tacitus. Yet it sat uneasily with the unconditional obedience the ideology also demanded. Tacitus himself had recognized the drawbacks of Germanic independence: Warriors arrived too late at meetings, sometimes by a day or two; required regulations to maintain peace between clans; and often fought one another instead of the Romans. Unbridled independence caused dissociation. They would serve as mercenaries, guaranteeing an enemy's victory and another Germanic tribe's defeat. Heinrich Bebel, as early as the sixteenth century, did not doubt that *Germanen* yielded to no one but other, deserted *Germanen*. Himmler now pronounced it an unquestionable racial truth that "only our own blood [fighting on the other side] poses a real danger to us."[85] He went on to qualify the will for freedom as a high virtue, yet dangerously flawed, and renarrated two thousand years of German history as a jolting "path to obedience": It found its final destiny in the Führer. Carried away into the thin air of paradox, he demanded obedience that "springs from blood, honor, and the will for freedom and is voluntary and therefore even more binding." Absolute freedom expressed itself in unconditional obedience: The veteran prattler had indulged himself once again.

As a young man Himmler repeatedly scolded himself for being a "wretched babbler.[86] In office he continued to chatter—now unabashedly. In secret speeches to his SS lieutenant generals, wielding a rhetoric of repetition, anecdotal digression, and chummy intimations, he pronounced his shibboleths: honor, history, the Führer, and comradeship. He also addressed faults inside his organization with casual brutality. On one such occasion he confessed (in the intimacy of shared beliefs) that, unfortunately, dealing with homosexuals as their Germanic forefathers had—sinking them into quicksand, clothes and all—was no longer an option. Instead of this ancient practice (which Tacitus had described and Günther discussed), he intended the incriminated SS men be shot during a staged escape. He must have felt this ratified in 1941 when Hitler decreed the death penalty for homosexual contacts among members of the SS and the police.[87] As with the Law for the Protection of German Blood and German Honor and the Law for the Organization of National Labor, National Socialist legislation harked back to the alleged Germanic past as found in—and more often between—the lines of Tacitus.

WHEN HIMMLER learned that there existed an old manuscript of the *Germania* in Italy, he ordered a subdivision of his SS, the Ahnenerbe, to look into the matter. *Ahnenerbe* literally signifies "ancestral heritage." It cropped up in the *völkisch* movement, then burgeoned in National Socialist parlance, evoking hereditary racial characteristics and the *Volk*'s traditional customs. In 1935 Himmler, Darré, and Herman Wirth—the latter an enlightened prehistorian to some; to most, however, a benighted crank—founded an institution by this name. Having subsequently changed in name and size, the Forschungs- und Lehrgemeinschaft das Ahnenerbe (Research and Teaching Community the Ancestral Heritage) in 1939 merged with the hypertrophying organization of the SS. In "its intellectual efforts and its intellectual struggles" it aimed at lifting Aryan-Germanic achievements of times long past from oblivion. More often than not Nazis gathered under its banner for their ideologically driven attack on the natural sciences and humanities.[88] Charlatans worked side by side with well-respected scientists on far-reaching expeditions: to Sweden to unearth evidence of a prehistoric Nordic alphabet; to the Middle East to substantiate the theory that in the Roman Empire the Nordic race had been challenged by the Semitic race for supremacy; and to the Himalayas in order to prove Günther's hypothesis of an Aryan conquest of the East. Results and discoveries appeared in the organization's monthly, *Germanien*; more comprehensive studies were published in special series. Their motto came from the organization's president: "A people will live happily in present and future times as long as it remembers its past and its ancestors' greatness." Himmler's authoritative words also greeted those readers who in 1943 opened the *Palaeographical Studies of Tacitus's* Agricola *and* Germania *Along with a Photocopy of the Codex Aesinas.*

The Codex Aesinas had been rediscovered by Marco Vattasso in the presence of Cesare Annibaldi, a priest, philologist, and teacher at the Liceo Ginnasio in Jesi, a medieval town by the river Esino in the Marches, fifteen miles west of the Adriatic Sea. On September 29, 1901, they crossed the town's Piazza Federico Secondo toward the abutting Palazzo Balleani with its marble Balcony, which—supported by four telamones—still dominates the white facade in local baroque style. Through double-wing doors set in heavy marble frames, they walked across multicolored tiles, dulled by generations of boots since the early eighteenth century. Passing under vaulted white ceilings stuccoed with gold, they reached the private library of Count Baldeschi-Balleani. There, among other precious items, they found a long-forgotten miscellaneous manuscript of the fifteenth century. It bundled together three works: the *Dictys Cretensis*, a chronicle of the Trojan War, purporting to be a Latin translation of the Greek original; Tacitus's *Agricola*; and the text that commenced in capitals, inked in red and black: DE ORIGINE ET MORIBUS GERMANORUM (see page 18). Annibaldi noticed that several folia of the first two works were written in Caroline minuscule, dating back to the ninth century, whereas the other folia and all of the *Germania* appeared to be in a humanist's hand. He would suggest in the publication of this sensational find that the Caroline section of the *Agricola* had once belonged to the famous Codex Hersfeldensis that Enoch of Ascoli had brought to Rome in 1455. When Enoch encountered difficulties in his attempt to make a profit on his toilsome discovery, he cut the precious parchments into parts to sell the texts individually. After Enoch's death in 1457, Stefano Guarnieri somehow secured a portion of the famous manuscript for himself, filled in lacunae, and added a copy of the *Germania* in his own hand (probably from the Hersfeldensis itself). A legal scholar, diplomat, and chancellor of Perugia, he was from a distinguished family in Osimo (about fifteen miles farther east of Jesi). He and his brother had received a humanistic education and later in life collected and skillfully copied manuscripts, assembling an assorted private library. It remained within the family until Sperandia Guarnieri, the last descendant, married Gaetano Balleani in 1793. The couple set up house in the palazzo in Jesi, which would also house the library of the wife's ancestor, Stefano. Thence, more than one hundred years later, Annibaldi brought the codex he named Aesinas to public attention.

Annibaldi's revelatory publication of the oldest extant copy of the Germans' alleged ur-text stirred Germanic enthusiasm. Pilgrimages to Italy followed. However, leading National Socialists desired more than a viewing (and not because the manuscript was indecipherable to anyone but highly trained palaeographers). In 1936, the year of the Berlin Olympics, Hitler himself approached Mussolini, who readily agreed that the Codex Aesinas be handed back to the descendants of the *Germanen*. Yet it did not change hands so much as Il Duce changed his mind. Some Nazis went themselves or sent Italian intermediaries to the Baldeschi-Balleani. At one point two anonymous men from Rome visited the palazzo in Osimo and offered money on behalf of undisclosed Germans. "Although it was lying on a table in the same room, wrapped in an old newspaper, [Countess Baldeschi-Balleani] denied knowing anything about it and said that in the absence of her husband she could give no information."[89] They left, came back, to no avail.

Rudolph Till had better luck. Appointed to the Ahnenerbe in February 1938 and shortly after to full professor at the University of Munich (possibly due to the intervention of Himmler himself), he chaired the Department of Classical Philology and Historical Studies, which was charged with investigating Italy and Greece for their Indo-Germanic and Aryan aspects.[90] When Count Baldeschi-Balleani yielded to the exhortations of the Italian minister of education Giuseppe Bottai and the German ambassador in Rome, SS-Gruppenführer Hans Georg von Mackensen, Till was allowed to study the codex in the months before the war broke out. It had been transported to Rome, where the Instituto di Patologia del Libro photographed it. In 1943 Till, then with the Wehrmacht, published a facsimile along with the results of his palaeographical study as the first volume in the Ahnenerbe series. Its preface reserves the greatest gratitude for the institution's president, from whom came "the decisive impulse and continuous, purposeful support." No reader would have suspected that Till (for unknown reasons) had not wanted to thank Himmler at all. But the correspondence between the publishing house of the Ahnenerbe and Wolfram Sievers, its managing director, reveals that Till had omitted him in his original preface. It was Sievers who insisted that the Reichsführer be acknowledged, "since it was he who made the Ahnenerbe aware of the Codex Aesinas in the first place."[91]

Himmler stayed on the alert for an opportunity to get his coveted manuscript. When Mussolini was forced to resign in the summer of 1943, and the Allies' Operation Husky had secured Sicily and made a successful beginning of the invasion of mainland Italy, he saw his chance amid the chaos. He sent troopers on their mission to the Villa Fontedàmo, where they performed their search. But they failed. The coveted codex remained out of reach, and all the Reichsführer could hold in his hands was Till's facsimile.

EPILOGUE

Another Reading, Another Book

I cannot contain my wonder about those overeager eulogists
of the *Germanen* who strive to attribute to *Germanien* [other
peoples'] lustrous triumphs.

—Beatus Rhenanus, 1531, abbrev.

WATER ACCOMPLISHED what Heinrich Himmler's SS
troops had not: It found the Codex Aesinas. After
World War II, Count Aurelio Baldeschi Guglielmi Balleani put the codex in a safe-deposit box at the Banco di Sicilia
in Florence. When the Arno burst its banks in November 1966,
spilling more water into the city than it had since the 1550s, the
codex was among the many damaged objects of art. It was taken to
the monastery of Santa Maria di Grottaferrata (also known as the
Abbazia di San Nilo) near Rome, where monks skilled in handling
manuscripts inserted absorbent paper. The operation succeeded.
Damaged but not destroyed, it was returned to Florence.

Even partially defaced, the codex continued to attract attention.
An interest in its acquisition was taken not only by the library at
Wolfenbüttel, where Justus Georg Schottelius had worked several
centuries before, but also on this side of the Atlantic. Mason Hammond, a professor of classics at Harvard, relates in a letter to the
chairman of the department at the time how he had met Count
Baldeschi-Balleani over dinner in the late summer of 1979. During

the conversation Hammond had the impression that the count was thinking about liquidating some of his possessions, and that the university might be able to secure the historic codex. This transaction never materialized, which was ultimately of little consequence, as Harvard's Widener Library already possessed a set of photographs of the manuscript (to which a copy of Hammond's letter was appended). But the parchment was a burden: The Baldeschi-Balleani did not have the facilities to store it properly, and showings to interested scholars caused inconveniences for all involved. After the count's death the family decided to bequeath it to the Italian government. Since 1992 it has been in the Biblioteca Nazionale in Rome, where it is now cataloged as the Codex Vittorio Emanuele 1631. Most recently, in the summer of 2009, it was on loan for an exhibition in the German city of Detmold in recognition, if not celebration, of the two thousand-year-anniversary of Arminius's victory over Varus's Roman legions.[1]

The metallic silence of the safe-deposit box at the Banco Siciliano may symbolize the sudden silence that engulfed Tacitus's text in the wake of the collapse of the National Socialist regime in 1945. The *Germania*—after decades of prominence in *völkisch* and National Socialist adaptations inside and especially outside academic presses—disappeared from popular culture and made only the most sporadic appearances in academic journals. When classicists hesitantly and tentatively approached again the only extant ethnographic monograph of ancient times, they had to recover it from under the debris of ideology, not as the founding document of the German people worthy of worship nor as an ethical or racial guidebook toward a better future but as an object of philological and historical study. They became increasingly interested in understanding the *Germania* as a product of its culture and its time: what it revealed about Latin in general and Tacitus's style in particular, whether here or there the transmitted text might be faulty, what light it might shed on Roman attitudes to foreign people, and how its information relates to other historical and archae-ological sources. This sober, scholarly approach, which since the 1980s has flourished and led to a new and largely ideology-free appreciation of Tacitus's text (as evidenced by three thorough commentaries within a decade), valued judiciousness over enthusi-asm. But this approach did not open up suddenly after 1945. In fact it had coexisted with the ideological approach almost ever since the rediscovery of the Codex Hersfeldensis in the middle of the fifteenth century.

A FRIEND of Erasmus of Rotterdam, Beatus Rhenanus lived his life (1485–1547) in pursuit of his studies. Contemporaries com-mented on his devotion, quipping on his name that Beatus (which means "happy" in Latin) was *beatus*—at least by himself. Born in Schlettstadt in Alsace and rigorously trained in the classics, he soon commanded a philological acumen in both Latin and Greek and a historical knowledge that would enable him to contribute to the first standard edition of Tacitus's works in the late summer of 1519. Earlier that same year he had already published the *Germania* separately, along with a brief commentary on "the ancient names of the people in *Germanien*." It was the first commentary in the German-speaking lands.[2]

While his contemporaries studied the *Germania* for what it might tell them about their present and the prospect of a better future, Rhenanus was interested in it as a document of the past. In this early phase of the reception of the *Germania*, he stands apart from his humanistic cohorts, most of whom wanted Tacitus to speak to the greatness of their past and serve as primary witness in their own panegyrical and pedagogical histories. Rhenanus was not free of patriotic fervor either, but the occasional trip notwithstand-ing, he refused to submit his scholarly conscientiousness to his patriotism. Philologically rigorous and historically circumspect, he focused on retrieving Tacitus's own words: what he had written and what he had meant. Tacitus writes that "scarcely anybody—maybe one or two—has a helm of metal or hide [*cassis aut galeae*]." In the transmitted Latin text of the manuscript, the two helmets occur in different numbers: first in the singular (*cassis*), then in the plural (*galeae*). Rhenanus took issue with this variation. There was "no doubt in [his] mind that it must be *galea*," which is the singular form, and that the mistake was caused by "the subsequent word, which begins with the letter *e*." Tacitus's following comment on horses (*equi*) had led the scribe who produced this copy of the *Germania* to write the letter *e* twice (a common scribal error known as dittography).[3] Rhenanus's motivation for this emendation is very different from Celtis's, whose tinkering with Tacitus's text, as we have seen, made Germanic human sacrifices disappear.

Rhenanus extended this rigor to his study of ancient historical information as well. The past, he advocated, should be understood on its own terms. "It is impossible to say how big are the changes that affected kingdoms and nations [from then until now]. . . . Consider the following questions again and again: When was the text you are reading written, by whom and on what; then [only] compare recent times with old ones."[4] In other words Tacitus's *Germania* should not be simply applied to the present. Rhenanus's admonition stands in marked contrast to the one uttered by Johann Eberlin von Günzburg, who used Rhenanus's commentary in his translation of Tacitus. He also encouraged his readers' special attention, even inserting a "note" here and there in the text, but in order to point out the contemporary relevance. The ancient Germans, Tacitus writes, are slow in gathering for an assembly, which provokes Eberlin's "take note" (*Merke*): It was exactly the same in his day at the diet.

The past was indeed a different country: While most of his contemporaries were concerned with similarities—real and forced—between their present and the past, Rhenanus focused on the differences. In his three-volume *Res Germanicae*, published in 1531, he took this thought to its natural end. He separated ancient *Germanien* (*Germania vetus*) from modern Germany. He rejected the practice, criticized in this section's epigraph, of attributing foreign accomplishments to the *Germanen* (whose record, he added in a moment of pride, did not need such tricks). And, most dramatically, he even questioned the view in which a regional population was uncritically held to be the descendants of a tribe Julius Caesar and Tacitus had mentioned. "If anybody wishes to ascribe what Tacitus . . . writes about the Suevi to today's Swabians, he has erred."[5] Rhenanus's lesson was that the German present could not simply claim the Germanic past.

THE PHILOLOGICAL and historical reading of the *Germania*, which Rhenanus began so compellingly and competently, developed over the centuries alongside and in partial interaction with the ideological one. Again and again voices could be heard that criticized the simple identification of the *Germanen* as the Germans' ancestors or, even more simplistically, as Germans. Heinrich Heine, whose sarcastic Q&A was mentioned in the introduction to this book, enjoys the company not only of many lesser knowns but also of Christoph Martin Wieland. The tetrarch of Weimar classicism (1733–1813) drily remarked that it did not seem "recommendable," what with the changes that had occurred over the centuries, "to regard eighteenth-century Germans as descendants of Tuiskon."[6] Would anybody seriously want to speak Hermann's language and embrace the ways of the Germanic tribes, Wieland queried? These critical voices were joined by those who contended that the *Germanen* the *Germania* described were primitive barbarians, as Cardinal Faulhaber had, and by those who, like Eduard Norden, questioned the authenticity of Tacitus's description. But they were drowned out by the countless enthusiasts who celebrated the Germanic past as the promise of the German future and the *Germania* as a "golden booklet"—until 1945.

Yet, even though the Germanic myth and its single most important sourcebook lost its moral authority after 1945, it did not lose its appeal. In 1979 Heinrich Böll, the German Nobel laureate in Literature who dealt critically with the Nazi legacy in his work, published an essay on the *Germania* in the weekly *Die Zeit*. He confessed that Tacitus's text struck him as "surprisingly up-to-date."[7] But even if it were not, he continued, it would still be worth any German's while: "It is one of the oldest if not the oldest document about our ancestors." Savoring Tacitus's description of Germanic songs, Böll commented that "it sounded rather familiar, [and that] now and then in a German man's resonating chest something truly Germanic could have been preserved!" The rest of the essay is in the same vein.

Böll's reading of the *Germania*, quickly and rightly condemned as naive by a leading classicist of the time, is, of course, understandable; after all, it had a long history. But it is precisely that fraught history that reveals such a naive reading as dangerous. In the end the Roman historian Tacitus did not write a most dangerous book; his readers made it so.

NOTES

Introduction: The Portentous Past

1 This episode was first narrated by Simon Schama, *Landscape and Memory* (London: HarperCollins, 1995), 75–81. I have followed him to the extent that I was able to verify details in conversation with Giovanni Baldeschi-Balleani (the count's son), to whom I am deeply grateful for his hospitality and generosity. The manuscript was actually discovered by Marco Vattasso, but Cesare Annibaldi, said priest, was present and subsequently published the first edition of the codex: *L'Agricola e la Germania di Cornelio Tacito; nel ms. latino n. 8 della biblioteca del Conte G-Balleani in Iesi* (Città di Castello: S. Lapi, 1907). Further information and documentation can be found in Francesca Niutta, "Sul codice Esinate di Tacito, ora Vitt. Em. 1631 della Biblioteca Nazionale di Roma," *Quaderni di Storia* 43 (1996): 173–202, esp. 178–79, 189–202; see also the end of chap. 8 with its n. 89. For the quotation, see n. 11.

2 Rudolf Stampfuss, "Der Kampf um den Rhein," *Der Schulungsbrief* 2 (1935): 169.

3 There is a good summary of the issues (with further literature) in J. B. Rives, *Tacitus. Germania* (Oxford: Clarendon Press, 1999), 1–11, 68–71.

4 Jacob Grimm is quoted fully in chap. 7, n. 20.

5 Bundesarchiv Koblenz, NL Himmler, N 1126/9, no. 218. On Campano see chap. 3, section 2, *Indigenous German Warriors*.

6 Richard Geuß, "Deutsche Vorgeschichte und deutsche Schule," *NS Bildungswesen* 1 (1936): 38.

7 Friedrich Nietzsche, *Jenseits von Gut und Böse* (Leipzig: C. G. Naumann, 1886), 201. For the issues discussed here see J. J. Sheehan, "What is German History? Reflections on the Role of the Nation in German History and Historiography," *Journal of Modern History* 53 (1981): 2–23, and Richard Löwenthal, "Geschichtszerrissenheit und Geschichtsbewußtsein in Deutschland," in *Sozialismus und aktive Demokratie: Essays zu ihren Voraussetzungen in Deutschland* (Frankfurt am Main: S. Fischer, 1974), 155–76.

8 I am using Benedict Anderson's title (*Imagined Communities: Reflections on*

the *Origin and Spread of Nationalism*, rev. ed. [London: Verso, 2006]), but this imagined community is different from his. I have suggested elsewhere (in A. J. Woodman, ed., *The Cambridge Companion to Tacitus* [Cambridge: Cambridge University Press, 2009], 280–89) that many of his observations already applied to the community of German humanists.

9 E. M. Arndt, "Geist der Zeit," orig. 1809, in *Deutsche Volkwerdung, Sein politisches Vermächtnis an die deutsche Gegenwart: Kernstellen aus seinen Schriften und Briefen*, ed. Carl Petersen and P. H. Ruth (Breslau: F. Hirt, 1940), 62.

10 Heinrich Heine, "Ludwig Börne. Eine Denkschrift," orig. 1840, in *Werke und Briefe*, ed. Hans Kaufmann (Berlin: Aufbau-Verlag, 1961–64), vol. 6, 171. For the Germanic myth and its development see the seminal study by Klaus von See, *Deutsche Germanen-Ideologie: Vom Humanismus bis zur Gegenwart* (Frankfurt am Main: Athenäum Verlag, 1970). The constitutive role of the past is a feature of nationalism in general rather than German nationalism in particular; see, e.g., David McCrone, *Understanding Scotland: The Sociology of a Stateless Nation* (London: Routledge, 1992), esp. 6.

11 Arnaldo Momigliano, *Studies in Historiography* (New York: Harper & Row, 1966), 112–13. For the following comparison to the Bible see chap. 8, n. 15.

12 Karl Gabler, "Sind die Germanen bei Tacitus Barbaren?" *Nationalsozialistisches Bildungswesen* 1 (1936), 41.

13 See Richard Dawkins, "Viruses of the Mind," *Free Inquiry* 13 (1993): 34–41.

14 Maximilian Schlossarek, *Die Taciteische 'Germania' als Künderin eines urdeutschen Heroismus* (Breslau [Wrocław]: Frankes Verlag, 1935), 18–19. On reception studies see Charles Martindale, "Introduction: Thinking through Reception," in *Classics and the Uses of Reception*, ed. Charles Martindale and R. F. Thomas (Malden, MA: Blackwell, 2006), 1–13.

15 The last quotation is from Eugen Fehrle, *Germania*, 4th ed. (Munich: J. F. Lehmanns, 1944), xv. Methodologically I am following Quentin Skinner, "Meaning and Understanding in the History of Ideas," reprinted in *Meaning and Context: Quentin Skinner and His Critics*, ed. James Tully (Princeton: Princeton University Press, 1988), 29–67. On *Begriffsgeschichte* as different from intellectual history, see Melvin Richter, *The History of Political and Social Concepts: A Critical Introduction* (Oxford: Oxford University Press, 1995). "Nazification of the past": Ernst Bloch, *Politische Messungen* (Frankfurt am Main: Suhrkamp, 1977), 300. For a first impression of the huge influence of the *Germania* on British writers see Jane Rendall, "Tacitus Engendered: 'Gothic Feminism' and British Histories, c. 1750–1800," in *Imagining Nations*, ed. Geoffrey Cubitt (Manchester: Manchester University Press, 1998), 57–74. For French writers see esp. Catherine Volpilhac-Auger, *Tacite en France de Montesquieu à Chateaubriand* (Oxford: Voltaire Foundation at the Taylor Institution, 1993), 291–402.

1. The Roman Conquest of the Germanic Myth

1 Pliny the Younger, *Panegyricus* 48.3. Domitian's predilection for killing flies is attested in Suetonius, *Domitian* 3.1. Translations from the Latin (usually as given by the respective *Oxford Classical Text*) are my own unless specified otherwise.

2 Tacitus, *Agricola* 3.2. My description in this paragraph is based on the *Agricola* (esp. 1–3 and 43–46). Other evidence seems to cast Domitian's reign in a significantly better light.

3 Tacitus, *Germania* 1.1. This order of Tacitus's minor works has recently been contested.

4 For the famous (and not unanimously accepted) reconstruction see Geza Alföldy, "Bricht der Schweigsame sein Schweigen? Eine Grabinschrift aus Rom," *Mitteilungen des Deutschen Archäologischen Instituts, Römische Abteilung* 102 (1995): 251–68. On Tacitus's *praenomen* see R. P. Oliver, "The Praenomen of Tacitus," *American Journal of Philology* 98 (1977): 64–70. A convenient summary of known facts about Tacitus's life can be found in A. R. Birley, "The Life and Death of Cornelius Tacitus," *Historia* 49 (2000): 230–47. On Tacitus's life and work there is the monumental (and somewhat problematic) work by Ronald Syme, *Tacitus* (Oxford: Clarendon Press, 1997 [orig. 1958]). Shorter, less controversial, and more accessible is R. H. Martin, *Tacitus and the Writing of History* (Berkeley: University of California Press, 1981).

5 Pliny the Elder, *Natural History* 3.31.

6 Tacitus, *Annals* 16.5.1, which I have slightly modified.

7 Seneca, *Apocolocyntosis* 4.

8 Tacitus, *Annals* 14.1.1.

9 Ibid., 15.38.1.

10 Suetonius, *Nero* 39.2 (modified) and 31.2 (for Nero's comment).

11 Ibid., 37.1.

12 Tacitus, *Dialogue* 17.3; the following quotation: *Histories* 1.50.2.

13 Tacitus, *Histories* 1.50.3.

14 Ibid., 1.4.2.

15 Suetonius, *Nero* 23.2.

16 Tacitus, *Agricola* 7.2.

17 Tacitus, *Dialogue* 36.8.

18 Pliny the Younger, *Letters* 2.1.6 and 2.11.17.

19 Suetonius, *Titus* 10.

20 Suetonius, *Domitianus* 3.1.

21 Tacitus, *Agricola* 39.1.

22 Adapted from Tacitus, *Histories* 1.2.1.

23 Juvenal, *Satire* 4.38, and Suetonius, *Domitian* 13.2.

24 Tacitus, *Annals* 11.11.

25 Tacitus, *Agricola* 45.1.
26 Lucilius, *Carminum Reliquiae*, ll. 1337–38 (Marx).
27 Tacitus, *Agricola* 1.4; the following quotation: 42.4.
28 Tacitus, *Histories* 1.1.4.
29 Ibid., 4.42.6.
30 Tacitus, *Agricola* 3.1. For the following see Edward Gibbon, *The History of the Decline and Fall of the Roman Empire* (New York: Heritage Press, 1946 [orig. 1776]), 1.
31 Martial, *Epigrams* 10.7.8–9.
32 Virgil, *Aeneid* 6.853.
33 Tacitus, *Germania* 33.2. The expression *urgentibus fatis*, which occurs in the immediate context, is one of the most discussed in Tacitean scholarship; see Rives (introduction, n. 3), 258–60. I have discussed the politics of the Roman debate about the Germanic north in C. B. Krebs, *"Borealism*: Caesar, Seneca, Tacitus, and the Roman Discourse about the Germanic North," in *Cultural Identity and the Peoples of the Ancient Mediterranean*, ed. E. S. Gruen (Los Angeles: Getty Research Institute Publications, 2010), 212–31.
34 Tacitus, *Germania* 2.1; the following quotations: 5.1, 2.2.
35 The Codex Aesinas offers *Tuisconem* where most other manuscripts have *Tuistonem*.
36 Tacitus, *Germania* 6.2; the following quotations: 5.2, 19.1, 19.3. On German humanism see chap. 4.
37 Tacitus, *Germania* 19.1; the following quotations: 22.3, 9.3, 14.1. On Himmler's SS see chap. 8.
38 Tacitus, *Germania* 14.2; the following quotations (with the exception of Campano, for whom see chap. 3): 13.1, 37.3 (heavily modified).
39 Tacitus, *Germania* 15.1. The views on the *Germania* presented here are fully developed in C. B. Krebs, *Negotiatio Germaniae: Tacitus' Germania und Enea Silvio Piccolomini, Giannantonio Campano, Conrad Celtis und Heinrich Bebel* (Göttingen: Vandenhoeck & Ruprecht, 2005), 81–110.
40 Tacitus, *Germania* 4. Karl Trüdinger, *Studien zur Geschichte der griechisch-römischen Ethnographie* (Basel: E. Birkhäuser, 1918). Eduard Norden, *Die Germanische Urgeschichte in Tacitus' Germania* (Leipzig: B. G. Teubner, 1920). For Norden see also chap. 7.
41 Many modern readers disagree. For a discussion of this issue see Krebs (n. 33).
42 The tenth book of the curator's epistles provides singularly illuminating insights into the administration of the Roman Empire and the attitude of an emperor who did not wish to be respected on the grounds of "either fears or anxieties, or charges of treason." For his treatment of Christians see Pliny the Younger, *Letters* 10.96 and 10.97, along with the comments in A. N. Sherwin-White, *The Letters of Pliny: A Historical and Social Commentary* (Oxford: Clarendon Press, 1966), 690–712.

43 Pliny the Younger, *Letters* 10.1.1.

44 Eutropius, *Abridgment of Roman History* 8.5.

45 Tacitus, *Histories* 1.2.1; the following quotations: 1.5.2, 1.49.4, 1.3.2. As for the number of books, all we know is that *Histories* and *Annals* amounted to a total of thirty. For a discussion see Syme (n. 4), 686–87 (Appendix 35, "The Total of Books").

46 Tacitus, *Histories* 1.4.1; the following quotations: *Agricola* 3.1; *Annals* 6.8.4, 15.37.4. For the *Annals* I have often made use of A. J. Woodman's excellent translation (Indianapolis: Hackett, 2004), which gives the reader a thorough impression of Tacitus's style.

47 Tacitus, *Annals* 6.27.1; the following quotation: 1.6.3.

48 *The Works of John Milton*, ed. F. A. Patterson, trans. Samuel Lee Wolff, vol. 7 (New York: Columbia University Press, 1932), 317–18.

49 Tacitus, *Annals* 1.5.1 (my emphasis); the following quotations: 3.3.1, 15.37–38.

50 Syme (n. 4), 624.

51 Tacitus, *Annals* 2.66.1; and the following quotation: 14.1.1.

52 Tacitus, *Annals* 3.76.2. See also *Oxford English Dictionary*, 2nd ed., s.v. "conspicuous."

2. Survival and Rescue

1 Poggio Bracciolini, *Epistolae*, ed. Tommaso Tonelli, 3 vols. (Florence: Marchini, 1832–61), 2.34 (abbrev.).

2 Pliny the Younger, *Letters* 7.20.1. I assume that in writing and releasing the *Germania* Tacitus followed common practice, as outlined in R. J. Starr, "The Circulation of Literary Texts in the Roman World," *Classical Quarterly* 37 (1987): 213–23. Pliny the Elder (*Natural History* 13.74–82) gives a detailed account of the ancient production of a papyrus roll.

3 Pliny the Younger, *Letters* 1.2.6. See also Peter White, "Bookshops in the Literary Culture of Rome," in *Ancient Literacies: The Culture of Reading in Greece and Rome*, ed. W. A. Johnson and Holt N. Parker (Oxford: Oxford University Press, 2009), 268–87. Tacitean echoes are listed by Gerhard Perl, *Tacitus: Germania, Lateinisch und Deutsch* (Berlin: Akademie Verlag, 1990), 50.

4 Pliny the Younger, *Letters* 7.33.1.

5 *Historia Augusta*, Tacitus 10.3. On the false lineage see Edmund Groag and Arthur Stein, *Prosopographia Imperii Romani*, pars II (Berlin: Walter de Gruyter, 1936), 251, no. 1036. For the transmission of classical texts see L. D. Reynolds, "Introduction," in *Texts and Transmission: A Survey of the Latin Classics*, ed. L. D. Reynolds and N. G. Wilson (Oxford: Clarendon Press, 1983), xiii–xliii.

6 Here I am relying on probabilities rather than facts.

7 "*Admonitio Generalis*," in *Monumenta Germaniae Historica, Capitularia*

regum Francorum, ed. Alfred Boretius (Hannover: Impensis Bibliopolii Hahniani, 1883), vol. 1, 52–62, 60. For an overview of the linguistic complexity see Rosamond McKitterick, *Charlemagne: The Formation of a European Identity* (Cambridge: Cambridge University Press, 2009), 315–20.

8   "*De litteris colendis*," in *Monumenta Germaniae Historica* (n. 7), 78–80, 79. Michel Banniard, "Language and Communication in Carolingian Europe," in *New Cambridge Medieval History, Vol. II*, ed. Rosamond McKitterick (Cambridge: Cambridge University Press, 1995), 695–708. Generally on "Die geistige Erneuerung unter Karl dem Großen" see Franz Brunhölzl, *Geschichte der lateinischen Literatur des Mittelalters*, 2 vols. (Munich: Fink, 1975–92), vol. 1, 243–315.

9   On Rudolf, see Brunhölzl (n. 8), vol. 1, 343–45.

10 Bruno Krusch, ed., "Translatio sancti Alexandri," *Nachrichten von der Gesellschaft der Wissenschaften zu Göttingen*, Phil.-Hist. Kl. 4 (1933): 405–37.

11 See Hannes Kästner, "Der großmächtige Riese und Recke Theuton," *Zeitschrift für Deutsche Philologie* 110 (1991): 68–97.

12 Poggio (n. 1), *Letters* 1.5. A great deal has been written about the rediscovery of the *opera minora* (see Perl [n. 3], 56–60, and the literature cited there), but no single account seems to present all the evidence.

13 Poggio (n. 1), *Letters* 1.21. The most comprehensive biography of Poggio is still Ernst Walser, *Poggius Florentinus. Leben und Werke* (reprint, Hildesheim: G. Olms, 1974 [orig. 1914]).

14 *Sub specie antiquitatis* is the happy phrase by which Gerald Strauss, *Historian in an Age of Crisis: The Life and Work of Johannes Aventinus* (Cambridge: Harvard University Press, 1963), 14, captures this sentiment.

15 Giannantonio Campano is quoted from the appendix in Di Bernardo (chap. 3, n. 20), 414. For humanism see Nicholas Mann, "The Origins of Humanism," in *The Cambridge Companion to Renaissance Humanism*, ed. J. Kraye (Cambridge: Cambridge University Press, 1996), 1–19.

16 Poggio's letter to Franciscus Piccolpassus is quoted from the translation by P. W. G. Gordan, *Two Renaissance Book Hunters* (New York: Columbia University Press, 1974), 205.

17 Leonardo Bruni (Florence, September 15, 1416) is quoted from Gordan (n. 16), 191.

18 Poggio, as in n. 1.

19 Heinrich was identified by Ludwig Pralle, *Die Wiederentdeckung des Tacitus: Ein Beitrag zur Geistesgeschichte Fuldas und zur Biographie des jungen Cusanus* (Fulda: Verlag Parzeller, 1952), 15–62.

20 The letter can be found in Remigio Sabbadini, *Storia e critica di testi latini* (reprint, Hildesheim: G. Olms, 1974 [orig. 1914]), 264–65.

21 Poggio (n. 1), *Letters* 2.40. On Antonio Panormita (Beccadelli), see *Dizionario Biografico degli Italiani* (Roma: Istituto della Enciclopedia Italiana, 1960–2009), vol. 7 (1965), 400–406.

22 The letter is reprinted in Sabbadini (n. 20), 267–70, esp. 270. For the library in Fulda see Paul Lehmann, "Die alte Klosterbibliothek Fulda und ihre Bedeutung," in *Erforschung des Mittelalters: Ausgewählte Abhandlungen und Aufsätze*, ed. Paul Lehmann (Stuttgart: A. Hiersemann, 1959–62), 1.213–31.

23 Poggio (n. 1), *Letters* 3.1.

24 Poggio (n. 1), *Letters* 3.12. For the Ciceronian but originally Greek expression see Cicero's letter to Lentulus, *ad Familiares* 1.6.2.

25 Poggio (n. 1.), *Letters* 3.14 and 3.19. Wordplay on Tacitus's name has a precedent in Sidonius Apollinaris, *Letters* 4.22.2.

26 Poggio (n. 1), *Letters* 3.29. For Jacopo's letter and its significance see Nicolai Rubinstein, "An Unknown Letter by Jacopo di Poggio Bracciolini on Discoveries of Classical Texts," *Italia medioevale e Umanistica* 1 (1958): 383–400.

27 R. P. Robinson, "The Inventory of Niccolò Niccoli," *Classical Philology* 16 (1921): 251–55.

28 See Remigio Sabbadini, *Le scoperte dei codici latini e greci ne' secoli XIV e XV* (Florence: Sansoni, 1967), vol. 2, 18, and C. W. Mendell, "Discovery of the Minor Works of Tacitus," *American Journal of Philology* 56 (1935): 113–30.

29 Decembrio's note is reprinted in Sabbadini (n. 20), 279.

30 Poggio's letter is reprinted in Georg Voigt, *Die Wiederbelebung des classischen Alterthums* (Berlin: Georg Raimer, 1893), vol. 2, 200, n. 1. The bibliographical information on Enoch is based on *Dizionario* (n. 21), vol. 24 (1993), 695–99.

31 Tortello's praise of the pope is reprinted in Voigt (n. 30), vol. 2, 199, n. 2.

32 The *breve*, found in the archives of Königsberg, is reprinted in Voigt (n. 30), vol. 2, n. 3.

33 Poggio (n. 1), *Letters* 10.17.

34 Cincius Romanus's letter (summer 1416) is quoted from the translation by Gordan (n. 16), 188–89.

35 Potano's colophon is reprinted in Georg Wissowa's edition of the *Codex Leidensis Perizonianus phototypice editus* (Leiden: A. W. Sijthoff, 1907), fol. 1ᵛ.

36 Sigismund Meisterlin, *Cronographia Augustensium: Cronik der Augspurger*, orig. 1456, ed. Hans Gröchenig (Klagenfurt: Armarium, 1998), 36 (the conversation), 26–32 (indigenousness). This argument has recently been made by Dieter Mertens, "Die Instrumentalisierung der 'Germania' des Tacitus durch die deutschen Humanisten," in *Zur Geschichte der Gleichung "germanisch-deutsch": Sprache und Namen, Geschichte und Institutionen* (Ergänzungsbände zum Reallexikon der germanischen Altertumskunde 34), ed. Heinrich Beck et al. (Berlin: Walter de Gruyter, 2004), 37–102, 65–67.

37 The letters were found in the Florentine archives and published by Vittorio Rossi, "L'indole et gli studi di Giovanni di Cosimo de' Medici,"

Rendiconti della R. Accademia dei Lincei, classe di scienze morali, ser. 5, vol. 2 (1893): 129–150, esp. 130–35.

38 Cf. Rubinstein (n. 26), 391–92.

3. The Birth of the German Ancestors

1 E. S. Piccolomini, *Libellus dialogorum*, is quoted in the translation from C. M. Ady, *Pius II, the Humanist Pope* (London: Methuen, 1913), 79.

2 Lorenzo Valla, *Elegantiarum libri sex* (Paris: Ex officina cursoria Simonis Colinaei, 1527), *Praefatio*, aiiʳ.

3 "*De legatione Germanica*," in *Rerum Germanicarum scriptores aliquot insignes*, ed. Marquard Freher and B. G. Struve (Strasbourg: J. R. Dulssecker, 1717), vol. 2, 288. Poggio's words: chap. 2, n. 13. For the Italian attitude toward Germans see Peter Amelung, *Das Bild des Deutschen in der Literatur in der italienischen Renaissance (1400–1559)* (Munich: M. Heuber, 1964).

4 E. S. Piccolomini, *Opera omnia* (Basel: Ex officina Henricpetrina, 1551), epistle 162, fol. 716.

5 On the reception of the *Germania* in this period see Jacques Ridé, *L'image du Germain dans la pensée et la littérature allemandes de la redécouverte de Tacite à la fin du XVIe siècle* (Lille: Atelier Reproduction des thèses, 1977). Also see Mertens (chap. 2, n. 36). For rhetorical analyses of Piccolomini's and Campano's works, see Krebs (chap. 1, n. 39), 111–90.

6 E. S. Piccolomini, *Commentarii rerum memorabilium que temporibus suis contingerunt*, ed. Adrianus van Heck (Vatican City: Biblioteca apostolica vaticana, 1984), vol. 2, 518. Biographical information is taken from Ady (n. 1) and Georg Voigt, *Enea Silvio de' Piccolomini als Papst Pius II und sein Zeitalter*, 3 vols. (Berlin: G. Reimer, 1856–63).

7 This self-characterization is quoted from Stefan Sudmann, "Das Basler Konzil im Konflikt mit Rom und Reich," in *Rom und das Reich vor der Reformation*, ed. Nikolaus Staubach (Frankfurt am Main: Peter Lang, 2004), 53–70, esp. 54.

8 Piccolomini's letter is reprinted in Georg Voigt, "Die Briefe des Aeneas Sylvius vor seiner Erhebung auf den päpstlichen Stuhl," *Archiv für Kunde österreichischer Geschichtsquellen* 16, no. 146 (1856): 358. For the following comparison with Ovid see Rudolf Wolkan, ed., *Der Briefwechsel des Eneas Silvius Piccolomini* (Vienna: A. Hölder, 1909–12), vol. 1, 542–43.

9 All following quotations are from the *Oratio de clade Constantinopolitana et bello contra Turcos congregando*, as printed in the *Opera omnia* (n. 4), fol. 678–89.

10 Johannes Helmrath, "Pius II. und die Türken," in *Europa und die Türken in der Renaissance*, ed. Bodo Guthmüller and Wilhelm Kühlmann (Tübingen: Niemeyer, 2000), 9–137, esp. 94.

11 Piccolomini, *Commentarii* (n. 6), vol. 1, 93–94.

12 For the letter see Adolf Schmidt, ed., *Germania [von] Aeneas Silvius, und*

Jakob Wimpfeling: Responsa et replicae ad Eneam Silvium (Cologne: Böhlau, 1962), 9–10. For an overview on the *gravamina*: Eike Wolgast, "*gravamina*," *Theologische Realenzyklopädie* 14 (1985): 131–34.

13 Piccolomini is quoted from his dedicatory letter in Schmidt (n. 12), 11.

14 *De ritu, situ, moribus et condicione Germaniae descriptio* is the title of the edition of Strasbourg (1515), instigated by Jacob Wimpfeling, and of the popular edition of Basel (1551); both make reference to Tacitus. The *editio princeps* (Leipzig, 1496) has *Teutonie* instead of *Germanie* (Piccolomini himself did not give a title to his epistolary work).

15 All subsequent unspecified quotations are taken from Piccolomini's *Germania* (n. 12). For a discussion of his usage of Tacitean passages see Mertens (chap. 2, n. 36, 67–71) and Krebs (chap. 1, n. 39, 123–29).

16 Piccolomini, *Germania* (n. 12) 2.4. There is a textual variant: *sororia* ("similar") instead of *ferociora*. The gist is not affected.

17 Tacitus, *Germania* 19.3.

18 Jacob Wimpfeling, *Responsa et replicae ad Eneam Silvium*, in Schmidt (n. 12), 127–46, esp. 127. For the following calculation see Mertens (chap. 2, n. 36), 61.

19 Michele Ferno, *Vita Campani*, in *Opera omnia Campani* (Venice: Bernardinus de Vianis, 2nd ed., 1495), fol. viii^v–xvi^v, here fol. xi^v. On Paul II: J. F. D'Amico, *Renaissance Humanism in Papal Rome* (Baltimore: Johns Hopkins University Press, 1983), 92–97.

20 This characterization by Alessandro Braccesi is quoted from F.-R. Hausmann, "Giovanni Antonio Campano (1429–1477)," *Römische Historische Mitteilungen* 12 (1970): 125–78, esp. 131. Biographical information is also taken from Flavio di Bernardo, *Un vescovo umanista alla corte pontificia: Giannantonio Campano* (Rome: Università gregoriana, 1975).

21 *Vita Campani* (n. 19), fol. xi^v. For his familiarity with Piccolomini's work: *Opera omnia* (n. 19), *Epistles* 1, fol. ii^r.

22 *In conventu Ratisponensi ad exhortandos principes Germanorum contra Turcos et de laudibus eorum oratio*, in *Opera omnia* (n. 19), fol. xc^r–xcv^r. This printed version of the *Oratio* is faulty, and subsequent quotations may reflect my corrections: xciii^r, ibid., xcv^r (slightly abbreviated).

23 Jacques Perret, *Recherches sur le texte de la "Germanie"* (Paris: Les Belles Lettres, 1950), 151, n. 5, gives a helpful collation of parallel passages in Tacitus and Campano.

24 Tacitus, *Germania* 33.2.

25 *Orat. Ratis.* (n. 22), fol. xciii^v. On "Etymology as a Category of Thought," see E. R. Curtius, *European Literature and the Latin Middle Ages*, trans. W. Trask (New York: Pantheon Books, 1953), 495–500.

26 *Orat. Ratis.* (n. 22), fol. xciii^r.

27 Campano, *Epistles* 6.2, (n. 19), fol. xlix^v. For his polish see the letter to Giacomo Ammannati, May 24, 1471 (ibid., fol. xlix^v). Indispensable for those interested in Campano's letters: F.-R. Hausmann, *Giovanni Antonio Cam-*

pano: Erläuterungen zu seinen Briefen (PhD diss., University of Freiburg, 1968).

28 *Vita Campani* (n. 19), fol. xi^v.

29 The *Oxford English Dictionary* defines "irrumator" with a delicate reference to Julius Rosenbaum's *Plague of Lust* (1901), where the term is identified as someone who "takes the *fellator* between his opened thighs." For Conrad Leontorius's rage, vented in a letter, see Joseph Schlecht "Zur Geschichte des erwachenden deutschen Bewußtseins," *Historisches Jahrbuch* 19 (1898): 351–58. For Leontorius's circle: I. D. Rowland, "Revenge of the Regensburg Humanists," *Sixteenth Century Journal* 25 (1994): 307–22.

30 For further reactions to Campano's letters, see Ulrich Paul, *Studien zur Geschichte des deutschen Nationalbewusstseins im Zeitalter des Humanismus und der Reformation* (Berlin: E. Ebering, 1936), 64. For his role in the dissemination of Germanic traits, see Tiedemann (chap. 4, n. 12), 43.

31 Giovanni Nanni, *Annio da Viterbo: Commentaria fratris Ioannis Annii Viterbiensis ordinis praedicatorum theologiae professoris super opera diversorum auctorum de antiquitatibus loquentium* (Rome: Eucharius Silber, 1498). All references to Annius's text will be to this edition.

32 Heinrich Bebel, *Germani sunt indigenae* (orig. 1509), in *Patriotische Schriften: sechs Schriften über Deutsche, Schweizer und Schwaben*, ed., trans., and with commentary and an introduction by Thomas Zinsmaier (Konstanz: Edition Isele, 2007), 65–86, 78.

33 Virgil, *Aeneid*, 1.1–2. See, e.g., E. S. Piccolomini, *Europa*, ed. Adrianus van Heck (Vatican City: Biblioteca apostolica vaticana, 2001), 148–50, for the Trojan descent of the Franci (to which I will return in the second section of chap. 4, *Since Time Immemorial*). On genealogical myths: Frantisek Graus, "Troja und die trojanische Herkunftssage im Mittelalter," in *Kontinuität und Transformation der Antike im Mittelalter*, ed. Willi Erzgräber (Sigmaringen: J. Thorbecke, 1989), 25–44. Jörn Garber, "Trojaner—Römer—Franken—Deutsche: 'Nationale' Abstammungstheorien im Vorfeld der Nationalstaatenbildung," in *Nation und Literatur im Europa der Frühen Neuzeit*, ed. Klaus Garber (Tübingen: M. Niemeyer, 1989), 108–63.

34 Roberto Weiss, "An Unknown Epigraphic Tract by Annius of Viterbo," in *Italian Studies Presented to E. R. Vincent* (Cambridge: W. Heffer, 1962), 101–20. On Annius: Roberto Weiss, "Traccia per una biografia di Annio da Viterbo," *Italia medioevale e umanistica* 5 (1962): 425–41. Annius's epigraphic forgeries have been doubted: Walter Stephens, "When Pope Noah Ruled the Etruscans: Annius of Viterbo and his Forged Antiquities," *Modern Language Notes* 119 (2004, Italian issue): 201–23.

35 For Annius's methods and his critics, see Walter Stephens, *Berosus Chaldaeus: Counterfeit and Fictive Editors of the Early Sixteenth Century* (PhD diss., Cornell University, 1979).

36 *Antiquitates* (n. 31), *Ioan. Annii Viterbiensis sacrae theologiae professoris in quinque libros Berosi, Praefatio*, fol. Nviii^r.

37 For the table of contents, see *Antiquitates* (n. 31), fol. Nviii^r. The following quotation: fol. Pi^v and again: fol. Pii^r.

38 *Antiquitates* (n. 31), fol. Piiii^r. Tacitus, *Germania* 2.2. My translation is based on *The Complete Works of Tacitus*, ed. Moses Hadas (New York: Modern Library, 1942), 709.

39 *Antiquitates* (n. 31), fol. Pii^r.

40 Sebastian Münster (*Cosmographey*) is quoted in Herfried Münkler et al., eds., *Nationenbildung: Die Nationalisierung Europas im Diskurs humanistischer Intellektueller* (Berlin: Akademie Verlag, 1998), 258.

41 *Antiquitates* (n. 31), fol. Nviii^r and again: fol. Qiii^r; territory: fol. Qv^r; the following quotation: fol. Tii^r.

42 Rhenanus is quoted in Anthony Grafton, "Traditions and Invention and Inventions of Tradition in Renaissance Italy: Annius of Viterbo," in *Defenders of the Text: The Traditions of Scholarship in an Age of Science, 1450–1800* (Cambridge: Harvard University Press, 1991), 76–103, esp. 93. But even Rhenanus had used Berosus in his *Commentariolus* (in 1519).

43 For the editions see Werner Goez, "Die Anfänge der historischen Methoden-Reflexion im italienischen Humanismus," in *Geschichte in der Gegenwart*, ed. Ernst Heinen and H. J. Schoeps (Paderborn: Schöningh, 1972), 3–21, esp. 12.

4. Formative Years

1 The *editio princeps* (Bologna: Azoguidi, 1472) is titled *Cornelii Taciti illustrissimi historici de situ, moribus et populis Germaniae libellus aureus*.

2 Jacob Wimpfeling, *Epitome rerum Germanicarum* (Hannover: apud G. Antonium, 1594 [orig. 1505]), *Praefatio*, A4. As "first history": Paul Joachimsen, *Geschichtsauffassung und Geschichtsschreibung in Deutschland unter dem Einfluss des Humanismus*, vol. 3 (Leipzig: Teubner, 1910), 66.

3 Ulrich von Hutten, *Opera quae reperiri potuerunt omnia*, 5 vols., ed. E. Böcking (Leipzig: Teubner, 1859–70), 117.

4 E. S. Piccolomini, *Historia Friderici III. Imperatoris*, is quoted from Ady (as in chap. 3, n. 1), 113. See also Hermann Wiesflecker, *Maximilian I: Die Fundamente des habsburgischen Weltreiches* (Vienna: R. Oldenbourg, 1991).

5 Andreas Althamer, *Scholia in Corneliu[m] Tacitu[m] Rom. historicu[m], De situ moribus, populisq[ue] Germaniae* (orig. Nuremberg, 1529), in Simon Schardius, *Rerum Germanicarum Scriptores varii . . . in quatuor [sic!] tomos collecti* (Gießen: Ex officina Seileriana, 1673), 1–37, 37. For a historical overview see: Geoffrey Barraclough, *The Origins of Modern Germany* (Oxford: Blackwell, 1952), 339–67.

6 Piccolomini, *Historia Friderici III*, is quoted in Ady (as in chap. 3, n. 1), 118. It was only under Maximilian I that "the German Nation" was officially included in the empire's standard nomenclature. See Barraclough (n. 5), 369. On nationalism before nationalism: R. Stauber, "Nationalismus vor

dem Nationalismus? Eine Bestandsaufnahme der Forschung zu 'Nation' und 'Nationalismus' in der Frühen Neuzeit," *Geschichte in Wissenschaft und Unterricht* 47 (1996): 139–65.

7 Bebel (chap. 3, n. 32), 70. See Rowland (as in chap. 3, n. 29).

8 Conrad Celtis, *Libri odarium quattuor, liber epodon, carmen saeculare,* ed. Felicitas Pindter (Leipzig: Teubner, 1937), od. 4.5.23. For the following humanists' names see L. W. Spitz, *Conrad Celtis. The German Arch-Humanist* (Cambridge: Harvard University Press, 1957), 49.

9 Conrad Celtis, *Quattuor libri Amorum secundum quattuor latera Germaniae. Germania generalis. Accedunt carmina aliorum ad libros Amorum pertinentia,* ed. Felicitas Pindter (Leipzig: Teubner, 1934), am. 1.1.16–22; am. 1.3.61–62.

10 Conrad Celtis, *Oratio in gymnasio in Ingolstadio publice recitata,* in *Selections from Conrad Celtis,* ed., trans., and comm. Leonard Forster (Cambridge: Cambridge University Press, 1948), section 26. On Celtis see Spitz (n. 8).

11 Heinrich Bebel, *Oratio ad regem Maximiliam de laude eius Germanorumque* (orig. 1501), in Zinsmaier (n. 7), 7–64, 20. For a discussion: Krebs (as in chap. 1, n. 39), 241–43.

12 Münster, *Cosmographey,* is quoted from Hans Tiedemann, *Tacitus und das Nationalbewusstsein der deutschen Humanisten am Ende des 15. und Anfang des 16. Jahrhunderts* (Berlin: Ebering, 1913), 19.

13 Althamer (n. 5), 4.

14 Aventinus, *Deutsche Chronik, Vorrede des Kaspar Brusch,* in *Johannes Turmair's genannt Aventinus Kleinere historische und philologische Schriften,* ed. Königliche Akademie der Wissenschaften, first half (Munich: C. Kaiser, 1880), 301.

15 Bebel, *Oratio* (n. 7), 34. And Bebel, *De laude, antiquitate, imperio, victoriis rebusque gestis veterum Germanorum,* in Schardius (n. 5), 117. The following quotation: Franciscus Irenicus, *Germaniae exegeseos volumina duodecim* (Hagenau: Thomas Anshelm, 1518), fol. a ii^r.

16 Trithemius's praise of Wimpfeling, which I am using more generally, is quoted from Ridé (as in ch. 3, n. 5), vol. 2, 304.

17 Celtis, *Oratio* (n. 10), section 39.

18 G. M. Müller, *Die Germania generalis des Conrad Celtis: Studien mit Edition, Übersetzung und Kommentar* (Tübingen: Niemeyer, 2001). The letter is quoted on p. 36, n. 16.

19 Bebel, *De laude* (n. 15), 127.

20 Bebel, *Oratio* (n. 11), 48. See Dieter Mertens, "Bebelius . . . patriam Sueviam . . . restituit: Der poeta laureatus zwischen Reich und Territorium," *Zeitschrift für württembergische Landesgeschichte* 42 (1983): 145–73. On Maximilian's historical interests: Jan-Dirk Müller, *Gedechtnus* (Munich: W. Fink, 1982), esp. 87.

21 Bebel, *Oratio* (n. 11), 48. On Bebel's life and works: C. J. Classen, *Hein-*

rich Bebels Leben und Schriften (Göttingen: Nachrichten der Akademie der Wissenschaften, 1997).

22 Bebel, *Indigenae* (n. 7), 66. E. S. Piccolomini, *De Europa*, ed. commentarioque instr. Adrianus van Heck (Vatican City: Biblioteca apostolica vaticana, 2001), 148.

23 Bebel, *Indigenae* (n. 7), 70 (and cf. 66: *corrupti*). The following quotation: Bebel, *Epitome laudum Suevorum*, in Schardius (n. 5), 139. Tacitus had explained the purity of the *Germanen* as a consequence of the hostile environment and the common ways of ancient travel. But according to Bebel aggressors had not been disgusted by wood-bristling and swamp-sodden Germany; rather they had always been fought off by his valiant ancestors. In line with his effort to aggrandize the past, the emperor's poet laureate turned a contingency into a credit.

24 For the Roman foundation myth see Livy, *The History of Rome*, book 1.8, esp. 5–6. On *colluvies* see *Thesaurus Linguae Latinae*, vol. 3.1665.79–1666.25.

25 Aventinus, *Bayerische Chronik* (orig. 1556), in *Sämmtliche Werke*, ed. Königliche Akademie der Wissenschaften, vol. 4 (Munich: C. Kaiser, 1880–1908), 191; cf. *Deutsche Chronik* (orig. 1541), vol. 1, 332 and 339–42. On Aventinus see Strauss (as in chap. 2, n. 14).

26 Aventinus (n. 25), vol. 4, 53; cf. vol. 1, 329.

27 Aventinus (n. 25), vol. 1, 302.

28 Aventinus (n. 25), vol. 1, 333, writing "Teutschenburg."

29 Aventinus (n. 25), vol. 1, 345. The following quotation: 346.

30 Aventinus (n. 25), vol. 1, 353.

31 This paragraph is based on Wimpfeling (n. 2), chap. vi.

32 Bebel, *Oratio* (n. 11), 40. Tacitus, *Germania* 37, is quoted, e.g., by Wimpfeling, Bebel, and Irenicus.

33 Suetonius, *Life of Augustus* 23.2.

34 Tacitus, *Annals* 2.88.2. On Arminius/Hermann and his myth: *Arminius und die Varusschlacht*, ed. Rainer Wiegels and Winfried Woesler (Paderborn: Schöningh, 1995).

35 Jacques Ridé, "Arminius in der Sicht der deutschen Reformatoren," in *Arminius und die Varrusschlacht* (n. 34), 239–48.

36 Wimpfeling (n. 2), chap. iii (but it is a commonplace).

37 Tacitus, *Germania* 13–15, esp. 14.1.

38 Tacitus, *Germania* 24.2. Irenicus (n. 15), fol. fii^v.

39 Celtis, *Germania generalis* (n. 18), verse 95. The characterization of Roman fickleness paraphrases Hutten (n. 3), vol. 3, 330.

40 Bebel, *Oratio* (n. 11), 32–34.

41 See Tiedemann (n. 12), 48–58. For Beatus Rhenanus's critical attitude, see the epilogue.

42 Campano (as in chap. 3, n. 22), fol. xcii^r.

43 Aventinus, *Annales Ducum Boiariae* (n. 25), vol. 3, 423. The following etymology is Wimpfeling's (n. 2), 203–4, as is the following quotation.

44 Aventinus, *Bayrischer Chronicon* (n. 25), vol. 1, 108.

45 *Dialogus Huttenicus quo homo patriae amantissimus patriae laudem celebravit,* 1529.

46 Hutten (n. 3), vol. 1, 355, is quoted from Hajo Holborn, *Ulrich von Hutten and the German Reformation* (New Haven, CT: Yale University Press, 1937), 125.

47 Hutten, *Ad Crotum Rubianum*, is quoted from Theodore Ziolkowski, *The Mirror of Justice: Literary Reflections of Legal Crises* (Princeton: Princeton University Press, 1997), 114. See Gerald Strauss, *Law, Resistance and the State: The Roman Law in Reformation Germany* (Princeton: Princeton University Press, 1986). The first half of the sixteenth century also saw the first prints of Germanic tribal laws: Johann Sichard, *Leges Riboariorum Baioariorumque quas vocant a Theodorico rege Francorum latae* (Basel, 1530), and B. J. Herold, *Originum ac Germanicarum antiquitatum libri* (Basel, 1557). See Karl Kroeschell, "Germanisches Recht als Forschungsproblem," in *Festschrift Thieme*, ed. Karl Kroeschell (Sigmaringen: J. Thorbecke, 1986), 3–20.

48 Hutten, *Inspicientes* (n. 3), vol. 4, 289.

49 Aventinus, *Deutsche Chronik* (n. 25), 345.

50 Bebel, *Epistula Henrici Bebelii iustingensis . . . de laudibus atque philosophia Germanorum veterum* (n. 7), 138–45, 142. Piccolomini (whom Bebel might be thinking of) is quoted in chap. 3, n. 15.

51 Illiteracy is only one possible reading of Tacitus, *Germania* 19.1. For Celtis's druids and Bebel's proverbs: Krebs (chap. 1, n. 39), 200, n. 17, and 241–48. For doubts about the authenticity: Leo Wiener, *Tacitus' Germania and Other Forgeries* (New York: Innes & Sons, 1920).

52 Wimpfeling (n. 2), 209–10 (the Tacitean snippets are given in parentheses): *pudicitia* (cf. *saepta pudicitia agunt*), *sincera ac pura* (cf. *propriam et sinceram et tantum sui similem gentem*), *nobilitas* (cf. *reges ex nobilitate*), *fortitudo* (cf. *praecipuum fortitudinis incitamentum*), *proceritas* (cf. *similis proceritas*), *libertas* (cf. *illud ex libertate vitium*, said in a context where Tacitus describes what Wimpfeling here has in mind), *fides* (cf. esp. *ea est in re prava pervicacia; ipsi fidem vocant*), *liberalitas* (cf. *principis sui liberalitate*), *constantia* (cf. *acies . . . labantes a feminis restitutas constantia precum*). In two instances Wimpfeling uses the word differently from Tacitus.

53 Tacitus, *Germania* 20.2. The number of instances is based on a search of the *Bibliotheca Teubneriana Latina* (Berlin: Walter de Gruyter, 2009). It occurs frequently in humanists' characterization of the German; see, e. g., *Epistula* (n. 50), 138–45, which follows Tacitus even more closely than Wimpfeling. The racist discussion is in Günther, *Rassengeschichte* (as in chap. 8, n. 59), 124.

54 Hutten, *Inspicientes* (n. 48), 282.

55 Bebel, *Epistula* (n. 50), 142.

56 "Martia Roma prius fuerat, Cythereia nunc est" is quoted in a letter by Jacob Wimpfeling, for which see Ernst Martin, "Ein Brief von Jacob Wimpfeling," *Zeitschrift für Kirchengeschichte* 7 (1885): 144–49, 147.

57 For the first conversation see Martin Luther, *Werke, kritische Gesamtausgabe, Tischreden*, vol. 3 (Weimar: H. Böhlau's Nachfolger, 1914), nos. 3803, 3807. The following quotation: vol. 4, no. 4555.

58 Althamer (n. 5), 19.

59 *Germania Cornelii Taciti. Vocabula regionum enarrata et ad recentes adpellationes accomodata. Harminius Ulrici Hutteni. Dialogus cui titulus est Julius. Recens edita a Philippo Melanthone* (Wittenberg: Johannes Luft, 1557 [orig. 1538]). The quotations are from the dedicatory letter, which can be found in *Philippi Melanchthonis opera quae supersunt omnia*, ed. C. G. Bretschneider, vol. 3, *Corpus reformatorum III* (Halle: C.A. Schwetschke, 1836), nr. 1708, 565–67. Celtis's *Germania generalis* was included only in the second edition. For *The Renaissance and Reformation Movements* see L. W. Spitz (Chicago: Rand McNally, 1971).

60 Johann Eberlin von Günzburg, *Ein zamengelesen buochlin von der Teutschen Nation Gelegenheit, Sitten und Gebrauche*, ed. Achim Masser (Innsbruck: Universität Innsbruck, 1986).

61 The reference to Celtis: Althamer (n. 5), 18. A significantly expanded version appeared in 1536 in Nuremberg under the title *Commentaria Germaniae in P. C. Taciti libellum de situ moribus & populis Germanorum*.

5. Heroes' Songs

1 J. G. Schottelius, *FriedensSieg* (orig. 1648), ed. F. E. Koldewey (Halle: Niemeyer, 1900), esp. 41. For the following: ibid., esp. 48–51. The description of the "stage *Germane*" (*Theatergermane*) Arminius is based on Conrad Buno's contemporary engraving, which can be found in Sara Smart, *Doppelte Freude der Musen: Court Festivities in Brunswick-Wolfenbüttel 1642–1700* (Wiesbaden: Harrassowitz, 1989), 19, fig. 5.

2 Jacob Balde, *Silvarum liber iv. Threni, sive lamentationis Videntis vastationem Germaniae* (1643). On Württemberg see Heinz Engels, *Die Sprachgesellschaften des 17. Jahrhunderts* (Gießen: W. Schmitz, 1983), 6. More generally for historical background see C. V. Wedgwood, *The Thirty Years War* (New York: New York Review Books, 2005 [orig. 1938]), esp. 34–69.

3 B. Ph. von Chemnitz's (written under a pseudonym) *Dissertatio de ratione status in imperio nostro Romano-Germanico* is quoted from E. H. Zeydel, *The Holy Roman Empire in German Literature* (New York: Columbia University Press, 1918), 62.

4 Paul Fleming, *Germaniae exsulis ad suos filios sive proceres regni epistola* (1631), verse 31. Tacitus, *Germania* 33.2.

5 J. G. Schottelius, *Lamentatio Germaniae Exspirantis. Der numehr hinterbenden Nymphen Germaniae elendeste Todesklage* is quoted from Sara Smart, "Justus Georg Schottelius and The Patriotic Movement," *Modern Language Review* 84 (1989): 83–98, 89.

6 Martin Opitz, *Aristarch*, in *Buch von der Deutschen Poeterey (1624)* . . ., ed. Herbert Jaumann (Stuttgart: Reclam, 2002), 77–78. On the Germanic myth: Wilhelm Frenzen, "Germanenbild und Patriotismus im Zeitalter des deutschen Barock," *Deutsche Vierteljahreszeitschrift für Literaturwissenschaft und Geistesgeschichte* 15 (1937): 203–19.

7 Philipp von Zesen, *Rosen=månd*, foreword, is quoted from Ferdinand van Ingen, "Die Sprachgesellschaften des 17. Jahrhunderts: Versuch einer Korrektur," *Daphnis* 1 (1972): 14–23, 19.

8 Conrad Celtis, *Germania generalis* (chap. 4, n. 18), verses 71–73. The quotation is from Celtis, *Panegyricus ad Maximilianum pro instituto & erecto collegio poetarum & mathematicorum*, v. 66–68. On Aventinus see his *Vorrede zur Bayrischen Chronik* (chap. 4, n. 25), vol. 4, 6.

9 See Wedgwood (n. 2) for this anecdote.

10 J. G. Schottelius, *Ausführliche Arbeit von der teutschen Haubtsprache* (Tübingen: M. Niemeyer, 1995 [orig. 1663]), 308. For the vivisection see J. M. Moscherosch, *Visiones de Don Quevedo: Wunderl. u. wahrhafftige Gesichte Philanders von Sittewalt* (Hildesheim: G. Olms, 1974 [orig. 1642–43]), 698.

11 *Teutscher vnartiger Sprach- Sitten und Tugend verderber*, is quoted from Kurt Wels, *Die patriotischen Strömungen in der deutschen Literatur des Dreissigjährigen Krieges* (Greifswald: H. Adler, 1913), 119.

12 J. G. Schottelius (n. 10), biiir. For a longer version of this chapter (and further documentation), see C. B. Krebs, ". . . *ihre alte Muttersprache . . . unvermengt und unverdorben*: Zur Rezeption der taciteischen *Germania* im 17. Jahrhundert," *Philologus* 154 (2010): 119–39.

13 See the full title of J. G. Schottelius, *Teutsche Sprachkunst* (Braunschweig: B. Grubern, 1641). See generally on "Sprachgesellschaften und nationale Utopien" Wilhelm Kühlmann, in *Föderative Nation: Deutschlandkonzepte von der Reformation bis zum Ersten Weltkrieg*, ed. Dieter Langewiesche and Georg Schmidt (Munich: Oldenbourg, 2000), 245–64.

14 For an overview of theories see W. J. Jones, "*König Deutsch zu Abrahams Zeiten*: Some Perceptions of the Place of German Within the Family of Languages, from Aventinus to Zedler," in *Das unsichtbare Band der Sprache*, ed. J. L. Flood et al. (Stuttgart: Hans-Dieter Heinz, 1993), 189–213. *Das Buch der hundert Kapitel und der vierzig Statuten des sogenannten Oberrheinischen Revolutionärs* is quoted from there, 191. The following quotation: Schottelius (n. 10), 24.

15 Genesis 11:1–9 is quoted from the King James Version, modified as needed to fit my syntax.

16 Philipp Clüver, *Germania antiqua* (Leiden: Elsevier, 1616), 41. This entire paragraph is a reconstruction of Clüver's argument with the exception of the age of the German language, for which see J. R. Sattler, *Teutschen Orthographey vnd Phraseologey* (Hildesheim: G. Olms, 1975 [orig. 1607]), 3.

17 The commentator is Althamer; see Friedrich Gotthelf, *Das deutsche Altertum in den Anschauungen des sechzehnten und siebzehnten Jahrhunderts* (Berlin: A. Duncker, 1900), 20. The following reconstruction follows Clüver (n. 16), 80.

18 The characterization is by Hermann Conring, *De moribus Germanorum cum notis criticis Hermanni Conringi cura*, 3rd ed. (Helmstedt: H. D. Müller, 1678), 48. On Nuremberg see Kästner (chap. 2, n. 11), 78.

19 Clüver (n. 16), *Lectori auctor S.* The preceding biographical sketch is based on Joseph Partsch, *Philipp Clüver, der Begründer der historischen Länderkunde* (Vienna: Olmütz 1891), 3–22.

20 Cf. Tacitus, *Germania* 22.1, 17.2, 13.1, 20.1. See Stephanie Moser, *Ancestral Images: The Iconography of Human Origins* (Ithaca: Cornell University Press, 1998), 85–90, for a brief discussion of this iconographic series.

21 Two such critical voices can be found in Theobald Bieder, *Geschichte der Germanenforschung. 1. Teil, 1500 bis 1806*, 2nd ed. (Leipzig: V. Hase & Koehler, 1939), 82.

22 Clüver's interpretation in several aspects reproduces theories by lesser-known predecessors. For a comprehensive survey see Arno Borst, *Der Turmbau von Babel: Geschichte der Meinungen über Ursprung und Vielfalt der Sprachen und Völker* (Stuttgart: A. Hiersemann, 1957–63).

23 Clüver (n. 16), 82. Clüver, in fact, prints "Tuitonem deum" in his own edition, believing that Tacitus most likely encountered that dialect variant of "Teuto" (ibid., 85). But since his subsequent argument is easier to follow if we assume "-eu," and others (like Schottelius) will embrace Clüver's ratiocination but prefer "Teuto," I have simplified the issue.

24 Clüver (n. 16), 84.

25 Schottelius (n. 10), 1018. The following quotation: Martin Opitz, *Briefwechsel und Lebenszeugnisse*, ed. Klaus Conermann (Berlin: Walter De Gruyter, 2009), vol. 2, 792.

26 Christoph Schorer's *Sittenverderber* (1644) is quoted from W. J. Jones, *Sprachhelden und Sprachverderber: Dokumente zur Erforschung des Fremdwortpurismus im Deutschen (1478–1750)* (New York: Walter De Gruyter, 1995), 305–45, 333.

27 Martin Opitz, *Trostgedichte* (1633), book 1, in *Dreißigjähriger Krieg: Eine Textsammlung aus der Barockliteratur*, ed. Wolfgang Popp (Münster: Lit, 1998), 103.

28 Martin Kempe, *Neugrünender Palm-Zweig der teutschen Helden-Sprache und Poeterey* (1664), in *Die Fruchtbringende Gesellschaft unter Herzog August von Sachsen-Weissenfels*, ed. Martin Bircher and Andreas Herz (Tübingen:

M. Niemeyer, 1997), 172, verse 281. Heinrich Bebel's treatise: *Commentaria de abusione linguae latinae apud Germanos* (Strasbourg, 1500).

29 G. P. Harsdörffer, *Frauenzimmer Gesprächspiele* (orig. 1644–49), ed. Irmgard Böttcher (Tübingen: M. Niemeyer, 1968–69), vol. 4, 519. See Erich Trunz, "Schichten und Gruppen in der deutschen Literatur," in *Deutsche Literatur zwischen Späthumanismus und Barock: 8 Studien* (Munich: Beck, 1995), 187–206.

30 For biographical information: Marian Szyrocki, *Martin Opitz*, 2nd ed. (Munich: Beck, 1974). See also Curt von Faber du Faur, "Der *Aristarchus*: Eine Neuwertung," *Proceedings of the Modern Language Association* 69 (1954): 566–90.

31 Opitz, *Aristarch* (n. 6), 78; the following quotations: ibid., ibid., 78–79.

32 Opitz, *Aristarch* (n. 6), 78; the following quotation: 94.

33 Opitz, *Buch von der Deutschen Poeterey (1624)* (n. 6), chap. 4, 23–24. The following quotation: ibid. On bards: Conrad Wiedemann, "Druiden, Barden, Witdoben. Zu einem Identifikationsmodell barocken Dichtertums," in *Sprachgesellschaften, Sozietäten, Dichtergruppen*, ed. Martin Birchner and Ferdinand van Ingen (Hamburg: Hauswedell, 1978), 131–50.

34 Schottelius (n. 10), 1018. The epigraph: D. C. von Lohenstein, *Großmüthiger Feldherr Arminius* (Hildesheim: G. Olms, 1973 [orig. 1689]), *Ehrengetichte*, d3ᵛ.

35 Johann Klaj, *Lobrede der Teutschen Poeterey*, in *Redeoratorien und "Lobrede der teutschen Poeterey,"* ed. Conrad Wiedemann (Tübingen: M. Niemeyer, 1965), Anhang, 412, with reference to Melchior Goldast, *Constitutiones imperiales* (Frankfurt am Main, 1607–13), 4 vols.

36 Schottelius (n. 1), 50.

37 Friedrich von Logau, *Sinngedichte* (Stuttgart: Reclam, 1984), 2.8.13, 115. See Ferdinand van Ingen, "Die Sprachgesellschaften des 17. Jahrhunderts: Versuch einer Korrektur," *Daphnis* 1 (1972): 14–23.

38 Schottelius, *Fruchtbringende Lustgarte. Kurzer Vorbericht An die Hochloeblichste Fruchtbringende Gesellschaft* (orig. 1647), ed. Marianne Burkhard (Munich: Kösel, 1967), iiiiʳ. See also Klaus Conermann, "Die Fruchtbringende Gesellschaft," *Veröffentlichungen des Historischen Museums für Mittelanhalt Köthen* 25 (2002): 26–56.

39 Logau (n. 37) is quoted from Hans Kohn, *The Idea of Nationalism: A Study in Its Origins and Background* (New Brunswick, NJ: Transaction Publishers, 2005 [orig. 1944]), 684, n. 21. Other strategies to justify inebriety are discussed in Nienke Lammersen-van Deursen, *Rhetorische Selbstporträts* (Amsterdam: VU University Press, 2007), 86–91. The translation: K. M. Grodnitz von Grodnau, *Tacitus, C. Cornelius (Lat.) . . . Beschreibung 2. Der Teutschen-Völcker Ursprunges . . .* (Frankfurt am Main: Humm, 1657).

40 Schottelius (n. 38), iiiiᵛ.

41 See Schottelius's entry in the *Köthener Gesellschaftsbuch* (no. 397). See also

J. J. Berns, "Der weite Weg des Justus Georg Schottelius von Einbeck nach Wolfenbüttel: Eine Studie zu den Konstitutionsbedingungen eines deutschen Gelehrtenlebens im 17. Jahrhundert," *Einbecker Jahrbuch* 30 (1974): 5–20. The full title of Schottelius's magnum opus: *Ausführliche Arbeit Von der Teutschen HaubtSprache. Worin enthalten Gemelter dieser HaubtSprache Uhrankunft/ Uhraltertuhm/ Reinlichkeit/ Eigenschaft/ Vermögen/ Unvergleichlichkeit/ Grundrichtigkeit/ zumahl die SprachKunst und VersKunst Teutsch und guten theils Lateinisch völlig mit eingebracht/ wie nicht weniger die Verdoppelung/ Ableitung/ die Einleitung/ Nahmwörter/ Authores vom Teutschen Wesen und Teutscher Sprache/ von der verteutschung/ Item die Stammwörter der Teutschen Sprache samt der Erklärung und derogleichen viel merkwürdige Sachen; Abgetheilet In Fünf Bücher* (Braunschweig: Zilliger, 1663).

42 The Roman Marcus Terentius Varro was a polymath; among his many books were twenty-five on the Latin language (of which only five remain). Schottelius's honorary name reflects the recognition he enjoyed among his contemporaries. But it also reveals the continuous paradigmatic status the Romans occupied among those who promoted the national. German greatness at least partly continued to be measured by (Greek and) Roman standards.

43 Friedrich Gundolf, "Justus Georg Schottelius," in *Deutschkundliches*, ed. Hans Teske (Heidelberg: C. Winter, 1930), 72.

44 Schottelius (n. 10), 123.

45 Klaj (n. 35), 403, and Logau (n. 37), 3.5.43, 164. See Andreas Gardt, *Sprachreflexion in Barock und Frühaufklärung: Entwürfe von Böhme bis Leibniz* (Berlin: Walter De Gruyter, 1994), 148–50.

46 *Heldensprache*: G. P. Harsdörffer, *Poetischer Trichter* (Hildesheim: G. Olms, 1971 [orig. 1648–53]), part 3, 5.

47 Schottelius (n. 10), 5, and the following: ibid., 166.

48 Schottelius (n. 1), 15.

6. The Volk of Free-Spirited Northerners

1 This episode and the communications can be found in *Huit Dissertations que M. le Comte de Hertzberg a lues dans les assemblèes publiques de l'Académie Royale des Sciences & Belles-Lettres de Berlin, dans les années 1780–87* (Berlin: G. J. Decker, 1787), 39–44. For a biography of Hertzberg see A. T. Preuss, *Ewald Friedrich Graf von Hertzberg* (Berlin: Voss, 1909). For historical background I have here and elsewhere relied on Rudolf Vierhaus, *Germany in the Age of Absolutism*, trans. J. B. Knudsen (Cambridge: Cambridge University Press, 1988).

2 The full title runs *Dissertation tendant à expliquer les causes de la supériorité des Germains sur les Romains & à prouver que le Nord de la Germanie ou Teutonie entre le Rhin & la Vistule, & principalement la présente Monarchie*

Prussienne, est la patrie originaire de ces nations héroiques, qui dans la fameuse migration des peuples ont détruit l'Empire Romain, & qui ont fondé & peuplé les principales monarchies de l'Europe. All quotations are from the edition cited in n. 1.

3 Biographical data are taken from Robert Shackleton, *Montesquieu: A Critical Biography* (London: Oxford University Press, 1961).

4 Louis de Jaucourt, "Germanie," in *Encyclopédie, ou Dictionnaire raisonné des sciences, des arts et des métiers* (Paris: Briasson, 1751–65), vol. 7, 644–46. Generally on *Tacite en France de Montesquieu à Chateaubriand* see Volpilhac-Auger (introduction, n. 15).

5 See Leon Poliakov, *The Aryan Myth: A History of Racist and Nationalist Ideas in Europe*, trans. Edmund Howard (New York: New American Library, 1977 [orig. 1971]), 17–36, for the *querelle des races*; Montlosier and Sieyès are quoted on pp. 30 and 28, respectively.

6 All quotations from *The Spirit of the Laws* are taken from the translation by Thomas Nugent (rev. J. V. Prichard [London: G. Bell & Sons, 1918]), which is in the public domain (www.constitution.org/cm/sol.htm). I have occasionally modified them. References are to book and chapter; see *Spirit* 1.1 and 19.4.

7 *Spirit* (n. 6), 19.14. See Shackleton (n. 3, 307) for Montesquieu's copy of the treatise, and G.-L. Fink, "Von Winckelmann bis Herder: Die deutsche Klimatheorie in europäischer Perspektive," in *Johann Gottfried Herder, 1744–1803*, ed. Gerhard Sauder (Hamburg: F. Meiner, 1987), 156–76, for the popularity of the theory.

8 Johann Heumann von Teutschbrunn, *Der Geist der Geseze der Teutschen* (Nuremberg, 1761), 9.

9 *Spirit* (n. 6), 30.2. My count of Tacitean references is based on Catherine Volpilhac-Auger, *Tacite et Montesquieu* (Oxford: Voltaire Foundation at the Taylor Institution, 1985), 190.

10 *Spirit* (n. 6), 11.6; see also 18.30, 28.2, 31.4.

11 Sebastian Franck (*Chronicon Germaniae*, 1538, fol. 6b), whom I cite from Erwin Hölzle, *Die Idee einer altgermanischen Freiheit vor Montesquieu* (Munich: R. Oldenbourg, 1925), 18.

12 Tacitus, *Germania* 11.1. "Verderbliche Staatsmaximen" is the characterization by Heumann (n. 8), fol. 2ᵛ.

13 "Commentaire sur l'esprit des lois," in *Oeuvres complètes de Voltaire* (Paris: L. Hachette, 1876–1900), vol. 31, 297, 307; my paraphrase follows the original closely. The expression "in the woods" became common currency: see Poliakov (n. 5).

14 For the review see *Göttingische Zeitungen von gelehrten Sachen* 90 (1749): 715–18. Kästner (*Vorrede*, xi–xiii) is cited from Frank Herdmann, *Montesquieurezeption in Deutschland im 18. und beginnenden 19. Jahrhundert* (Hildesheim: G. Olms, 1990), 85. For *Der Geist der Geseze der Teutschen* see n. 8. J. H. G. von Justi, *Die Natur und das Wesen der Staaten* (Berlin: Johann

Heinrich Ruedigers, 1760), had already spoken of the "Geist der Gesetze" in his (unpaginated) preface.

15 F. K. von Moser, *Von dem deutschen Nationalgeist* (Nuremberg: Notos, 1976 [orig. 1765]), 5, 7, 33. For biographical information see *Allgemeine Deutsche Biographie* (Leipzig: Duncker & Humblot, 1885), vol. 22, 764–83.

16 F. C. K. v. Creutz, *Versuch einer pragmatischen Geschichte von der merkwuerdigen Zusammenkunft des teutschen Nationalgeistes und der politischen Kleinigkeiten* (Frankfurt am Main: Varrentrapp, 1766), 24, 6.

17 H. W. v. Bülow, *Noch etwas zum deutschen Nationalgeiste* (Lindau: Thierbach, 1766), 35, 92.

18 J. H. Eberhard, *Freie Gedancken über einige der neuesten Staats-Strittigkeiten*, (1767), is quoted from Nicholas Vazsonyi, "Montesquieu, Friedrich Karl von Moser, and the 'National Spirit Debate' in Germany, 1765–1767," *German Studies Review* 22 (1999): 225–46, esp. 236.

19 The two quotations are by Friedrich Nicolai (1765, cited in Kohl [n. 43], 112) and N. S. Nothanker (1773, cited in Ergang [n. 44], 143). Goethe and Schiller are quoted in Conrad Wiedemann, "The Germans' Concern about Their National Identity in the Pre-Romantic Era: An Answer to Montesquieu?" in *Concepts of National Identity*, ed. Peter Boerner (Baden-Baden: Nomos, 1986), 141–52, esp. 143. The following two journals are *Der Teutsche Merkur* and *Allgemeine Deutsche Bibliothek*.

20 *Herder's Sämmtliche Werke*, ed. Bernhard Suphan (Berlin: Weidmann, 1877–1913), vol. 13, 384. On Herder's experiencing Germany see A. J. La Vopa, "*Herder's Publikum*: Language, Print, and Sociability in Eighteenth-Century Germany," *Eighteenth-Century Studies* 29 (1996): 5–24. *SW*=*Sämmtliche Werke*.

21 *Spirit* (n. 6), 1.3, 28.1, 18.22.

22 Montesquieu, *Persian Letters*, trans. Margaret Mauldon (Oxford: Oxford University Press, 2008), no. 103.

23 Heumann (n. 8), fol. 2^r, 5. He returns to the problem later, e.g., when discussing "die einheimischen und Hülfs-Rechte[n]" (101).

24 Hermann Conring (1606–81), the influential seventeenth-century historian of German law, published in 1643 his treatise *On the Origin of German Law* (for which he is credited with the foundation of the history of German law). He gratefully points to Tacitus, who attributed to the German ancestors a "well-ordered community and praiseworthy mores" (*De origine juris germanici* [Helmstedt, 1643], 18–19). Unfortunately laws could not be found in his account, and the *Germania*, of which he produced his own edition (*De moribus Germanorum cum notis criticis Hermanni Conringi cura* [Helmstedt, 1652]), merely provided the historical context for those interested in German law in general and its origins in particular.

25 G. C. Gebauer, *Vestigia iuris Germanici antiquissima in Cornelii Taciti Germania obvia* (Göttingen: Vandenhoeck, 1766), basically a collection of previously written essays. Tacitus's remark: *Germania* 12.2.

26 Justus Möser, "Zwei Recensionen über 'Von dem deutschen Nationalgeiste (Frankfurt a. M. 1765)' und 'Noch Etwas zum deutschen Nationalgeiste (Lindau 1766),'" in *Sämmtliche Werke*, ed. B. R. Abeken (Berlin: Nicolai, 1843), vol. 9, 240–45, 241 (abbrev.).

27 Friedrich Nicolai, *Leben Justus Möser's*, in *Sämmtliche Werke* (n. 26), vol. 10, 47. More recently on Möser's time: J. B. Knudsen, *Justus Möser and the German Enlightenment* (Cambridge: Cambridge University Press, 1986).

28 Herder, "An das Lief- und Estländische Publikum" (orig. 1772), in *SW* (n. 20), vol. 5, 347. See also *Der Teutsche Merkur* 2 (1773): 259.

29 Möser, *SW* (n. 26), vol. 6, esp. ix–x.

30 Ibid., 40–41. Cf. Tacitus, *Germania* 12.3. Möser's critical reader: J. Ch. Gatterer, "Rezension zu 'Justus Mösers Oßnabrueckische Geschichte. Allgemeine Einleitung,'" *Allgemeine historische Bibliothek* 9 (1769): 111.

31 Tacitus, *Germania* 26.3 (cf. 14.5, 15.1). Montesquieu, *Spirit* (n. 6), 18.21. See K. H. L. Welker, "Altes Sachsen und koloniales Amerika: Naturrechtsdenken und Tacitusrezeption bei Justus Möser," in R. Wiegels and W. Woesler (chap. 4, n. 34), 323–44, on property as qualification; and (despite occasional Nazi jargon) Horst Kirchner, *Das germanische Altertum in der deutschen Geschichtsschreibung des achtzehnten Jahrhunderts* (Berlin: E. Ebering, 1938), 46–56, on the controversy about farming among the *Germanen*.

32 Möser's letter to Thomas Abbt (ca. 10 Aug. 1765), in *Briefe*, ed. Ernst Beins and Werner Pleister (Hannover: Selbstverlag der Historischen Kommission, 1939), 195–98, is discussed in Peter Schmidt, *Studien über Justus Möser als Historiker* (Göppingen: Kümmerle, 1975), 118.

33 Möser, *SW* (n. 26), vol. 5, 202.

34 Jacob Grimm, "Vorrede Deutsches Wörterbuch I," in *Kleinere Schriften*, vol. 8, *Vorreden*, ed. Eduard Ippel (Gütersloh: C. Bertelsmann, 1871), 338.

35 J. C. L. de Simonde, *De la vie et des écrits de P. H. Mallet* (Genève: J. J. Paschoud, 1807), 12.

36 The titles of Mallet's two volumes are *Introduction à l'histoire de Dannemarc, où l'on traite de la religion, des loix, des moeurs & des usages des anciens Danois*; and *Monuments de la mythologie et de la poesie des Celtes et particulierement des anciens Scandinaves: pour servir de supplement et de preuves a l'Introduction a l'histoire de Dannemarc*. I have used Bishop Percy's translation, *Northern Antiquities* (rev. ed., London: H. G. Bohn, 1847), abbreviated as *NA*. On the Nordic Renaissance, see F.-X. Dillmann, "Frankrig og den nordiske fortid—de første etaper af genopdagelsen," in *The Waking of Angantyr: The Scandinavian Past in European Culture*, ed. Else Roesdahl and P. M. Sørensen (Århus: Århus University Press, 1996), 13–26.

37 I paraphrase the preface, *NA* (n. 36), 55–59; the quotation: 122.

38 Gottfried Schütze, *Der Lehrbegriff der alten deutschen und nordischen Völker von dem Zustande der Seelen nach dem Tode überhaupt* (Leipzig: Langenheim, 1750), 65.

39 Mallet deals with religion primarily in *NA* (n. 36), chaps. 3–6; the quotations: 122, 83. The reinterpretation is in Schütze (n. 38), 227. For a modern study of "Tacitus' *Germania* als religionsgeschichtliche Quelle" see Dieter Timpe in *Germanische Religionsgeschichte: Quellen und Quellenprobleme*, ed. Heinrich Beck (Berlin: Walter De Gruyter, 1992), 434–58.

40 *NA* (n. 36), 221–23 (runes), 158 and 235–39 (bards).

41 Otto Fischer, ed., *H. W. v. Gerstenbergs Rezensionen in der Hamburgischen Neuen Zeitung 1767–1771* (Berlin: Behr, 1904), 269. For the reception of the Nordic mythology see Lutz Rühling, "Das deutsche Bild Skandinaviens: Von barocker Poeterey bis zum wilden Norden," in *Grenzgänge: Skandinavisch-deutsche Nachbarschaften*, ed. Heinrich Detering (Göttingen: Wallstein-Verlag, 2001), 60–77.

42 Klopstock (to Denis, 8 Sept. 1767), in *Briefe*, vol. 5, ed. Klaus Hurlebusch, in *Werke und Briefe*, ed. Horst Gronemeyer et al. (Berlin: Walter De Gruyter, 1974–), no. 19, p. 24. Klopstock's portrait of the ancient Germans is discussed in Jean Murat, *Klopstock: Les thèmes principaux de son oeuvre* (Strasbourg: Les Belles Lettres, 1959), 255–311, esp. 293–96.

43 Klopstock's letter to Tscharner (13 Sept. 1750) is quoted in K. M. Kohl, *Friedrich Gottlieb Klopstock* (Stuttgart: Metzler, 2000), 41. For the following see more generally Klaus Düwel and Harro Zimmermann, "Germanenbild und Patriotismus in der deutschen Literatur des 18. Jahrhunderts," in *Germanenprobleme in heutiger Sicht*, ed. Heinrich Beck (Berlin: Walter De Gruyter, 1986), 358–95.

44 Herder's dictum is quoted from Dieter Lohmeier, "Kopenhagen als kulturelles Zentrum der Goethezeit," in *Grenzgänge* (n. 41), 78–95, 78. The final characterization of Klopstock is de Staël's, quoted from Robert Ergang, "National Sentiment in Klopstock's Odes and Bardiete," in *Nationalism and Internationalism*, ed. E. M. Earle, (New York: Columbia University Press, 1950), 120–43, 122.

45 Klopstock, *Die deutsche Gelehrtenrepublik*, ed. R. M. Hurlebusch (Berlin: Walter De Gruyter, 1975), 144.

46 Klopstock, *Hermanns Schlacht*, ed. M. E. Amtstätter (n. 42), Abteilung *Werke*, vol. 6.1, 77, 151. The letter to Johann Friedrich Boie (24 Nov. 1767) is quoted in Harro Zimmermann, *Freiheit und Geschichte: F. G. Klopstock als historischer Dichter und Denker* (Heidelberg: C. Winter, 1987), 234.

47 Klopstock's ode is quoted in Bernd Fischer, *Das Eigene und das Eigentliche* (Berlin: Erich Schmidt, 1995), 146. The poem is titled "Unsere Sprache." For the comparison to Zesen, see Kohl (n. 43), 53.

48 Klopstock, *Briefe 1776–1782*, ed. Helmut Riege (n. 42), vol. 7.2, 435. The letter to Ebert (18 Feb. 1769) is quoted in Kohl (n. 43), 106.

49 Herder, "Eine Erscheinung," *SW* (n. 20), vol. 29, 333. See also Dieter Lohmeier, *Herder und Klopstock* (Bad Homburg: Gehlen, 1968), esp. 15–28.

50 "Auf meinen ersten Todten": Herder, *SW* (n. 20), vol. 29, 282. Biographi-

cal data are taken from Wulf Koepke, *Johann Gottfried Herder* (Boston: Twayne, 1987), esp. 1–8.

51 Herder, *Iduna*, in *SW* (n. 20), vol. 18, 488. The following quotation: *Fragments on Recent German Literature*, in *SW* (n. 20), vol. 1, 366.*

52 Herder, ibid. vol. 1, 366. The following quotation: ibid., 185. Tacitus's remark: *Germania* 4.1.

53 Herder, ibid., vol. 2, 32 (the parts in italics are my translations of the original Latin that Herder quotes: *informem terris, asperam coelo, tristem cultu adspectuque,* and *nec tam voces illae, quam virtutis concentus videntur.* The following: *Zusatz zu der neuen Ausgabe,* in *SW* (n. 20), vol. 2, 246. For Herder's interest in folklore see W. A. Wilson, "Herder, Folklore and Romantic Nationalism," *Journal of Popular Culture* 6 (1973): 819–35. When Herder published a collection of such songs, he tellingly titled them *Stimmen der Völker in Liedern (Peoples' Voices in Songs).*

54 Herder, *Von deutscher Art und Kunst, Stimmen der Völker, Vorrede,* is quoted in Otto Dann, "Herder und die Deutsche Bewegung," in *Johann Gottfried Herder, 1744–1803,* ed. Gerhard Sauder (Hamburg: F. Meiner, 1987), 308–40. On "Das Wort 'Volk' im Sprachgebrauch Johann Gottfried Herders" see Wulf Koepke, *Lessing Yearbook* 19 (1987): 207–20.

55 Herder, *SW* (n. 20), vol. 2, 42.

56 Herder, *SW* (n. 20), vol. 13, 252, 257, is quoted in F. M. Barnard, *Herder's Social and Political Thought* (Oxford: Clarendon Press, 1965), 70. On the reception of Herder see Bernhard Becker, "Phasen der Herder-Rezeption von 1871–1945," in Sauder (n. 54), 423–36.

7. White Blood

1 Jacob Grimm, *Geschichte der deutschen Sprache,* is quoted from Ludwig Denecke, *Jacob Grimm und sein Bruder Wilhelm* (Stuttgart: J. B. Metzlersche Verlagsbuchhandlung, 1971), 97. For historical background: David Blackbourn, *History of Germany, 1780–1918: The Long Nineteenth Century,* 2nd ed. (Malden, MA: Blackwell, 2003).

2 *Deutschlands Zukunft: In sechs Reden* (Elberfeld: Büschler, 1814). His autobiography: *Erinnerungen aus meinem Leben* (Hannover: Hahn'sche Hofbuchhandlung, 1863).

3 Friedrich Kohlrausch, *Die deutsche Geschichte für Schule und Haus,* is normally quoted from the ninth edition (Elberfeld: Büschler, 1829), but this passage is from the second edition (1816), 30 (as it seems omitted in later editions). I have occasionally used the English translation by J. D. Haas, *A*

---

* My translation of this and the following passage follows but modifies the text available at the *Internet Modern History Sourcebook* (www.fordham.edu/halsall/mod/1784herder-mankind.html).

History of Germany: From the Earliest Period to the Present Time (New York: D. Appleton, 1856).

4 Fichte is quoted from *J. G. Fichte: Addresses to the German Nation*, ed. G. A. Kelly (New York: Harper Torchbooks, 1968), 3, 211.

5 Jacob Grimm, "Preface to the *German Dictionary* of 1854," is quoted from Peter Ganz, *Jacob Grimm's Conception of German Studies* (Oxford: Clarendon Press, 1973), 11.

6 Biographical information is taken from W. G. Jacobs, *Johann Gottlieb Fichte* (Hamburg: Rowohlt, 1984). On his stay in Berlin see Stefan Reiß, "Fichte in Berlin," in *Fichte in Berlin*, ed. Ursula Baumann (Hannover-Laatzen: Wehrhahn, 2006), 9–46, esp. 11.

7 J. G. Fichte, *Gesamtausgabe der Bayerischen Akademie*, ed. Reinhard Lauth and Hans Jacob (Stuttgart: Friedrich Frommann, 1962–) I, 9, 289.

8 All quotations are taken from Kelly (n. 4), 92, 122, 81, 88. It is Fichte's son (*Fichtes Leben und litterarischer Briefwechsel* [Sulzbach: Seidel, 1830], vol. 1, 538) who mentions Tacitus (mostly, he adds, the books of the *Annals* that deal with Arminius).

9 Fichte (n. 4), 228. See Aira Kemilainen, *Auffassungen über die Sendung des deutschen Volkes um die Wende des 18. u. 19. Jahrhunderts* (Helsinki: Finnish Academy, 1956).

10 See Gregory Moore, ed., *Fichte: Addresses to the German Nation* (Cambridge: Cambridge University Press, 2008), xx–xxiii, esp. xx.

11 Fichte (n. 4), 45, 47, and the following: 47.

12 Stein is quoted from G. S. Ford, *Stein and the Era of Reform in Prussia, 1807–1815* (Princeton: Princeton University Press, 1922), 144.

13 Heinrich Heine, *Geständnisse*, in *Sämtliche Werke*, ed. Oskar Walzel (Leipzig: Insel, 1910–15), vol. 10, 151.

14 Friedrich L. Jahn, *Deutsches Volkstum*, orig. 1810 (Berlin: Aufbau-Verlag, 1991), 26. The following quotation: 22. See *Deutsches Wörterbuch von Jacob und Wilhelm Grimm* (Leipzig: S. Hirzel, 1854–1960), vol. 26, col. 500, on "Volksthum, volksthümlich und -keit."

15 Jahn (n. 14), 157. For the following: *Deutsches Wörterbuch* (n. 14), vol. 22, col. 1876, on "Turnen."

16 Freiherr vom Stein's words on the *Monumenta* are quoted from Walter Goetz, *Historiker in meiner Zeit* (Cologne: Böhlau Verlag, 1957), 92. On the significance of the *Germania* in the field of *Deutsche Altertumskunde*, see Mario Mazza, "La 'Germana' di Tacito: etnografia, storiografia e ideologica nella cultura tedesca dell' ottocento," *Studi Urbinati di Storia, Filosofia e Letteratura* 53 (1979): 167–217.

17 See Grimm's *Selbstbiographie*, in J. u. W. Grimm, *Werke*, part 1, *Die Werke J. Grimms*, vol. 1, *Kleinere Schriften*, 2nd ed. (Hildesheim: G. Olms, 1991), 1–24, esp. 18. See also Denecke (n. 1), 140. The following quotation: Hermann Engster, *Germanisten und Germanen* (Frankfurt am Main: P. Lang, 1986), 16.

18 K. F. Eichhorn, *Deutsche Staats- und Rechtsgeschichte* (Göttingen: Vanden-hoeck & Ruprecht, 1808–12), Vorrede.

19 See Kroeschell (as in chap. 4, n. 47).

20 Jacob Grimm, *Deutsche Mythologie*, (Hildesheim: Olms-Weidmann, 2003 [orig. 1835]), Vorrede, vi.

21 Fichte (n. 4), 90. Biographical information on Kohlrausch is taken from his *Erinnerungen* (n. 2).

22 *Jenaische Allgemeine Literatur-Zeitung* (1817), vol. 1, no. 16. The laudatory notes are mentioned by Kohlrausch (n. 2), 168. On school reform: K.-E. Jeis-mann's introduction in K.-E. Jeismann and Peter Lundgreen, eds., *Handbuch der deutschen Bildungsgeschichte* (Munich: C. H. Beck, 1987), vol. 3, 1–9.

23 Information about publication and editions is taken from Ernst Wey-mar, *Das Selbstverständnis der Deutschen* (Stuttgart: E. Klett, 1961), 22 (nn. 21–22).

24 See n. 3.

25 Kohlrausch (n. 3), 17. F. A. Eckstein, *Lateinischer und griechischer Unter-richt* (Leipzig: Fues' Verlag, 1887), 238–43, in his survey of the pedagogical debate about the suitability of the *Germania* as a school text, asserted that no German youth should leave the Gymnasium without acquaintance of it; this, he added, lay in the interest of the fatherland.

26 All quotations: Kohlrausch (n. 3), 24, 56, 19 (emphasis added).

27 Robert Bernasconi, "Who Invented the Concept of Race? Kant's Role in the Enlightenment Construction of Race," in *Race*, ed. Robert Bernasconi (Malden, MA: Blackwell, 2001), 11–36, 11.

28 Linnaeus is quoted from Lisbet Koerner, *Linnaeus: Nature and Nation* (Cambridge: Harvard University Press, 1999), 25. "Mismeasure" is bor-rowed from S. J. Gould, *The Mismeasure of Man* (New York: W. W. Nor-ton, 1981).

29 M.-J.-P. Flourens, "Eloge historique de Jean-Frédéric Blumenbach," in *The Anthropological Treatises of Johann Friedrich Blumenbach*, ed. Thomas Bendyshe (Boston: Longwood Press, 1978 [orig. 1865]), 47–64, esp. 50–51.

30 *De generis humani varietate nativa* first appeared in 1775, in a revised edi-tion in 1781, and then again in 1795 greatly enlarged. I am quoting from *Anthropological Treatises* (n. 29), 71, 202, 233, 72. On degeneration: S. J. Gould, "Geometer of Race," *Discover* 15 (1994): 65–69.

31 Blumenbach, *Variety* (n. 29), 269; cf. 224, 226, where he attributes Cauca-sian characteristics to "the inhabitants of ancient Germany." On him and the Caucasian race, see B. D. Baum, *The Rise and Fall of the Caucasian Race* (New York: New York University Press, 2006), esp. 80–81, 89. For the feud see F. W. P. Dougherty, "Christoph Meiners und J. F. Blumenbach im Streit um den Begriff der Menschenrasse," in *Die Natur des Menschen*, ed. Gunter Mann and Franz Dumont (Stuttgart: G. Fischer, 1990), 89–112.

32 Jahn, *Volkstum* (n. 14), 34. Upon closer reading, Fichte, Arndt, and Jahn

himself held more pluralistic views; see Brian Vick, "The Origins of the German Volk: Cultural Purity and National Identity in Nineteenth-Century Germany," *German Studies Review* 26 (2003): 241–56. On Gall see Gunter Mann, "Franz Joseph Gall (1758–1828) und Samuel Thomas Soemmerring: Kranioskopie und Gehirnforschung zur Goethezeit," in *Samuel Thomas Soemmerring und die Gelehrten der Goethezeit*, ed. Gunter Mann and Franz Dumont (Stuttgart: G. Fischer, 1987), 149–89. For Kohlrausch's studies with Blumenbach see his *Erinnerungen* (n. 2), 48.

33 Kohlrausch, *Erinnerungen* (n. 2), 165.

34 E. M. Arndt, *Reisen, Dritter Teil*, 2nd ed. (Leipzig: Heinrich Gräff, 1804), 85. Stein is quoted from A. G. Pundt, *Arndt and the Nationalist Awakening in Germany* (New York: Columbia University Press, 1935), 92.

35 Arndt, *Fantasien zur Berichtigung der Urteile über künftige deutsche Verfassungen* (orig. 1815), is quoted in the translation by Hans Kohn, "Arndt and the Character of German Nationalism," *American Historical Review* 44 (1949): 787–803, esp. 791–92. On Arndt's racism see Brian Vick, "Arndt and German Ideas of Race: Between Kant and Social Darwinism," in *The Problematic Legacies of Ernst Moritz Arndt*, ed. Walter Erhart and Arne Koch (Tübingen: Niemeyer, 2007), 65–76.

36 *Essai sur l'inégalité des races humaines* (Paris: Librairie de Firmin Didot, 1853–55). The English translation by Adrian Collins, *The Inequality of Human Races* (New York: G. P. Putnam's Sons, 1915), comprises only vol. 1; other translations are mine and marked by a reference to volume, book, and page of the French edition. For biographical information see Jean Boissel, *Gobineau: Biographie: Mythes et réalité* (Paris: Berg International, 1993). On the publication of the *Essai*: Michel Lemonon, "Gobineau, père du racisme? La diffusion en Allemagne des idées de Gobineau sur les races," *Recherches Germaniques* 12 (1982): 78–108.

37 All quotations are taken from the *Essai* (n. 36): 205, 2.3.101 (2x), 53, 209 (modified), xiv (2x). For Gobineau's theory in the context of racist ideas see E. J. Young, *Gobineau und der Rassismus: Eine Kritik der anthropologischen Geschichtstheorie* (Meisenheim am Glan: A. Hain, 1968).

38 *The Works of Sir William Jones* (London: J. Stockdale and J. Walker, 1807), vol. 2, 268.

39 Friedrich M. Müller, *Three Lectures on the Science of Language and Its Place in General Education* (Chicago: Open Court Publishing, 1890), 70.

40 R. G. Latham, one of the most-cited advocates for the European origin, pronounced on this "Aryan question" in his *The* Germania *of Tacitus with Ethnological Dissertations and Notes* (London: Taylor, Walton, and Maberly, 1851), cxlii. For the use of the term "Aryan" see Hans Siegert, "Zur Geschichte der Begriffe 'Arier' und 'arisch,'" *Wörter und Sachen: Zeitschrift für indogermanische Sprachwissenschaft, Volksforschung und Kulturgeschichte* 4 (1941–42): 73–99. The German reviewer is quoted in Lemonon (n. 36), 90.

41 *Essai* (n. 36), 4.6.350, 2.3.105f (2x), 4.6.72–73.

42 *Essai* (n. 36), 4.6.74, 4.6.80.

43 *Essai* (n. 36), 4.6.92. Gobineau's article "Ce qui se fait en Asie" is quoted from Ludwig Schemann, *Gobineaus Rassenwerk* (Stuttgart: F. Frommanns, 1910), 484.

44 The excerpt from Wagner's letter (1 March 1871) is quoted in Winfried Schüler, *Der Bayreuther Kreis von seiner Entstehung bis zum Ausgang der wilhelminischen Ära* (Münster: Aschendorff, 1971), 1–2.

45 For this episode see Young (n. 37), 235.

46 For this observation see Lemonon (n. 36), 92–93.

47 Schemann (n. 43), 333.

48 H. S. Chamberlain, "Dilettantismus, Rasse, Monotheismus," foreword to 4th ed. of *Grundlagen des xix. Jahrhunderts* (Munich: Bruckmann, 1903), 18.

49 Thomas Nipperdey's characterization is quoted from Roger Chickering, *We Men Who Feel Most German: A Cultural Study of the Pan-German League, 1886–1914* (London: George Allen & Unwin, 1984), 25.

50 The program of the Deutschbund is quoted from Uwe Puschner, "Die Germanenideologie im Kontext der völkischen Weltanschauung," *Göttinger Forum für Altertumswissenschaften* 4 (2001): 85–97, esp. 88–89.

51 Otto Ammon, *Die natürliche Auslese beim Menschen: Auf Grund der Ergebnisse der anthropologischen Untersuchungen der Wehrpflichtigen in Baden und anderer Materialien* (Jena: G. Fischer, 1893), 1.

52 See Detlev Rose, *Die Thule-Gesellschaft* (Tübingen: Grabert, 1994), 90–91, for a facsimile of the recruitment flyer.

53 The program of the *Allgemeiner Deutscher Sprachverein* is quoted (slightly modified) from Chickering (n. 49), 36.

54 Gustaf Kossinna, *Altgermanische Kulturhöhe* (Munich: Lehmann, 1927), whence the following quotations (12, 14, 65) are taken. Gustaf Kossinna, *Die deutsche Vorgeschichte: Eine hervorragend nationale Wissenschaft* (Leipzig: Curt Kabitzsch Verlag, 1912). On the Germanic myth around the turn of the century see Rainer Kipper, *Der Germanenmythos im Deutschen Kaiserreich* (Göttingen: Vandenhoeck & Ruprecht, 2002).

55 H. S. Chamberlain, *Lebenswege meines Denkens*, 2nd ed. (Munich: Bruckmann, 1922), 37.

56 Chamberlain's letter is quoted in G. G. Field, *Evangelist of Race: The Germanic Vision of Houston Stewart Chamberlain* (New York: Columbia University Press, 1981), 77.

57 For an outline of the project see H. S. Chamberlain, *The Foundations of the 19th Century*, 2nd ed. (New York: J. Lane, 1912), lxii. The damnation is Oaksmith's (*Race and Nationality* [London: William Heinemann, 1919], 58).

58 All quotations are taken from *Foundations* (n. 57), 320, 494.

59 *Foundations* (n. 57), lxv. The following: 257 (emphasis added), 496 (I have changed the English translation), 574.

60 *Foundations* (n. 57), 256–57, 335, 253.

61 H. S. Chamberlain, *Rasse und Persönlichkeit* (Munich: Bruckmann, 1925), 74. The following: "Dilettantismus" (n. 48), 24.

62 *Foundations* (n. 57), 266 n. The following: ibid., 537.

63 "Deutsche Grundschriften," in *Iduna: Weimarisches Taschenbuch auf 1903*, ed. Ernst Wachler (Berlin: H. Costenoble, 1903), 183.

64 Ludwig Wilser, *Cornelius Tacitus: Germanien. Herkunft, Heimat, Verwandtschaft und Sitten seiner Völker*, 3rd ed. (Steglitz: Hobbing, 1917), vii. The following quotation: v.

65 Wilhelm Schwaner, ed., *Germanen-Bibel, aus heiligen Schriften germanischer Völker*, preface to 4th ed. (Stuttgart: Deutsche Verlags-Anstalt, 1934).

66 For the prize, see *Gnomon* 2 (1926): 688. Norden (chap. 1, n. 40), preface.

67 Hermann Nollau, ed., *Germanische Wiedererstehung* (Heidelberg: C. Winter, 1926), introduction.

68 R. G. Sebottendorff, *Bevor Hitler Kam: Urkundliches aus der Frühzeit der nationalsozialistischen Bewegung* (Munich: Grassingen, 1933). The translation is from R. H. Phelps, "Before Hitler Came: Thule Society and Germanen Orden," *Journal of Modern History* 35 (1963): 245–61, 245. For the classical study of National Socialism as a *völkisch* movement, see G. L. M. Mosse, *The Crisis of German Ideology* (New York: H. Fertig, 1998 [orig. 1964]).

8. A Bible for National Socialists

1 "Das katholische Deutschland spricht," *Baseler Nachrichten*, Jan. 4, 1934.

2 Quoted in Georg Moenius, *Kardinal Faulhaber* (Wien: Reinhold-Verlag, 1933), 10–11.

3 The Security Service (SD) is quoted in Susanne Kornacker, "Die Adventspredigten 1933: 'Judentum, Christentum, Germanentum,'" in *Kardinal Michael von Faulhaber 1869–1952*, ed. Thomas Forstner, Susanne Kornacker, and Peter Pfister (Munich: Generaldirektion der Staatlichen Archive Bayerns, Archiv des Erzbistums München und Freising, 2002), 330. Michael von Faulhaber, *Judaism, Christianity, and Germany*, trans. G. D. Smith (New York: Macmillan, 1934), 8. The title of the fifth sermon is misleadingly translated as "Christianity and Germany" (instead of "Germanicness").

4 Schulhoff's letter can be found in Kornacker (n. 3), 332–33.

5 All quotations in this paragraph are from Faulhaber (n. 3), 94–99.

6 Volker Losemann, "Aspekte der nationalsozialistischen Germanenideologie," in *Alte Geschichte und Wissenschaftsgeschichte*, ed. Karl Christ, Peter Kneissl, and Volker Losemann (Darmstadt: Wissenschaftliche Buchgesellschaft, 1988), 268 (and n. 63). See ibid., 267–68 (and n. 59), and Kornacker (n. 3), 328 for the newspaper articles.

7 Michael von Faulhaber, *Sieben Briefe an den unbekannten Deutschen: Ein*

Nachwort zu den Adventspredigten (Munich: Erzbischöfliches Archiv München, Kardinal-Faulhaber-Archiv, NL 9128), quotes this (p. 6) from an article by Count E. Zu Reventlow in *Reichswart*, Jan. 14, 1934.

8 Quoted in Otto Suffert, "Die Germanen in der Silvesterpredigt des Kardinals Faulhaber," *Germanien* 6 (1934): 67.

9 Faulhaber (n. 7), 14, refers to *Volksgemeinschaft*, Heidelberg, March 23, 1934.

10 Faulhaber (n. 7), 10. The three anonymous pamphlets are *Abraham a S. Clara an Kardinal Faulhaber, Teut an Faulhaber,* and *Der Fürsterzbischof Kohn an seinen geliebten Bruder, den Fürsterzbischof Faulhaber*; all appeared in 1934, published by Deutscher Hort Verlag Dessau. The more voluminous refutations are *Blut und Boden, Ehre und Freiheit! Das Vermächtnis Wittekinds und seine Antwort auf die politischen Predigten des Kardinals Faulhaber* (Hannover: C. V. Engelhard, 1934); and J. v. Leers, *Der Kardinal und die Germanen* (Hamburg: Hanseatische Verlagsanstalt, 1934). The former (p. 8) also mentions Enea Silvio Piccolomini.

11 "Declaration": Suffert (n. 8), 66. "Understanding": Herrmann Schneider, "Die germanische Altertumskunde zwischen 1933 und 1938," *Forschungen und Fortschritte* 15 (1939): 1–3.

12 Zimmermann, *Diesterweg-Erläuterungen,* 4th ed. (1943), is quoted in A. A. Lund, *Germanenideologie im Nationalsozialismus: Zur Rezeption der "Germania" des Tacitus im "Dritten Reich"* (Heidelberg: Universitätsverlag C. Winter, 1995), 33, n. 10.

13 Richard Geuß, as in introduction, n. 6.

14 Eugen Fehrle, as in introduction, n. 15.

15 Rudolf Benze, *Nationalpolitische Erziehung im Dritten Reich* (Berlin: Junker und Dünnhaupt Verlag, 1936), 20.

16 Hans Mommsen's thesis is discussed by Hermann Weiß, "Der 'schwache' Diktator: Hitler und der Führerstaat," in *Der Nationalsozialismus: Studien zur Ideologie und Herrschaft,* ed. Wolfgang Benz et al. (Frankfurt am Main: Fischer Taschenbuch Verlag, 1993), 64–77.

17 Dieter Schenk, *Hans Frank: Hitlers Kronjurist und Generalgouverneur,* (Frankfurt am Main: Fischer Verlag, 2006), 236.

18 Werner Maser, *Adolf Hitler: Mein Kampf,* 6th ed. (Esslingen: Bechtle, 1981), image 6.

19 J. C. Fest, *Das Gesicht des Dritten Reichs,* 5th ed. (Munich: Piper, 1963), 171.

20 Adolf Hitler, *Mein Kampf,* trans. R. Mannheim (Boston: Houghton Mifflin, 1943), 360–61. Henry Picker, *Hitlers Tischgespräche im Führerhauptquartier 1941–42,* 2nd ed. (Stuttgart: Seewald Verlag, 1965), 446. See more generally Bernard Mees, "Hitler and Germanentum," *Journal of Contemporary History* 39, no. 2 (2004): 255–70.

21 Ernst Piper, *Alfred Rosenberg. Hitlers Chefideologe* (Munich: Blessing, 2005), 418.

22 Hans-Dietrich Loock, "Zur 'Großgermanischen Politik' des Dritten Reichs," *Vierteljahrshefte für Zeitgeschichte* 8 (1960): 53, n. 83.

23 Quoted in Piper (n. 21), 228.

24 Quoted in Bolko Freiherr von Richthofen, *Die Vor- und Frühgeschichtsforschung im neuen Deutschland* (Berlin: Junker und Dünnhaupt, 1937), 44.

25 Piper (n. 21), 195.

26 For a description of the Germanic room, see Liebetraut Rothert, "Deutsche Vorgeschichte auf dem Reichsparteitage 1936 in Nürnberg," *Germanenerbe* 1 (1936): 194. The following journals are *Der Schulungsbrief, Das Schwarze Korps, Nationalsozialistisches Bildungswesen, Germanenerbe, Volk und Rasse,* and *Das Nationalsozialistische Monatsheft.*

27 Walther Schulz, "Germanien von der Familie zum Reich," *Der Schulungsbrief* 2 (1935): 208. See also Richard von Hoff, "Die nordischen Wurzeln des Nationalsozialismus," *Rasse* 2 (1935): 81–94.

28 Hitler (n. 20), 414, and Georg Vogel, *Die Deutsche Frau,* vol. 1, *Die germanische Frau* (Breslau [Wrocław]: Handel, 1935 [?]), 2.

29 Georg Tidl, *Die Frau im Nationalsozialismus* (Vienna: Europaverlag, 1984), 73.

30 Falk Ruttke, "Rassen und Erbplege in der Gesetzgebung des Dritten Reichs," *Der Schulungsbrief* 1 (Oct. 1934): 16.

31 "Deutsche Volksgesundheit aus Blut und Boden," *Der Stürmer* 3 (1935): 1.

32 Rose Woldstedt-Lauth, *Mädel von heute—Mütter von morgen: Gespräche zwischen Mutter und Tochter über das Liebesleben der Menschen* (Stuttgart: Strecker und Schröder, 1940), 12 (abbrev.).

33 Hans F. K. Günther, *Mein Eindruck von Adolf Hitler* (Pähl: Franz von Bebenburg, 1969), 94.

34 M. H. Kater, *Hitler Youth* (Cambridge: Harvard University Press, 2004), 1–12.

35 Ibid., 1. The phrase is a translation of an autobiographical comment by Hermann Graml.

36 International Council for Philosophy and Humanistic Studies, *The Third Reich* (New York: Praeger, 1955), 742.

37 Hitler (n. 20), 408–10.

38 Tacitus, *Germania* 24.1. See, e.g., Schulz (n. 27), 199.

39 Dietrich Klagges, "Geschichte und Erziehung," *Nationalsozialistisches Bildungswesen* 2 (1937): 83. Cf. Reichsministerium für Wissenschaft, Erziehung und Volksbildung, *Erziehung und Unterricht in der Höheren Schule* (Berlin: Weidmannsche Verlagsbuchhandlung, 1938), 11.

40 Hans Strider, "Deutsche Erzieher, deutsche Erzieherinnen," *Nationalsozialistisches Bildungswesen* 1 (1936): 2.

41 Hitler (n. 20), 427.

42 Alfred Rosenberg, "Germanische Lebenswerte im Weltanschauungskampf," *Germanenerbe* 1 (1936): 198–99.

43 Klagges (n. 39), 81–98, esp. 85.

44 Eugen Fehrle, "Die Germania des Tacitus als Quelle für deutsche Volkskunde," *Schweizerisches Archiv für Volkskunde* 26 (1925): 253.

45 Gerhard Röttger, "Die taciteische Germania im heutigen Lateinunterricht," *Neue Jahrbücher für Antike und deutsche Bildung* 2 (1939): 267–82.

46 All quotations are from Carl Schütte and Otto Gaede, *Geschichtsbuch für die Jugend des Dritten Reiches*, 2nd ed. (Halle: H. Schroedel, 1934): esp. 3, 10, 11–14. See also Reichsministerium für Wissenschaft, Erziehung und Volksbildung, "Richtlinien für den Geschichtsunterricht in der Volksschule, 1939," in *Erziehung und Unterricht in der Volksschule* (Berlin: Eher, 1939), 13–14; and the *Stoffverteilungsplan* and *Richtlinien*, as reprinted in Horst Gies, *Geschichtsunterricht unter der Diktatur Hitlers* (Cologne: Böhlau, 1992), 28, 156.

47 This and the following quotation: Gabler (introduction, n. 12), 41–47.

48 All quotations from: Martin Staemmler, *Volk und Rasse* (Berlin: Verl. für soziale Ethik und Kunstpflege, 1933).

49 For Mrs. Best see Peter Padfield, *Himmler: Reichsführer-SS* (London: Macmillan, 1990), 377. I have expanded Himmler's reply by a few words to make it less impenetrable.

50 Quoted in Elvira Weisenburger, "Der 'Rassepapst': Hans Friedrich Karl Günther, Professor für Rassenkunde," in *Die Führer der Provinz: NS-Biographien aus Baden und Württemberg*, ed. Michael Kissener and Joachim Scholtyseck (Konstanz: Universitätsverlag Konstanz, 1997), 161–200, esp. 188–89; cf. 162.

51 Quoted in ibid., 165.

52 Hans F. K. Günther, *Ritter, Tod und Teufel* (Munich: J.F. Lehmann, 1937), 109–10.

53 Slight abbreviation of the quotation in Josef Ackermann, *Heinrich Himmler als Ideologe* (Göttingen: Musterschmidt, 1970), 111.

54 G. D. Stark, *Entrepreneurs of Ideology: Neoconservative Publishers in Germany, 1890–1933* (Chapel Hill: University of North Carolina Press, 1981), 197.

55 Hans F. K. Günther, *Kleine Rassenkunde des deutschen Volkes* (Munich: J. F. Lehmann, 1934), 11. The next quotation: Günter, *Ritter* (n. 52), 189f.

56 The description of the Nordic race is in part quoted, in part adapted from *Günther, Rassenkunde* (n. 55), 21–25.

57 Heinrich Himmler, *Geheimreden 1933 bis 1945 und andere Ansprachen* (Berlin: Ullstein, 1974), 127.

58 Piper (n. 21), 584.

59 All quotations in this paragraph are taken from Hans F. K. Günther, *Herkunft und Rassengeschichte der Germanen* (Munich: J. F. Lehmann, 1935), 149, 152, 139, and 123f.

60 Hitler's library: R. H. Phelps, "Die Hitler Bibliothek," *Deutsche Rundschau* 80 (1954): 923–31. His borrowing from Günther: Lund (n. 12), 22, n. 70.

61 On this law see Karl Kroeschell, "Führer, Gefolgschaft und Treue," in *Die deutsche Rechtsgeschichte in der NS-Zeit*, ed. Joachim Rückert and Dietmar Willoweit (Tübingen: Mohr Siebeck, 1995), 55–76.

62 Schlossarek (introduction, n. 14), 18f. See also K. A. Eckardt, "Widernatürliche Unzucht ist todeswürdig," *Das Schwarze Korps* 1 (22 May 1935): 13.

63 Heinrich Himmler, *Die Schutzstaffel als antibolschewistische Kampforganisation* (Munich: F. Eher Nachführung, 1936), 28–29.

64 Goebbels's entry is quoted from Anna Bramwell, *Blood and Soil: Walther Darré and Hitler's Green Party* (Bourne End, England: Kensal Press, 1985), 54.

65 Richard Walther Darré, *Erkenntnisse und Werden: Aufsätze vor der Zeit der Machtergreifung* (Goslar: Verlag Blut und Boden, 1940), 158f. See also by the same author *Blut und Boden—ein Grundgedanke des Nationalsozialismus* (Berlin: Reichsdruckerei, 1936) and *Um Blut und Boden: Reden und Aufsätze*, 4th ed. (Munich: F. F. Eher Nachführung, 1942), 180–81.

66 Gabler (n. 47), 47.

67 Darré, *Erkenntnisse* (n. 65), 160.

68 Schlossarek (n. 62), 10.

69 Julius Weisweiler, *Tacitus: Germania—Von Blut und Boden, Sitte und Brauch im germanischen Raum* (Leipzig: Velhagen & Klasing, 1936), 8–9 (abbrev.). Hans Naumann, "Die Glaubwürdigkeit des Tacitus," *Bonner Jahrbücher des Rheinischen Landesmuseums* 139 (1934): 21–33 (well discussed in Lund [n. 12], 36–37).

70 Strasser's characterizing comment is quoted in Padfield (n. 49), 80. For biographical information I have also turned to Bradley Smith, *Heinrich Himmler—A Nazi in the Making 1900–1926* (Stanford, CA: Hoover Institution Press, 1971). For Himmler's ideology: Ackermann (n. 53).

71 For Himmler's comments on Jews see Ackermann (n. 53), 28–30.

72 Himmler's letter is quoted from Smith (n. 70), 165.

73 Bundesarchiv Koblenz, NL Himmler, N 1126/9, no. 218.

74 Himmler at a *Führerbesprechung der SS-Gruppe Ost*, quoted in Padfield (n. 49), 101.

75 Himmler (n. 63), 20, whence the following quotation also is taken.

76 Felix Kersten (*Totenkopf und Treue: Heinrich Himmler ohne Uniform* [Hamburg: Robert Mölich Verlag, 1952], 181) learned in 1943 that "the racially pure blood of German heroes [would thus] be transmitted to as many offspring as possible." See also the anonymous articles "Zum neuen Ehescheidungsrecht," "Das Kind heiligt die Ehe," and "Im Mittelpunkt: das Kind," *Das Schwarze Korps* 3 (21 Oct. 1937): 6.

77 Kersten (n. 76), 92–104, 120. Tacitus, *Germania* 8.2, quoted, e.g., in Schulz (n. 27), 193; Margarete Schaper-Haeckel, *Die Germanin: Körper, Geist und Seele* (Berlin: Engelhard, 1943), 89.

78 Padfield (n. 49), 83.

79 Albert Forster, "Vernehmungsprotokoll des Reichssicherheitshauptamtes" (25 May 1943), quoted in Ackermann (n. 53), 36, n. 103.

80 Horst Wagenführ, *Gefolgschaft—Der germanische Kampfbund* (Hamburg: Hanseatische Verlagsanstalt, 1935), from which all following unspecified quotations are drawn. On the Hitler Youth see Kater (n. 34).

81 A clip of one such ceremony can be seen on YouTube ("Die SS Vereidigung am 9 November"), www.youtube.com/watch?v=3necLq4Ynoo. "The loyal Heinrich," as Hitler called Himmler, when the time of trial came, failed his leader. Though he had reaffirmed in front of his men that "there was no mercy for disloyalty among us, *Germanen*" (quoted in Fest [n. 19], 173), he deserted after months of flirtation with oppositional groups and the Allied leadership in the west. See Ian Kershaw, *Hitler 1936–45: Nemesis* (New York: W. W. Norton, 2000), 716–17, 817–19.

82 Himmler (n. 57), 27.

83 Der Reichsführer SS, *Der Weg zum Reich* (Berlin, 1942), 20. SS-Hauptamt, *Lehrplan für die weltanschauliche Erziehung in der SS und Polizei* (Berlin, 1940 [?]), 14. SS-Briga[de]f[ührer] Hermann, "Warum Sport in der SS?" *SS Leitheft* 2, no. 12 (1936): 41–42.

84 Cf. Padfield (n. 49), 204–5.

85 Himmler (n. 57), 38, 127.

86 Himmler is quoted in Padfield (n. 49), 51.

87 Himmler (n. 57), 97. Tacitus, *Germania* 12.1. The practice had also been discussed in the SS journal *Das Schwarze Korps*: Eckhardt (n. 62), 13. For Hitler's decree see Burkhard Jellonnek, *Homosexuelle unter dem Hakenkreuz: Die Verfolgung der Homosexuellen im Dritten Reich* (Paderborn: F. Schöningh, 1990), 30–31.

88 Himmler (n. 57), 29. For the organizational changes see M. H. Kater, *Das "Ahnenerbe" der SS 1935–1945: Ein Beitrag zur Kulturpolitik des Dritten Reiches?* (Munich: R. Oldenbourg, 1997), 59–91. For the three expeditions see Heather Pringle, *The Master Plan: Himmler's Scholars and the Holocaust* (New York: Hyperion, 2006), 63–75, 99–120, 145–63. For the rediscovery of the Codex Aesinas see also Niutta (as in introduction, n. 1) and Schama (as in introduction, n. 1) as well as Marco Vattasso's brief account of his discovery in *Bollettino di Filologia Classica* 9 (1902): 107.

89 Letter dated September 3, 1979, from Prof. Mason Hammond to Prof. Zeph Stewart (Widener Medieval Studies Lib Z105.5.A47 C64 1900z).

90 Kater (n. 88), 72.

91 The correspondence: Bundesarchiv Berlin, Akten NS 21/439 and 381; letter 10/9/1942.

Epilogue

1 Letter dated September 3, 1979 (chap. 8, n. 89). On Wolfenbüttel's interest see Egert Pöhlmann, "Codex Hersfeldensis und Codex Aesinas: Zu Tacitus' Agricola," *Würzburger Jahrbücher für die Altertumswissenschaft* 27 (2003): 153–60, 155, n. 15. I am once more grateful to Giovanni Baldeschi-Balleani for providing me with details pertaining to the codex.

2 Beatus Rhenanus, *Commentariolus uetusta Germaniae populorum uocabula paucis explicans et obiter alia quaedam*, in Schardius (as in chap. 4, n. 5), 70–77 (mistakenly attributed to Henricus Glarianus).

3 James Hirstein, "L'œuvre philologique de Beatus Rhenanus et le devenir de la 'philologie humaniste,'" in *Beatus Rhenanus (1485–1547) Lecteur et editeur des texts anciens*, ed. James Hirstein (Turnhout, Belgium: Brepols, 2000), 1–20, 19–20.

4 Rhenanus, *Commentariolus* (n. 2), 70.

5 Beatus Rhenanus, *Rerum Germanicarum libri tres* (orig. 1531), ed., trans., comm. Felix Mundt (Tübingen: Niemeyer, 2008), 194 and 614f. for a good summary. The second observation, as quoted, had already been made in the *Commentariolus* (n. 2), 70. On Beatus Rhenanus's method, see Ada Hentschke and Ulrich Muhlack, *Einführung in die Geschichte der klassischen Philologie* (Darmstadt: Wissenschaftliche Buchgesellschaft, 1972), 14–59.

6 C. M. Wieland, "Wenn Sie fortfahren die Teutschen des achtzehnten Jahrhunderts für Enkel Tuiskons anzusehen," *Der Deutsche Merkur* 1 (1773): 183. Quoted from Wieland, *Werke*, ed. Fritz Martini and H. W. Seiffert (Munich: Hanser, 1964–68), vol. 3, 273.

7 Heinrich Böll, "Germania," *Die Zeit*, March 2, 1979. All following quotations are taken from there. Manfred Fuhrmann, "Die *Germania* des Tacitus und das deutsche Nationalbewußtsein," in *Brechungen*, ed. Manfred Fuhrmann (Stuttgart: Klett-Cotta, 1982), 113–28, esp. 115, was rightly critical.

INDEX

Page numbers in *italics* refer to illustrations.
References to works cited in the notes are not included.